D1714900

Mending Fences

Mending Fences

Confidence- and Security-Building Measures in South Asia

EDITED BY

Šumit Ganguly
and Ted Greenwood

WestviewPress
A Division of HarperCollins*Publishers*

Copyright © 1996 by Westview Press, A Division of HarperCollins Publishers, Inc.

Published in 1996 in the United States of America by Westview Press, 5500 Central Avenue, Boulder, Colorado 80301-2877, and in the United Kingdom by Westview Press, 12 Hid's Copse Road, Cumnor Hill, Oxford OX2 9JJ

A CIP catalog record for this book is available from the Library of Congress.
ISBN 0-8133-8995-X

The paper used in this publication meets the requirements of the American National Standard for Permanence of Paper for Printed Library Materials Z39.48-1984.

10   9   8   7   6   5   4   3   2   1

Contents

Acknowledgments

The original idea for this project grew out of a series of lunchtime conversations at Columbia University. Relying on our respective intellectual backgrounds and professional interests, we came to the conclusion that lessons and propositions about CSBMs derived from other regions of the world, notably Western Europe and the Middle East, could be usefully applied to South Asia. We found prompt research support for the project from George Perkovich, the director of the Secure Society Program at the W. Alton Jones Foundation in Charlottesville, Virginia.

The assistance and cooperation of a range of other individuals and organizations made this project possible. Two individuals deserve particular mention for their unstinting efforts to organize the meetings in New Delhi and Islamabad, at which early drafts of this book's chapters were presented as papers: Rajesh Rajagopalan, a Ph.D. candidate in the Department of Political Science at the City University of New York, and Nazir Husain, Assistant Professor of International Relations at Quaid-i-Azam University in Islamabad. We are grateful for the assistance, with a myriad of issues from arranging visas to providing background briefings, provided by Indian and Pakistani consulates in New York City, the Ministries of External and Home Affairs in New Delhi, the Ministry of Foreign Affairs in Islamabad, and the Inter Services Public Relations (ISPR) bureau of the Pakistan army in Lahore. Finally, without the tireless efforts of Traci Nagle, this book would not have been completed. To her our heartfelt thanks.

Šumit Ganguly
Ted Greenwood

Mending Fences

Introduction: The Role and Prospects of CSBMs in South Asia

Šumit Ganguly and Ted Greenwood

Few regions of the world have been as unaffected by the end of the cold war as South Asia. The region was rife with intrastate[1] violence and fraught with the possibilities and all too often the reality of interstate violence while the cold war raged around it; the same is true today. During the twenty-five years immediately after British India gave birth to the independent states of India and Pakistan, South Asia witnessed four interstate wars—three between India and Pakistan (1947–48, 1965 and 1971) and one between India and China (1962). Since then, there have been no further wars, but confrontations, crises, incidents, and low-level interstate violence have been intermittent from 1947 to the present.

Sino-Indian relations remained strained from the 1962 war until recently. During the 1965 Indo-Pakistani conflict, for example, the People's Republic of China (PRC) issued an ultimatum to India threatening offensive action unless it dismantled certain fortifications along the Sino-Indian border and returned several hundred sheep and a certain number of yaks that had been putatively misappropriated.[2] In 1967 India and China exchanged artillery barrages for several days at the strategic Nathu La pass. On the Himalayan front, a border clash between Indian and Chinese forces at Sumdurong Chu near the Nepal, India, and Bhutan trijunction in 1986 nearly precipitated a larger crisis.[3]

Several crises have also punctuated Indo-Pakistani relations. The most notable recent ones arose from mutual misperceptions of intent stemming from Indo-Pakistani military exercises in 1987 and India's concerns over Pakistan's support for the insurgency in the Indian-held portion of Kashmir in 1990.[4]

Despite this dismal history of conflict and discord, the Sino-Indian and Indo-Pakistani relationships have not been bereft of cooperative efforts and endeavors. Both Indian and Pakistani armed forces observed tacit and explicit constraints on the extent and targets of their attacks during all three Indo-Pakistani conflicts. Both sides did not bomb population centers, avoided attacking irrigation facilities such as dams and barrages and, more generally, limited the use of air power in certain contexts. Furthermore, they adhered to the Geneva Conventions in the treatment of prisoners of war despite the popular passions that surrounded the conflicts.

Given this history of both conflict and cooperation, can the adoption of confidence-and security-building measures (CSBMs)[5] that have been used successfully in other regional contexts have any relevance to the situation in South Asia? That is the central question on which this volume is intended to shed light. CSBMs are devices that are designed to serve one or more of four purposes: 1) providing mutual security pledges; 2) providing transparency between the military establishments of hostile states in order to reduce the possibilities of inadvertent conflict and to provide warning of and thereby deter impending attack; 3) managing dangerous and potentially dangerous military activities; and 4) crisis management.

In the early to mid-1990s the Indo-Pakistani relationship became particularly acrimonious following the sudden eruption of secessionist sentiment in Kashmir in 1989. Yet following the 1990 crisis, in the wake of U.S. Deputy National Security Adviser Robert Gates's mission to both capitals, New Delhi and Islamabad proceeded to develop a series of CSBMs. Among other matters, they agreed to prevent airspace violations, to engage in regular consultations on a pre-existing "hotline" between their directors-general of military operations, to provide prior notification of military exercises, and not to attack designated nuclear facilities. They also issued a declaration banning the use, production, and stockpiling of chemical weapons and agreeing not to assist others to acquire such weapons.[6]

In the Sino-Indian context, after a decade of careful negotiations, the two sides signed a range of CSBM agreements in September 1993 designed to limit the possibilities of inadvertent conflict along the Sino-Indian border. Among other issues covered in the agreements were prior notification of troop movements along the border, the establishment of hotlines between local commanders, and periodic meetings of military officials along the border. Furthermore, India unilaterally moved two mountain divisions away from the northeastern sector of the Sino-Indian border. More recently, despite their continuing border dispute, India and China are considering expanding their relations in a number of other areas, including defense cooperation.[7]

CSBMs cannot serve in South Asia, any more than elsewhere, as substitutes for tackling underlying sources of conflict. They are also of limited value when states deliberately choose to go to war. Nevertheless, as the experiences of and evidence from other regions of the world have shown, CSBMs can provide the psychological benefit of increasing confidence, where it is justified, and can improve security by helping prevent unintended or accidental conflict and by strengthening deterrence by ensuring that a party about to be attacked receives enough warning to be able to defend or attack preemptively. As a result, CSBMs can also help create a climate of expectations more conducive to the conduct of negotiations of underlying issues and to normal interstate relations.

The differences between India and Pakistan and those between India and the PRC, in all likelihood, can only be resolved through sustained negotiations leading to carefully crafted political compromises. Until such compromises are achieved, however, the insights gained from other regions' employment of CSBMs can to some extent be utilized in the South Asian context to improve security, to ease the psychological burden of continuing disharmony, and even to help create an environment in which fruitful negotiations can occur. Cognizance must always be given, but CSBMs usually tend toward stabilization of the status quo and therefore are likely to be less attractive to revisionist than to status quo states.

Review of Literature

A small but growing body of literature exists on the role and utility of CSBMs in South Asia. A brief review of this literature is in order before proceeding to a discussion of the findings of the present study.

United Nations conferences and publications on CSBMs are most memorable for having drawn the attention of governments and academic specialists to the possibility that confidence-and security-building measures developed primarily in the U.S.-Soviet and European contexts, but also in other regional contexts, might be usefully applied in other regions of the world and to naval forces.[8] The papers are of mixed quality and tend to be either purely historical or prospectively exhortatory, but are generally light on analysis.

All three studies produced by the Stimson Center are useful but necessarily limited in scope.[9] A. G. Noorani's analysis of three contentious issues in Indo-Pakistani relations—the Siachen Glacier, Sir Creek, and the Wular Barrage disputes—is historically sound. However, it is also extremely legalistic. Above all, it carefully analyzes the disputes but does not propose viable CSBMs for alleviating them. Nor is it entirely clear, based upon his own analysis, that these disputes, with the possible exception of the Siachen Glacier conflict, are amenable to resolution through the uses of CSBMs.

Michael Krepon and Mishi Faruquee's carefully edited transcript of a discussion of senior American officials who were involved in attempts to resolve the 1990 crisis between India and Pakistan points to the crying necessity for CSBMs in the region. Although not an analysis of the crisis, it is nevertheless an extremely useful form of oral history.

Pervez Hoodbhoy's study dwells upon the possibilities of CSBMs in the nuclear arena. Hoodbhoy questions the robustness of deterrence as a strategy in general. More specifically, he casts doubts on the reliability of command and control of nuclear weapons in the region. However, he recognizes the enormous political hurdles in both India and Pakistan in terms of proceeding towards denuclearization. Accordingly, he suggests that Pakistan maintain its current posture of "nuclear ambiguity." Simultaneously, he argues for the development of a more robust system of command and control over the existing nuclear forces in the region. Additionally, he exhorts the decision makers in India, Pakistan, and China to consider a possible deployment ban on intermediate range ballistic missiles.

Moonis Ahmar's paper is an attempt to draw lessons from European CSBMs and apply them within the historical and cultural context of South Asia.[10] However, it ends up being a combination of wishful thinking and the claim that small steps toward CSBMs cannot be taken without first solving the underlying political problems. As a result, it is not very helpful in a practical sense for those who believe that incremental progress in complex situations is better than none.

John Sandrock and Michael Maldony's study provides a careful recapitulation of all the CSBMs and their precursors in South Asia along with useful commentaries.[11] It is particularly useful as a readily accessible compendium.

A multi-authored study by Bajpai et al. of the 1987 Indian military exercise Brasstacks and its consequences in the subcontinent, though not explicitly focused on CSBMs, has some relevance to the topic at hand.[12] This study, the first of its kind, attempts to trace the origins, evolution, and ultimate resolution of the 1987 Brasstacks crisis. Its relevance lies in that it clearly underscores the important role that a range of CSBMs could play in preventing future crises in South Asia.

Finally, Raju G. C. Thomas's study of South Asian security in the 1990s is conspicuous in its failure to discuss the possible role of CSBMs in promoting security and stability in the subcontinent.[13]

What This Study Adds

One thing that has not been previously available in the literature is a realistic appraisal of the limitations and possible values of CSBMs in South Asia that both draws from the experience elsewhere—notably the U.S.-Soviet, European, and Middle Eastern contexts—and considers the actual historical and political context of South Asia as it is found today, not as authors would wish it to be. This volume fills that void. It begins with a systematic treatment of the security contexts as seen from India, Pakistan and China and adds a speculative chapter that asks what, if anything, might have been different in the past if CSBMs had been in place in the years of the region's major conflicts. The experience of CSBMs in the U.S.-Soviet relationship, in Europe, and in the Middle East are treated next, with explicit efforts to draw lessons for South Asia. Finally, each of the four categories of CSBMs are examined in turn to assess the potential value and limitations of each for the Sino-Indian and Indo-Pakistani relationships. Along the way, the special issues related to the gradually emerging nuclear capabilities of India and Pakistan are addressed.

Lessons Learned

What broad propositions can we derive from our study? A number of issues, of varying significance, emerge. To begin with, CSBMs are easier to accomplish among countries that recognize the legitimacy of each other's existence and territorial integrity and are therefore willing to talk with each other, and when borders have at least a de facto acceptance. For example, the countries of South Asia, for all their disputes and conflicts, have never questioned the legitimacy of each other's existence and have been willing to talk with each other about security issues as well as other items on the usually interstate agenda. (In the view of some Pakistanis, among them Shireen Mazari, the author of chapter 2, some groups within Indian society still have not accepted the legitimacy of the Pakistani state. This is not a widely accepted view, however.) As Mark Heller's paper emphasizes, this fact, although often taken for granted in South Asia, as it was in Europe, is of utmost importance. The same is true for acceptance of territorial integrity. Long before Rajiv Gandhi launched his China initiative in December 1988 the Chinese had stopped supporting the Mizo and Naga rebels in northeastern India. By the same token, during Rajiv Gandhi's visit to Beijing he unequivocally reaffirmed India's position that Tibet is an "integral part of China."

With respect to borders, although that between China and India remains in dispute, neither side is likely to resort to force to change the de facto line of control. The Chinese achieved their territorial objectives in the 1962 war. India, though obviously distressed with that outcome, has for all practical purposes abjured its territorial claims. Consequently, both sides find it expedient to pursue a series of CSBMs to avoid inadvertent conflict, even as a final resolution continues to be postponed. The Sino-Indian accords of September 1993 in effect signified the willingness of both sides to place their border dispute into indefinite cold storage.[14] The contrast between this and the Indo-Pakistan case is clear. The line of actual control in Kashmir has not been accepted either de facto or de jure. Hence the slower progress toward meaningful CSBMs in the latter case.

A corollary proposition is that CSBMs become easier to achieve as the threat of war recedes. Again, the Sino-Indian case is apposite. In 1986, owing to an Indian "limited probe" at Sumdurong Chu near the Nepal-Bhutan-India trijunction, the two antagonists almost stumbled into another full-scale conflict, which neither side wanted or was prepared to accept.[15] Military-to-military discussions were initiated after the Sumdurong Chu episode and the dangers of inadvertent conflict have been substantially reduced. As the willingness to accept war between them and therefore the threat of war receded, India and China have gradually adopted more extensive CSBMs with the intent of averting both planned and inadvertent conflict and of increasing confidence on both sides that this mind-set will endure. The India-Pakistan case illustrates the same point: Only with the de facto nuclearization of South Asia has war between India and Pakistan become virtually unthinkable. Hence, the ability to make small progress toward CSBMs in recent years.

A related proposition is that it is possible to achieve meaningful CSBMs between potentially hostile states without first having resolved the underlying issues. This has been true between the United States and Soviet Union, in Europe and, to some degree, even in the Middle East. There is no reason to think that it could not be true also in South Asia. Indeed, the CSBMs already agreed to between India and Pakistan, despite the continuing dispute over Kashmir, and between India and China, despite conflicting territorial claims along the border, attest to that point. But how far the development of CSBMs can go while underlying issues remain unresolved and the degree to which the existence and evolution of CSBMs can contribute to a readiness to reach accommodations on larger issues remains to be seen. To the extent that the U.S.-Soviet and European cases provide relevant guidance, we would be tempted to speculate that the answers would be quite far and to a considerable degree. It is this possibility, of course, that helps make CSBMs in South Asia a subject of great contemporary interest.

Contrary to the assertions of some, though by no means all, regional analysts and policy makers, we find that external actors can sometimes play a catalytic role in promoting CSBMs. The significance of Robert Gates's mission to New Delhi and Islamabad in dampening the 1990 crisis may well be contestable. However, a number of CSBMs between India and Pakistan were agreed upon following the Gates mission.

In a similar vein, the South Asian experience with CSBMs is not *sui generis*. All the three nations embroiled in conflicts—India, Pakistan, and China—are cognizant of developments in other regions of the world and have been quite willing to draw on experience elsewhere when doing so has seemed appropriate. Otherwise, even the limited number of CSBMs in the Indo-Pakistani context and the more extensive array along the Sino-Indian border would not likely have emerged so quickly and at least some of them might have had a different character.

As with most aspects of foreign and defense policy, policy makers' considerations of CSBMs cannot be unconstrained by the vagaries of domestic politics. Presently, the weak regime of Prime Minister Benazir Bhutto perceives little or no advantage in pursuing additional CSBMs with India. Her political opposition would promptly seize upon any attempt to engage in dialogue with India and portray it as pusillanimity. Similarly, the widespread belief in India that Pakistan is aiding and abetting the Kashmiri insurgents in their undiminishing struggle to be freed from India, and the high cost to India of containing this insurgency, are constraining India from moving too far or too fast with additional CSBMs.

Civil-military relations are markedly different in India, Pakistan, and China. In India, owing to a well-established democratic tradition, there is firm civilian control over the military. In Pakistan, however, despite the return of democracy, the military has emerged as one of the three centers of political power along with the elected representatives and the civilian bureaucracy.[16] In China, the power and preservation of the ruling oligarchy continues to depend heavily on support from the military. Despite these differences, the military establishments of all three states wield considerable influence in the pursuit of CSBMs. Unless the professional military is convinced of the utility of CSBMs, they will not be agreed and implemented. For example, the Indian military has been more than willing to steadily expand the range of CSBMs with their Chinese counterparts. Both military establishments see distinct advantages in pursuing CSBMs. The Chinese military are reassured that India will not seek to foment trouble in Tibet or its environs. The Indian military, by the same token, can better deploy its limited resources in Kashmir and elsewhere for internal security duties. A similar willingness has not been demonstrated with regard to Pakistan, however. The overall conflictual nature of Indo-Pakistani relations does not provide either military establishment enough incentives for reducing the present scope of armed conflict on the Siachen Glacier. The costs of maintaining forces in this inhospitable terrain are seen as tolerable by both sides.

Although no aspect of creating CSBMs is easy, institutional arrangements appear to be the most difficult to accomplish and, more importantly, to sustain. In the Sino-Indian case, efforts were made in the border talks to improve relations on a spectrum of issues with varying degrees of success. The Joint Working Group (JWG) was created only after nine rounds of talks had taken place and in the wake of a major political initiative, Rajiv Gandhi's visit to the PRC. Although, contrary to the initial intention, the JWG has not always been central to the creation or implementation of CSBMs. Nevertheless, so far it has continued to function meaningfully. In contrast, the Indo-Pakistani Joint Commission, a CSBM-like structure empowered to deal with a range of issues, is in desuetude owing to the precipitous decline in Indo-Pakistani relations since 1989.[17]

The South Asian Association for Regional Cooperation (SAARC) has played no role to date in the development of CSBMs. At one level this is because, so far, all CSBMs in South Asia have been bilateral and SAARC's charter states that no "bilateral and contentious" issues will be discussed under the aegis of SAARC. Of course, at another level, SAARC could be used for discussion of multilateral CSBMs, if states found those attractive, and the charter could be changed if the states involved thought that SAARC could be helpful with bilateral CSBMs. Either the states involved do not think SAARC could be useful or they fear opening up a debate on whether CSBMs in South Asia should continue to be solely bilateral or take on a more multilateral, regional character.

This leads directly to the final proposition worth emphasizing here. The reason CSBMS have not been attempted at a regional level in South Asia, despite the proposals by many analysts do so, is simple: India, the principal power in the region, prefers to conduct its relations with its neighbors along bilateral lines, so as to use its size and power to greatest advantage. Moreover, the interests and concerns of the other major players, namely Pakistan and China, have not been sufficiently parallel to give them any incentive to work in common cause to build CSBMs with India.

Future Directions

The results of this study are certainly sobering. It is important to note, however, that in the Sino-Indian relationship CSBMs have already made a small but meaningful difference. This is much less true in the Indo-Pakistani context. There, the agreements have been very limited and only fitfully or half-heartedly implemented.

Despite this decidedly mixed record, CSBMs are emerging in South Asia during the 1990s as a middle course between using force and resolving fundamental issues. Absent a willingness to resolve fundamental issues, such as the future and Kashmir and the Sino-Indian border, and reluctant to use force in a nuclearized South Asia, India and China and, to a lesser degree, India and Pakistan have now chosen bilateral CSBMs almost by default as their preferred approach to conflict resolution. Although Šumit Ganguly's historical analysis in chapter 4 suggests that the existence of CSBMs would have been of little to no value in avoiding past conflict, this might not be the case for future conflicts. By appropriately expanding the nascent network of bilateral CSBMs, the three largest states of South Asia could probably improve their security, increase their confidence in that security, foster a climate of expectations more conducive to normal interstate relations, and perhaps eventually become willing to negotiate resolutions to the fundamental issues that divide them. The analyses in the succeeding chapters suggest, in each of the four categories of CSBMs, which might be most appropriate for the near-to-medium term.

Mutual security pledges are neither necessary as a basis for making progress in other areas nor sufficient to resolve the security problems of South Asia. Nonetheless, they can contribute to both. The Simla Agreement, although an existing mutual security pledge between India and Pakistan, should not be given much credence. Not only is it interpreted quite differently by the two countries and did not prevent two major crises in 1987 and 1990, but Pakistan also regards it as illegitimate, having been forced to sign it after losing the 1971 war. The Indo-Pakistani agreements not to attack each other's declared nuclear facilities and to refrain from obtaining chemical weapons are likely to be more useful. Neither goes as far, however, as the Sino-Indian pledge that outstanding border issues would be solved only by peaceful means and, in the meantime, to respect the line of actual control. Although, as a revisionist power, Pakistan should not be expected to agree easily to a mutual pledge with India to refrain from the use or threat of force to settle outstanding issues, such a mutual security pledge would probably provide as great an assurance as is possible in still-volatile South Asia. Of less but still considerable value would be mutual pledges between India and Pakistan and between India and China not to be the first to use nuclear weapons against the other. The reluctance of India and Pakistan to acknowledge fully their nuclear weapons capabilities need not be a significant impediment here. Diplomats in both countries are surely up to the task of finding a formulation of such a pledge that would not require either side to acknowledge what it prefers to leave ambiguous. Whether the nuclearization of India and Pakistan can be reversed or halted through joint accession to the Nuclear Nonproliferation Treaty or by some other means of mutually eschewing nuclear weapons, or even whether their mutual security would be best served by this course, are matters on which our authors disagree.

Transparency measures can enhance deterrence and lengthen warning times of hostile intentions, thus enhancing security, and can reassure potential enemies that the other is not preparing for war or coercive military action, thus enhancing confidence. Because of these dual functions, transparency measures might be the most useful CSBMs. Some requirements now exist for prior notification of military exercises along the Indo-Pakistani and Sino-Indian borders, and regular, although limited, military-to-military contacts are required. China and India even exchange information about military positions along their line of actual control. These are all useful initial steps. A longer period for advanced notification, publication of an annual calendar of exercises, enlargement of the set of exercises requiring advanced notification, and advanced notice of all troop movements would all be useful extensions of current agreements. Inviting observers to witness exercises and expanding military-to-military contacts through exchange visits of senior strategists and planners and cross-attendance at military training institutions would further enhance transparency. So would fuller disclosure of military budgets, weapons inventories and purchases, force deployments, and construction of militarily relevant infrastructure, especially by Pakistan and China. Open-skies agreements, allowing reconnaissance overflights of each other's territory, would be an extremely useful transparency CSBM, but are unlikely to be agreed upon any time soon.

So long as mutual suspicions and the level of military activity at sea or along mutual borders and lines of actual control are high, agreements to manage dangerous and potentially dangerous military activities and accidents would be beneficial to all. Some beginnings have been made in the area of overflights and accidental air intrusions between both India and China and India and Pakistan. Also useful would be naval agreements regulating activities by the growing Indian and Chinese navies that might be regarded as hostile or threatening, agreements not to test missiles in the direction of another country, and agreements to prevent and limit the consequences of nuclear accidents.

For crisis management, some hotline communications exist between ground force headquarters and, in some instances, local commanders, but not yet between air force headquarters or between senior political authorities. Moreover, the communication mode in currently voice rather than text, which is less susceptible to misinterpretation and hasty judgment. The mechanisms now in place to prevent and mitigate crises along the Sino-Indian line of actual control could productively be carried over to the Indo-Pakistani relationship. However, this is unlikely to happen until, if ever, both sides are willing to accept this line as a de facto international border, as India and China essentially have. Pulling forces back from or limiting the size of force deployments and the types of weapons allowed along the lines of actual control would also be highly valuable crisis management CSBMs. Some progress in these areas has been made between India and China, but not yet between India and Pakistan. As the existence of nuclear capability gradually infuses thinking about South Asian security, ways should be found to avoid any state from having an incentive to launch a preemptive attack. This implies that each country should assure the others that its nuclear assets are neither excessively vulnerable nor capable of independent initiative outside of political control. There is much room here for unilateral action. However, mutual agreements through CSBMs might also be useful and feasible to a limited extent.

Notes

1. The many examples of intrastate violence will not be considered in this volume except where, as in the case of Kashmir, they had significant implications for actual or potential interstate violence.

2. Šumit Ganguly, *The Origins of War in South Asia*, 2nd ed. (Boulder, Co.: Westview, 1994).

3. Šumit Ganguly, "The Sino-Indian Border Talks, 1981–1989: A View from New Delhi," *Asian Survey* 29, no. 12 (December 1989), pp. 1123–35.

4. Šumit Ganguly, "Avoiding War in Kashmir," *Foreign Affairs* 69, no. 5 (winter 1990/91), pp. 57–73.

5. The earlier concept of confidence-building measures, of which Johan Joergen Holst, the late Norwegian foreign minister, is widely considered the progenitor, refers to measures that bolster the confidence that states have that other states are not intending or preparing to attack them. These do not necessarily improve the objective security of states, however. The now-common term "confidence- and security-building measures" is broader in its meaning. It includes measures that both bolster states' confidence *and* improve their objective security. It is this broader term that we will employ throughout this volume.

6. Bureau of South Asian Affairs, *The President's Report to Congress on Progress towards Nonproliferation in South Asia*, (Washington, D.C.: U.S. Department of State, April 1993).

7. Centre for Defence Studies, *International Security Digest* 1, no. 9 (August 1994).

8. The Department of Disarmament Affairs of the United Nations was among the first to focus attention on the possible utility of confidence- and security-building measures in regions of conflict where they had not yet been tried. Meetings were held in Kathmandu, Nepal, in January 1990 and Vienna, Austria, in February 1991. The published results of these meetings are, respectively, United Nations, Department of Disarmament Affairs, *Disarmament: Confidence and Security-Building Measures in Asia* (New York: United Nations, 1990); and United Nations, Department of Disarmament Affairs, *Confidence and Security-Building Measures: From Europe to Other Regions*, Disarmament Topical Paper 7 (New York: United Nations, 1991). Also see United Nations, Department of Disarmament Affairs, *Naval Confidence-building Measures*, Disarmament Topical Paper 4 (New York: United Nations, 1990); and Augustine P. Mahiga and Fidelis M. Nji, *Confidence-Building Measures in Africa* (New York: United Nations Institute for Disarmament Research, 1987).

9. The Henry L. Stimson Center in Washington, D.C., has published a series of monographs focused on CSBMs in South Asia. See A. G. Noorani, "Easing the Indo-Pakistani Dialogues on Kashmir: Confidence-Building Measures for the Siachen Glacier, Sir Creek, and the Wular Barrage Disputes," Occasional Paper no. 16 (April 1994); Michael Krepon and Mishi Faruqee (eds.), "Conflict Prevention and Confidence-Building Measures in South Asia: The 1990 Crisis," Occasional Paper no. 17 (April 1994); and Pervez Hoodbhoy, "Nuclear Issues Between India and Pakistan: Myths and Realities," Occasional Paper no. 18 (July 1994).

10. Moonis Ahmar, "Confidence-Building Measures in South Asia," PSIS Occasional Paper no. 3/1991 (Geneva: Program for Strategic and International Security Studies, 1991).

11. John H. Sandrock and Michael Maldony, "The History and Future of Confidence Building Measures in South Asia," background paper prepared for the U.S. Arms Control and Disarmament Agency, Science Applications International Corporation, McLean, Va., November 1994.

12. K. P. Bajpai, P. R. Chari, P. I. Cheema, S. P. Cohen, and Š. Ganguly, *Brasstacks and Beyond: Perception and Management of Crisis in South Asia* (New Delhi: Manohar, 1995).

13. Raju G. C. Thomas, *South Asian Security in the 1990s,* Adelphi Paper 278 (London: International Institute of Strategic Studies, 1993).

14. Šumit Ganguly, *Slouching Towards a Settlement: Sino-Indian Relations, 1962–1993,* Asia Program Occasional Paper no. 60 (Washington, D.C.: Woodrow Wilson International Center for Scholars, 1994).

15. Šumit Ganguly, "The Sino-Indian Border Talks."

16. Kanti Bajpai and Šumit Ganguly, "The Transition to Democracy in Pakistan," *In-Depth,* spring 1993, pp. 59–86.

17. Sandrock and Maldony, "The History and Future of Confidence-Building Measures in South Asia."

PART ONE

The Record of Conflict

1

Conflict, Cooperation, and CSBMs with Pakistan and China: A View from New Delhi

Kanti P. Bajpai

The end of the cold war has brought far-reaching changes in the international system, and has altered relationships and alliances in southern Asia. Nonetheless, India, Pakistan, and China continue to form a security complex, and many of their conflicts remain unresolved.[1] Throughout the cold war, conflict notwithstanding—and indeed as a function of past, present, and future conflict—the Indo-Pakistani and Sino-Indian relationships have featured cooperative efforts, episodes, trends, and real agreements. Cooperation in the 1980s and after the cold war has included a process of confidence-building. Confidence- and security-building measures (CSBMs), as explicit instruments for stabilizing military rivalries, have gained currency since the early 1970s, when they began to be discussed and deployed in Europe between cold war adversaries. Particularly since 1990, India, Pakistan, and China have used CSBMs as instruments for stabilizing, softening, and perhaps even terminating their own cold wars, and thus have avoided costly shooting wars.

States do not turn to measures such as CSBMs without analyzing the nature of conflict and cooperation with an adversary and how patterns of conflict and cooperation may be an incentive for stabilizing measures. This chapter will attempt to present India's view of its conflict and cooperation with Pakistan and China and to show how, by 1990, that view was hospitable to a CSBM process with both adversaries. The first two sections of this chapter will deal with New Delhi's record and view of conflict and cooperation with Islamabad and Beijing; the third section will ask why a CSBM process has become salient as an alternative or a supplement to other modes of conflict resolution, both cooperative and non-cooperative.

New Delhi sees Pakistan and China as "brother enemies"—potentially fraternal partners, but, by circumstance and choice, dangerous antagonists.[2] Both relationships have been marked by conflict culminating in war and by attempts to cooperate and avoid war. Indian policymakers see more conflict than cooperation, and war looms larger than the avoidance of war in New Delhi's memory. Indians also see an asymmetry in each relationship: Pakistan and China are more guilty than India of causing conflict and war, and India has more often offered cooperation and war-avoidance. There is little official admission of Indian culpability except as an acknowledgment that Indian gullibility or ineptitude led Pakistan and China to provoke war. This attitude has changed somewhat over the past five years, however. India's two massive military exercises in 1986–87, the Sumdurong Chu episodes with China, and the 1990 crisis with Pakistan heightened tensions with both rivals. These episodes have had a sobering effect on India's attitude and have raised questions about Indian responsibility, whether advertent or inadvertent, for provoking regional instability.

Indo-Pakistani Conflict and Cooperation

The record of conflict between India and Pakistan is long and continuous, and ranges over various issues. New Delhi's general view of this conflict can be summarized in the following propositions: first, as noted already, Pakistan, is the instigator of conflict and the user of force; second, Pakistan has stoked and abetted irredentist feeling in its portion of Kashmir, attempted to subvert Indian Kashmir, and used force to try to "liberate" Kashmir; third, in seeking parity with India Pakistan overreaches itself, thus leading to conflict and even war; fourth, outsiders—the United States, China, and various Muslim states—have for varying reasons contributed to Pakistan's quest for parity and in doing so have fueled conflict in South Asia; and fifth, the vulnerabilities and insecurities of Pakistani governments cause Islamabad to seek confrontation with India as a distraction from internal failings.

Despite their history of conflict, India and Pakistan do have a record of cooperation. New Delhi's view of cooperation is in large measure the obverse of its view of conflict: first, India, not Pakistan, instigates cooperation and is taken advantage of when it does so; second, although Pakistan may cooperate on lesser issues, it does not want to do so on Kashmir, partly because of the vulnerabilities of domestic politics; third, moments of cooperation are not a function of parity but of the extent to which India and Pakistan are intertwined in functional and economic areas; fourth, cooperation is more likely if it is pursued bilaterally rather than through the intervention of outside agencies or powers; and fifth, full cooperation and peace will occur only when Pakistan becomes stable, secular, and democratic, roughly in India's image.[3]

Given this as New Delhi's general view of conflict and cooperation, what are the specific conflicts and what cooperative efforts, episodes, trends, and agreements did these conflicts give rise to? A review of the record of conflict and cooperation shows that the two countries solved all of their disputes bar Kashmir by 1960; that from the point of view of India, the 1965 and 1971 wars "solved" even Kashmir, so that by 1972 the probability of war was sharply reduced; that thereafter, a number of tensions and disputes surfaced and intensified, so that since 1980 Indo-Pakistani relations have been at their worst and war once again has seemed a distinct possibility; and that the 1990s will feature the same disputes and tensions of the 1980s with one addition: a growing realization that nuclear and conventional capabilities on both sides, along with economic stagnation and debt, make war too costly a solution to those disputes.

The First Long Peace: 1948–65[4]

After partition, a number of disputes arose between India and Pakistan. These disputes covered a broad range of territorial, hydrological, economic, and political issues. Borders between the two countries had to be delineated. Agreements had to be reached about the sharing and development of the massive Indus rivers system, which was of great material importance to agriculture in both the Indian and the Pakistani Punjab. The remaining official assets from before partition had to be transferred. Each country had experienced an enormous influx of refugees from the other, and plans for compensating those refugees for property and other assets left behind had to be developed. Finally, and ironically given the fact of partition, the status and treatment of religious minorities in both states had to be normalized.

Contrary to the vision that the Indo-Pakistani relationship has been one of unremitting hostility, there were moments of cooperation. Over the seventeen years following the first Indo-Pakistani war, almost all of the conflicts that arose were approached cooperatively and solved cooperatively. Agreement was reached on refugee compensation (1950), the transfer of official assets (1948), and the position of minority communities (April 1950). In 1958, 1959, 1960, and 1963, the two countries settled territorial claims along the eastern and western borders. Negotiations were begun on the rationalization of borders and on the sharing of the Indus rivers; in 1960, with the help of the World Bank, they reached an agreement.[5]

The most troublesome disputes between India and Pakistan arose over the accession of some of the princely states. The accessions of Junagadh and Hyderabad were solved by 1948, when both were forcibly integrated into India. The fate of the state of Jammu and Kashmir, however, would not be solved so quickly. Almost immediately after partition, India and Pakistan had gone to war over Kashmir; the war ended with two-thirds of the state under Indian control and one-third controlled by Pakistan. The Kashmir dispute remains unresolved to this day, although not for lack of effort, and indeed the two sides came close to success. After the UN-aided cease-fire in 1948, multilateral efforts to solve Kashmir began at the request of New Delhi. Early UN efforts were unsuccessful, but in March 1950 India and Pakistan agreed to demilitarize Kashmir, hold a plebiscite, and continue with mediation. India began to make arrangements for the plebiscite, but when in February 1954 the United States announced military assistance to Pakistan, India moved away from the idea of a plebiscite and toward integration of the state with the rest of the Union. Bilateral negotiations continued. In 1956, when a solution again seemed close, Pakistan, fearing domestic protest, drew back. One final plan was rejected by India in 1958. This more or less brought to an end the UN's role in solving Kashmir.[6]

Attempts to find a solution continued. In January 1962 when Pakistan raised the issue in the UN, India agreed to bilateral—not UN-brokered—negotiations on all issues. After the Sino-Indian war in November 1962, India and Pakistan came under increasing U.S. and British pressure to make a deal on Kashmir. In 1963, the two met to discuss the issue but failed to reach agreement. In retrospect, this may have been another turning point: two years later, in early 1965, skirmishes broke out in the Rann of Kutch, an innocuous stretch of territory on the Gujarat-Sindh border. Although British mediation in March 1965 initially seemed to have stopped the drift to war, in September, partly as a result of the Rann episode, the second Kashmir war broke out.[7]

Punctuating the numerous exchanges on Kashmir were a series of attempts to negotiate a no-war/common defense pact (1949–50, 1953, 1956, 1959). In general, India sought no-war pacts as a means of stabilization, and Pakistan countered with offers of common defense. Pakistan rejected no-war pacts on the grounds that these would not solve the fundamental quarrel, which increasingly was Kashmir. India rejected common defense agreements out of fear that they would compromise non-alignment and embroil New Delhi in the cold war.[8]

From 1948 to the outbreak of war in 1965, then, conflicts between India and Pakistan related to the division of the subcontinent. Surprisingly, given the bitterness of partition, the extent of communal violence at independence, and the 1948 war over Kashmir, a substantial number of conflicts were solved the major exception being Kashmir. Nevertheless, one might suggest that by the early 1960s Kashmir had been solved to India's satisfaction: India had most of the state, including the Vale, and, at least constitutionally, Kashmir was increasingly integrated with the rest of India.

Postbellum Order-Building: 1966–71 and 1972–74

After the 1965 war, a number of issues relating to a post-bellum order were settled. Yet even as these were settled and a normalization process was set in motion, India and Pakistan found themselves in a crisis over developments in East Pakistan. By December 1971, the crisis had degraded into another war. India's victory brought the two sides back to negotiating a post-bellum order.

1966–71 The 1965 war had ended in stalemate, after which the United Nations, the United States, and Great Britain forced New Delhi and Islamabad to agree to a cease-fire. India could console itself on three counts, however: Pakistan had failed to get Kashmir; the lack of enthusiasm among Indian Kashmiris for the Pakistani attempt to win Kashmir seemed to indicate that the integration of the state, politically and psychologically, had proceeded further than many thought; and the Soviet-brokered Tashkent agreement (1966) formalized the end of the war but had not challenged New Delhi's control of its part of Kashmir. In addition, while Pakistan did not unequivocally abjure the use of force to settle Kashmir, India managed to avoid any sort of commitment to hold a plebiscite.

With the status quo on Kashmir assured, New Delhi once again initiated discussion on a no-war agreement (1968, 1969), again with no success. The Rann of Kutch issue—the precursor to the 1965 war—was solved through arbitration by the International Court of Justice (ICJ).[9]

In sum, as the two states closed out the decade, only the Kashmir problem remained. But even here, India could be reasonably satisfied: two wars had failed to resolve the dispute in favor of Pakistan.

1971–74 With Kashmir suspended, the focus of conflict unexpectedly shifted. Internal conflict in Pakistan headed the region toward war. The increasing unpopularity of the military dictatorship and economic problems were exacerbated by restiveness in East Pakistan. Civil war ensued. From New Delhi's point of view, the Pakistani government's response to demands for autonomy in East Pakistan was both a threat and an opportunity. The spillover of refugees and freedom fighters from East Pakistan posed a number of threats—demographic, economic, ethnic, and political—to the already-fragile Indian northeast.[10] But the civil war was also an opportunity to defeat Pakistan militarily and ideologically.

The war of December 1971 cut Pakistan in half and created a friendly state to India's east. India felt that its victory was two-fold. It had made the point that Islam could not be the basis of nationhood. But it had also bolstered its own position on the remaining dispute with Pakistan; if Pakistan could not stay together on the basis of Islam, surely the case for Kashmiri accession to Pakistan was weakened.[11]

After the 1971 war, a number of agreements were worked out relating to the post-bellum regional order. The Simla Accord (1972) affirmed two important principles: that neither party would use force to settle their disputes, and that Kashmir would be solved bilaterally.[12] More concretely, the two sides reached agreement on the release of and charges against Pakistani prisoners-of-war, as well as on Islamabad's recognition of Bangladesh (1974). New Delhi also got various subsidiary agreements on a more normalized relationship, which had been interrupted by the 1965 war. Ambassadorial-level representation, trade, travel, and communications were to be resumed. In November 1974, the two sides agreed to lift mutual trade embargoes and extend "most favored nation" status to each other.

The Second Long Peace: 1975–92

With a post-bellum regional order in place, South Asia embarked on what can be regarded as a second long peace, marked by three phases. The first phase, 1975–79, was a positive, mostly cooperative one, although by 1975 various problems were beginning to complicate relations. The second phase, 1980–89, saw stabilizing efforts struggle against growing conflict. The third phase, after the cold war, thus far shows mostly continuities with the preceding period despite structural changes at the global level, with one discontinuity: war appears increasingly unviable.

1975–79 At the very moment of post-bellum success, New Delhi confronted a new dispute, one that was symptomatic rather than central, but which acquired a life of its own: the nuclearization of the subcontinent. India's "peaceful nuclear explosion" (PNE) of 1974 led Pakistan directly to accelerate its own program. To ease Pakistani fears, New Delhi offered to sign a non-aggression treaty or enter into other security arrangements. Pakistani responded with the idea of a nuclear-weapons-free zone for South Asia (NWFZSA). This proposal was approved by the United Nations, and Islamabad has proposed and won passage of an NWFZSA resolution at the world body every year since 1974. India has consistently rejected NWFZSA on the grounds that it would address neither vertical proliferation nor Chinese weapons.[13]

After India's PNE and the initial attempts to deal with it, Pakistan offered a series of proposals, including a joint declaration renouncing nuclear weapons (1978), mutual inspection of nuclear facilities (1979), simultaneous accession to the Nuclear Nonproliferation Treaty (NPT) (1979), and simultaneous acceptance of IAEA safeguards (1979). India ignored or rejected all these proposals, primarily on the grounds that they were propagandistic, lacked credibility because they did not address Indian concerns about Chinese nuclear weapons, and, as regional agreements, were not universal in scope. The two countries did sign an accord on hotlines, however.[14]

The nuclear problem was compounded by war at the margins of the region, in Afghanistan. When the Soviet army invaded Afghanistan in December 1979, India and Pakistan took quite different stands. Pakistan lined up with the West against the Soviets, while India found itself uneasily poised between condemning the Soviets and maintaining an alliance-like relationship with Moscow.[15] From New Delhi's point of view, the earlier cold war patterns seemed to both form and threaten the relative stability and peace of the post-1971 period. Crucially, Indian and Pakistani weapons acquisitions—started before and therefore independently of the Afghan war—intensified as U.S.-Soviet cold war competitiveness returned to the region.[16] Both acquired enormous amounts of weaponry from the United States and Soviet Union respectively, and, for the first time since the 1954–65 period, a conventional arms race was on in South Asia.

By 1979, most of the security gains of the post-1971 war period had been lost. First, whereas the Simla accord formally regulated their relationship, the two sides held to different interpretations. For instance, Pakistan insisted that the reference to bilateralism was not as absolute as India claimed. Thus, Pakistan felt that it was not prevented from raising the Kashmir issue in international fora.[17] Second, the various normalization agreements had failed to deliver; Islamabad continued to subvert free trade, travel, and communications. Third, its new miliary relationship with the United States threatened to resuscitate Pakistani miliary power from its post-1971 status and restart the conventional arms race. The situation was now complicated by the possibility of nuclear weapons competition.

1980–89 After the Soviets invaded Afghanistan, India and Pakistan attempted to stabilize their relations against spillovers from the war. Another round of no-war pact negotiations occurred. While Pakistan urged force reduction negotiations leading to a no-war pact, India insisted on a broadened agenda that included increasing trade, travel, and cultural agreements to be codified in a treaty of friendship and cooperation. Not surprisingly, these also ended in failure.

Although the no-war/treaty of friendship and cooperation negotiations ran aground, cooperative efforts continued. Indian and Pakistani officials and leaders met regularly at meetings of the South Asian Association for Regional Cooperation (SAARC), which was launched officially in December 1985. While the SAARC charter prohibits the discussion of bilateral and contentious issues, India and Pakistan used the opportunities afforded by SAARC to hold informal bilateral meetings that would have been precluded by the norms of diplomatic conduct in the region. Under the cover of a SAARC summit, for example, Prime Ministers Rajiv Gandhi and

Mohammed Khan Junejo met in 1986 to try to defuse the incipient crisis over military exercises.

But India saw in SAARC a more subtle, indirect means of regional conflict management and resolution. New Delhi's view was that while high-level political contacts at summits were a benefit, low-level official and nongovernmental interaction in functional and economic areas was vital. Regional cooperation in the latter areas would in the long run foster habits of cooperation, tie South Asians into cooperative arrangements that would be too costly to jeopardize through conflict and war, and allow more extensive people-to-people or society-to-society interactions, which would change attitudes and constrain aggressive leadership.

By 1982, there was a new source of conflict: Pakistan's aid and shelter to Sikh militants in Indian Punjab. New Delhi protested, eventually threatening to pursue the militants and even to go to war if Islamabad did not curb its support. Islamabad, less formally and less frequently, accused India of involvement in the militancy in Sindh. In this heated environment, the Indian and Pakistani military exercises of 1986–87 rapidly escalated into armed confrontation. However, with conventional forces massed along the border, uncertainty over nuclear weapons capability and the availability of delivery systems, both sides realized that they were on the edge of war and of possible nuclear escalation. The crisis was defused in late January 1987, although it took several months of negotiations to conclude an agreement on the disengagement of forces and several more months to implement the agreement.

By 1989, the Kashmir problem had resurged. New Delhi charged that Pakistan was instigating and supporting the militancy in the Valley. Islamabad retorted that India had not fulfilled its undertaking to hold a plebiscite in Kashmir and that New Delhi's response to Kashmiri dissent violated human rights. By 1990, matters would come to a head, but from 1989 on, tensions over Kashmir were once more the primary conflict between India and Pakistan. The two states had come full circle since the 1960s.[18]

1990–92 In spite of the withdrawal of the Soviets from Afghanistan, ebbing U.S. support for Pakistan, greater U.S. support for India, and moves toward democracy in Pakistan, Indo-Pakistani relations have scarcely been worse. The problems of the 1980s have been carried over: nuclear and conventional arms racing and Pakistani involvement in Punjab and Kashmir.

Nuclear proliferation is evidently well advanced and seemingly immune to a "rollback," but New Delhi is more or less satisfied with the choice both sides have made, that of deterrence through ambiguity.[19] Despite New Delhi's concern about matching Pakistan's conventional weaponry, it recognizes that the conventional arms race works in India's favor—India is bigger and can always outproduce and outspend its neighbor. Further-more, although Pakistani missile development (the indigenously produced *Hatf* and Chinese-made M-11s) and its acquisition of F-16s, combined with its well-advertised nuclear weapons capability, are worrying because India has no defense against a nuclear attack, New Delhi recognizes that Pakistan also has no defense against missiles (the *Agni* and *Prithvi*) and strike aircraft (MiG 27s, MiG 29s, Mirages, and Jaguars) from India. Moreover, Islamabad must wrestle with the uncertainty over Indian nuclear capability.

Nevertheless, New Delhi appreciates that deterrence through ambiguity, like all other deterrence postures, is neither technically nor psychologically foolproof; technical malfunctions, command and control failures, and mis-perceptions can all undermine deterrence. Therefore, New Delhi has an interest in stabilizing South Asia's nuclear postures. As far back as 1988, India proposed exchanging lists of nuclear facilities as part of a no-attack accord. This proposal was finally instituted in January 1992, when such lists were exchanged—perhaps the first CSBM in the region.[20] In 1990, Prime Minister Nawaz Sharif of Pakistan proposed a five-nation nuclear prolif-eration conference to be held by the two South Asian states, the United States, the Soviet Union, and China. The three outside powers agreed, but New Delhi once again rejected the idea, even though the proposal seem-ingly addressed India's concern that South Asian nuclear issues be dis-cussed in a larger context that included China. Delhi countered that a phased but universalistic disarmament process of the sort envisaged in Rajiv Gandhi's United Nations proposals of 1988 was the only basis for Indian participation in nuclear talks.[21] Since rejecting Pakistan's proposal, India has held a series of talks with Washington on nuclear matters and has co-sponsored various UN resolutions, including a comprehensive test ban, a freeze on the production of fissile material, and no-first-use declarations by all nuclear and near-nuclear powers.

In the end, the nuclear issue remains a symptomatic one. Punjab and especially Kashmir, on the other hand, are substantive and central issues because they go to the heart of nationhood and political legitimacy. New Delhi has indicated that, given Pakistani involvement, it might be forced to widen its counterinsurgency operations to include militant facilities across the border, and thus to risk war. In 1990, with the situation in Kashmir deteriorating, an Indian military buildup along the border presaged just such a confrontation. Reputedly, Islamabad saw matters seriously enough to convey the first-ever nuclear threat in the subcontinent.[22]

India's proposal for confidence- and security-building measures origi-nated out of the 1986–87 and 1990 experiences. Robert Gates, in his 1990 "crisis" mission to the region, had suggested to New Delhi that this might be a useful initiative in averting hostilities. The diplomatic environment in South Asia was hospitable to a CSBM process. As noted, in the early 1980s,

India had proposed that the two sides agree not to attack each other's nuclear facilities. By 1990, when Gates came to the region, the two sides were in the process of preparing the lists of nuclear facilities that were to give the agreement operational utility. (These lists were finally exchanged in January 1992). Since mid-1990, India and Pakistan have embarked on a systematic course of confidence-building and further CSBMs have been concluded. These include an agreement on airspace violations and emergency landings and on prior notification of military exercises.[23]

Sino-Indian Conflict and Cooperation

The Sino-Indian record of conflict is shorter than the Indo-Pakistani record, and the range of issues is narrower. New Delhi's general view of conflict with China can be summarized in the following propositions: first, like Pakistan, China is the instigator of conflict and the use of force; second, China deceived India on the border dispute and, given its closed political system, may use strategic deception in the future; third, China has encouraged rebellion in India's northeast; fourth, China has interfered in South Asian quarrels, especially India's dispute with Pakistan; and fifth, China cannot abide the possibility that India may be an equal power.

New Delhi's view of cooperation once again is largely the obverse of its view of conflict: first, India is the instigator of cooperation and has been taken advantage of when it has offered cooperation; second, China's view of a cooperative solution of the border dispute is shallow and is based essentially on the notion of a swap, whereas India's view is moral and is based on well-established international law and practice; third, India has consistently avoided interfering in China's internal affairs, especially Tibet, even when the Chinese were fomenting rebellion in India; fourth, India has not interfered in China's relations with third parties and indeed has tried to advance or mend those relations;[24] and fifth, real cooperation will probably be impossible until India achieves military and economic parity with its northern neighbor.

Beyond this abstract view of conflict and cooperation, what are the specific areas of conflict and what cooperative efforts, episodes, trends, and agreements did conflict give rise to? A review of the record shows that in contrast with India's relationship to Pakistan, India had relatively few conflicts with China and that their one major source of difference, Tibet, was apparently solved by 1954; that from New Delhi's point of view, relations were cordial and broad-based enough until 1956;[25] that from 1957, the border conflict and the Tibetan issue rapidly eroded the relationship despite cooperative efforts; that after India's military defeat in 1962, those two issues were in large part suspended and a cold war ensued; that by 1976 a long peace had broken out, which featured détente, normalization of relations, and resumption of border talks, but also a rise in instabilities; and that the 1990s have brought India and China full circle in that the border and Tibet, a broadening of relations, and a wider competition for influence are sources of conflict. As with India's relationship with Pakistan, both sides increasingly realize that nuclear and conventional capabilities make war a very costly solution to their differences.[26]

Entente Cordiale: 1949–56

In contrast with its relationship with Pakistan, India's initial engagement with China was positive, even though New Delhi understood that there were points of friction. India was one of the first states to recognize the Chinese Communist government, even though it was clear that this move would harm relations with the West. New Delhi also led the move to induct Mao's China into the UN and oust the Taiwanese government. In 1950, as American-led UN troops in Korea approached Chinese territory and crossed the Yalu, India served as an intermediary between Beijing and Washington by passing on China's warning of intervention.[27] New Delhi also "introduced" China to a suspicious Third World; the Afro-Asian conference at Bandung (1955), organized by India and the other Colombo powers and stolen as it were by Zhou Enlai, was in part intended to bring China in from the cold.

Its support for China notwithstanding, New Delhi recognized that there were two major points of friction: Tibet and the border issue. In 1950, barely a year after the Communist party came to power in China, the Chinese army entered Tibet and integrated it forcefully with the rest of the country. New Delhi protested, but accepted that Tibet was an autonomous region of China. India had special ties with Tibet and a number of matters relating to its Tibetan presence and interaction had to be settled. This was accomplished four years later when India and China signed an agreement on "Trade and Intercourse between the Tibet Region of China and India." This agreement dealt with a number of diplomatic and trade issues, and contained the famous "Panchsheel" principles, or the "Five Principles of Peaceful Coexistence" that were to guide Sino-Indian relations: the mutual respect for each other's territory and sovereignty, mutual non-aggression, mutual non-interference in each other's domestic affairs, equality and mutual benefit, and peaceful coexistence.

The second problem issue was a settlement of the border, where the primary conflict was over the Aksai Chin. Some Indian officials had urged as early as 1950 that border problems be raised and negotiated with the new Chinese leadership. China eventually replied that it had not had time to revise old maps and that Beijing would deal with the matter in due course. Although India remained uneasy, it failed to push for talks. Not until 1957, when India discovered a road Beijing had build connecting Xinjian and Tibet, did the issue blow up.

Prebellum Border Conflict: 1957–62

Relations deteriorated after 1957. Tibet returned decisively to the agenda. In 1957, there was a dispute over grazing rights. The following year, Beijing formally accused India of allowing Kalimpong in West Bengal to be used by Tibetans, Americans, and Taiwanese to subvert Tibet.[28] In 1959, as fighting broke out in Tibet, the Dalai Lama fled for asylum in India.

On September 8, China once again proposed that the status quo be observed and provisional agreements be negotiated on specific disputed stretches of the border.[29] Nehru replied with the suggestion that Chinese forces should be withdrawn from several recently opened posts.[30] On November 7, Zhou Enlai proposed that both armies move back 20 km from the McMahon Line in the eastern sector and from the line of control (LOC) in the western sector. Beijing also suggested that a summit be held.[31] Nine days later, India responded by suggesting that certain patrolling limits be instituted to ease tensions. New Delhi agreed to an interim pullback of forces but disagreed on how far. It also conceded that Chinese civilian traffic could be permitted on the contested Aksai Chin road.[32] On December 17, Beijing rejected New Delhi's proposed pullback limits, but continued to press for an interim pullback, and agreed to stop forward patrolling. It also pressed for an immediate summit. India rejected the Chinese suggestions, including the idea of a summit.[33]

India soon changed its mind on the summit, however, and in January 1960 Zhou Enlai visited New Delhi. The only positive decision at the meeting arose from Zhou's suggestion that a joint border commission go to the frontier. India rejected this idea, contending that the frontier was for the most part adequately delimited. Instead, New Delhi proposed that officials meet to consider the documentary evidence. The Chinese agreed. Little changed with Zhou's visit or with the subsequent meetings of officials charged with resolving the boundary question.[34] The Indians soon implemented a "forward policy," which involved moving lightly armed patrols into disputed territory to reconnoiter and establish a presence, but not to challenge Chinese positions. The Chinese, according to the Indians, proceeded with "reconnaissance, probing, surveys, and road-building."[35]

The relationship worsened steadily until war broke out in September 1962. Two months later, after a victorious campaign, China declared a unilateral cease-fire and withdrew its troops to a point 20 km behind the LOC as it had existed on November 7, 1959. (This action was consistent with its proposal of that date and with the terms enunciated in the first cease-fire offer on October 24.) Beijing expected India to reciprocate or else China reserved the right to take further military action.[36]

Six Asian and African states—Burma, Cambodia, Ceylon, Ghana, Indonesia, and the United Arab Republic—put forward a set of proposals for the easing of tensions pending a final solution of the border conflict. These "Colombo Proposals" combined elements of the Indian and Chinese suggestions surveyed above: in the eastern sector, the LOC was to be a cease-fire line; in the western sector, China was to withdraw to a point 20 kilometers from the LOC as it had existed on November 7, 1959, and the Indians were to stay where they were before the fighting had broken out. Pending a final resolution of the border, the area vacated by China was to serve as a demilitarized zone without prejudice to either side's case. Both sides initially accepted the proposals in principle, but when China asked for certain modifications, India insisted on the original proposals.[37]

I rehearse the history of events surrounding the 1962 war in some detail at least in part to point to a feature that is important for contemporary CSBMs. Nested within these events were efforts by both sides to deploy CSBM-like measures in the interest of stability: provisional agreements on specific stretches of border, the withdrawal of forces to create a disengagement zone, patrolling limits, the use of roads for civilian but not military traffic, and crisis summitry as a kind of "hotline." These "precursor CSBMs" show that CSBMs as an idea are not necessarily new or alien to the subcontinent.

Postbellum Cold War: 1963–75

For the rest of the decade, relations remained tense. Although the shooting war had ended, clearly the state of war continued to exist in that both countries expected there could be war and therefore made the necessary preparations. Meanwhile, they conducted a cold war.

A number of trends and events worried New Delhi. The Chinese nuclear explosion at Lop Nor in 1964 increased concerns about Chinese military power. When India went to war with Pakistan in 1965, Beijing warned of Chinese intervention. Beginning in 1967, Beijing openly sided with secessionist groups in India's northeast and provided them with arms, money, training, and bases.[38] Also in 1967, at Nathu La in the eastern sector, a fierce artillery battle was fought. Indian forces held their own this time, but India was reminded of the fragility and fractiousness of the border.

After the shooting war of 1962, New Delhi had turned to the United States and Britain on the one hand and the Soviet Union on the other to prepare for the next round of hostilities should it occur. New Delhi resisted a formal alliance with either side, and in 1969, when the Soviets suggested an "Asian Collective Security" system, New Delhi showed little enthusiasm, at least in part because it did not want to be identified with an anti-Chinese grouping.[39]

In retrospect, it seems clear that this forbearance and demonstration of autonomy on India's part helped make possible the détente that slowly, discontinuously, and frequently recursively got underway in the 1970s. In 1970, Mao signaled the Chinese desire for better relations by approaching and greeting the Indian chargé d'affaires in a Beijing diplomatic line. Indian reaction was cautious: one response was to ask Beijing to restrain the Chinese news agency, Xinhua, in its reporting of the border issue. Following Mao's signal, Zhou Enlai congratulated Mrs. Gandhi on her landslide 1971 electoral victory.[40]

This rather modest start toward more normal diplomatic intercourse was interrupted by the Bangladesh crisis just weeks after Mrs. Gandhi's victory. Fearing Chinese intervention in the crisis, and confronting a U.S.-China rapprochement, New Delhi signed a twenty-five-year treaty of friendship and cooperation with the Soviet Union. Beijing warned New Delhi of the consequence of involvement in East Pakistan, but it was unable to prevent an Indian victory in the December war. Relations once again became glacial. Indeed, from 1972 to 1975, China and India reverted to a cold war, a large part of which was played out at the level of Chinese support for India's northeast rebels and for the small states of South Asia in their quarrels with New Delhi.[41]

The Long Peace: 1976–92

By 1976, however, a long-term change for the better began. India's long peace with China can be divided into three phases. The first, 1976–79, featured a continuation of the diplomatic normalization begun in 1970 and a reversal of Chinese intervention in Indian internal affairs and in regional affairs. In the second, 1980–89, border talks were resumed after a thirty-year hiatus and a more normalized relationship albeit with military instabilities, set in. The third, from 1990 on, promises to mirror the second, with the continuation of border talks and the broadening of relations, but also with the likelihood of new areas of competition and conflict. As with Pakistan, this last period has seen the institution of Indian-initiated confidence-building talks and various CSBMs, which reflect New Delhi's concern that the instabilities of the late 1980s be avoided.

1976–79 In 1976, Mrs. Gandhi proposed upgrading diplomatic representation to the ambassadorial level. India appointed an ambassador later that year and, six months later, China appointed its ambassador.[42] By this time, China had begun to alter its view of South Asia; it was now encouraging the smaller South Asian countries to settle their differences with New Delhi, and also stopped encouraging and aiding secessionist groups in India.[43]

In 1977, the newly elected Janata government attempted to normalize relations even further and to reopen the border issue. While Foreign Minister Vajpayee was in Beijing for talks in 1979, however, China opened its punitive military campaign against Vietnam. With Indian public opinion turning against Beijing, the opening to China was closed, as was the possibility of proceeding further with normalization and border talks.[44]

1980–89 The 1980s were the most positive period for Sino-Indian relations since the border war. In May 1980, Chinese Premier Hua Guofeng raised the possibility of reopening border talks. A joint communiqué stressed the need to avoid border clashes. In June 1980, Deng Xiaoping repeated China's interest in improving relations. Foreign Minister Huang Hua visited New Delhi in June 1981 and both sides made concessions at the talks. China eased its proposed "package deal," whereby the border conflict would be settled by minor adjustments along the LOC, by agreeing to consider alternatives if that was not acceptable. Hua also announced that China would open two ancient Hindu pilgrimage sites in Tibet—Mansarovar and Kailash. India, on the other hand, moved away from its refusal to discuss substantive issues until China withdrew from "Indian" territory.[45]

Yet various conflicts continued to pique tensions. India's conferral of full statehood to Arunachal Pradesh in 1987 elicited a sharp Chinese protest. In late 1986 and early 1987, Indian army units established a presence in the Sumdurong Chu Valley; the Chinese responded by doing the same. The ensuing confrontation threatened war. Following India's massive military exercise, Operation Checkerboard (1987), the Chinese began to reinforce the border, and once again relations became tense.[46]

Beyond these incidents, each side harbored concerns about the other. Beijing remained suspicious of India over Tibet; Indian reassurances on this issue are still sought at virtually every high-level meeting. Beijing continued to accuse India of "hegemonistic" designs in South Asia and of complicity in the grand designs of the Soviet Union, particularly in encircling China. New Delhi was concerned about Chinese arms sales and transfers to Pakistan, particularly of missiles and nuclear technology. Likewise, China watched with care the development of India's nuclear and missile programs and its conventional force modernization, which surpassed in sophistication that of the PLA.[47]

Despite these concerns and conflicts, the two sides conducted eight rounds of border talks over a period of seven years. Agreements were reached to continue the process of normalization. Trade, cultural, scientific, and other exchanges were to some extent separated from the ups and downs of the border talks and from the strategic and diplomatic disagreements listed above. While the talks progressed slowly, the two sides also held high-level meetings and reached various low-level agreements. Thus, the foreign ministers met in New York before the sixth round of talks, and

Prime Minister Rajiv Gandhi and Premier Zhao Ziyang held a brief summit in October 1985. The foreign ministers conferred again after the seventh round of talks, this time to discuss measures to avoid a confrontation in Sumdurong. Finally, Rajiv Gandhi made a state visit in December 1988.[48]

In short, from 1980, the two sides entered a phase of relatively continuous communications, in which low-level agreements were reached. This process clearly had its limits, but it was seen by both sides as part of a cooperative engagement that would lead up to dealing with the great outstanding issue, namely, the border conflict.

1990–92 In the 1990s, New Delhi confronts additional worries. First, it is concerned about the growth of the Chinese navy, particularly its increasing presence in the Indian Ocean. Chinese plans to acquire or build an aircraft carrier and to expand its navy to blue-water strength means that it will rub up against Indian units in the Indian Ocean. India has one of the world's largest Exclusive Economic Zones (EEZs) and it anticipates encroachments, including some from China. New Delhi is watching with interest how the Chinese behave over the Spratly Islands dispute.

Second, New Delhi is concerned about Beijing's growing technical, economic, and military relationship with Burma. India's relationship with Burma's military rulers has been particularly cold since Aung San Suu Kyi was first imprisoned; New Delhi protested her incarceration and the general level of political repression in Burma.[49] Increasingly, however, New Delhi is moving to improve relations with the military regime, in large part to balance Rangoon's deepening relationship with Beijing.[50] Chinese technicians have built roads in Burma, and Beijing is reputedly interested in trade through Rangoon, an outlet which is closer to its southeastern provinces such as Yunan than are Chinese ports. The Indians, however, view these roads not just as development infrastructure but also as potential military infrastructure. In addition, Chinese trade and investment in Burma has grown substantially as its military rulers turn to non-Western economic partners in the wake of Western criticism and sanctions. China is also selling military equipment in Burma and is refurbishing Burmese naval facilities and building new ones. In return, it has been rumored that China will get access to Burmese ports, including the Hangyyi Islands in the Bay of Bengal, from which Beijing could monitor India's rocketry range across the bay in Orissa.[51]

In spite of these worries, in 1990 India proposed CSBM talks with China. At the fourth meeting of the Joint Working Group, various CSBMs were negotiated, including hotline communications and meetings between local army commanders. Army commanders are scheduled to meet face-to-face at least twice a year in both eastern sector and the western sector, with additional meetings to be held if and when necessary. Both sides are now also committed to prior notification of army exercises,[52] although the specifics of notification (e.g., how much advance notice is due, exercises within what range of the border, with what kinds of weapons, etc.) have not been made public.[53]

During Prime Minister Narasimha Rao's visit in September 1993 the JWG-recommended measures were in effect affirmed and further measures were agreed upon; these have since been codified in a formal agreement. The September 7 agreement on "the maintenance of peace and stability along the line of actual control" (LOAC) contains six important measures. First, it pledges both sides to respect the LOAC and specifies steps to be taken in case of infringements. Second, it outlines reductions in military forces along the LOAC, with "the extent, depth, timing and nature" of the reductions to be determined by mutual consultation. Third, it prohibits military exercises of a certain level in specified zones, and requires prior notification of exercises of a certain level near the LOAC. Fourth, it specifies that in case of "contingencies or other problems" near the LOAC, border personnel will consult through meetings and channels to be mutually determined. Fifth, it pledges the two sides to take measures to prevent air intrusions across the LOAC and to consult on possible restrictions on air exercises near the LOAC. Finally, it requires the two sides to appoint diplomatic and military experts who will formulate measures to implement the agreement and resolve differences in the alignment of the LOAC.[54]

Conflict, Cooperation, and CSBMs

Under what circumstances do states choose CSBMs? In general, states have an incentive to pursue CSBMs under the following conditions:

1. When they are involved in an enduring dispute in which the stakes are high;
2. When there is a substantial probability or expectation that the dispute will lead to hostilities;
3. When military technologies and strategy favor the offense over the defense, i.e., when there are incentives to strike first;
4. When conventional and nuclear weaponry, which may be used offensively or defensively, make the costs of war disproportionate to any reasonable goals in the dispute;
5. When there is a fear that miscommunication, misperception, and misinterpretation—arising from various technical problems or cognitive failures—could lead to inadvertent war; and
6. When neither outright war nor a comprehensive peace seems plausible.

A combination of some or all of these conditions would make CSBMs attractive in a given situation. If these are the relevant test conditions for CSBMs, then the preceding review of Indo-Pakistani and Sino-Indian relations suggests that, from New Delhi's point of view, CSBMs are apt for the present.

1. Enduring Conflict

India finds itself locked into enduring conflict with two of its most powerful neighbors. With Pakistan, issues have come and gone over forty-five years, but there has scarcely been a time when the relationship has been dispute-free. At least one issue, Kashmir, has endured throughout, although at varying levels of salience. Moreover, the stakes in both Kashmir and Punjab are high; both issues and Pakistani involvement in them, from India's perspective, strike at the heart of Indian nationhood. They transcend any simple strategic reckoning figured in territorial losses or gains.

India is in a similar situation with China. The border conflict with China has endured, but, like Kashmir, it is not simply an issue of territorial loss or gain. Especially since the 1962 war, it has come to be seen as part of a long historical chain of defeat and humiliation at the hands of outsiders. This issue, too, strikes at the heart of Indian nationhood. However, it is more susceptible to a solution. For one thing, there are no third parties involved. For another, clearly, a border deal is easier to cut; a corpus of international law and practice on border settlements could help to evolve a solution (as India claims); and a swap involving concessions in the western sector for concessions in the eastern sector is plausible (as China claims).

In Kashmir, by contrast, this is not the case. An important third party is involved—the Kashmiris, who have shown a capacity for autonomous choice and action. Moreover, there is no comparable basis for a solution in international law or practice; and Kashmir is not amenable to a swap. Finally, the stakes are not as high; the far northern borderlands, many of them inaccessible and barren, do not figure in the Indian political and cultural imagination on the order of Kashmir.

2. Expectations of Hostility

Based largely on past experience but also on inferences from present behaviors and capabilities, New Delhi expects that India could once again go to war, particularly over Kashmir and less over the border dispute with China. India and Pakistan have already fought two wars over Kashmir (1948, 1965) and the 1971 war involved some hostilities in Kashmir. At great financial, material, and human cost, the two sides have also fought a mini-war in Siachen, a glacier in Kashmir, since 1986.[55] Siachen is of no strategic significance expect as a test of each side's commitment and pre-paredness, precisely why they have fought so hard. A more recent confron-tation over Kashmir threatened to escalate to war (1990). New Delhi is convinced, moreover, that Islamabad will continue its "low-intensity" operations in Kashmir, supplying the militants with money, guns, refuge, and training, and perhaps awaiting a chance to send in regular troops to wrest the state. India and Pakistan will therefore remain in "a state of war"—expecting one, preparing for one, and possibly fighting one.

With China, New Delhi fears war less but does not rule it out. The Indian government still sees the 1962 war as largely unprovoked. It sees China as unpredictable and as prone to saber-rattling. Since 1975–76, Beijing has refrained from encouraging India's northeast secessionists and has moder-ated its tone on India's regional disputes, but New Delhi feels that Chinese policy could easily be reversed.

More worrying, in the 1990s, is the prospect of three factors—ethnic conflict in China, particularly in Xinjiang and Tibet, regional disparities in the wake of economic liberalization, and a resurgent pro-democracy move-ment—combining to make Beijing more aggressive externally if only as a diversion from internal conflict. Instabilities in Tibet, in particular, could lead to tensions with India.[56]

3. Offense over Defense

New Delhi recognizes that India, China, and Pakistan all possess technolo-gies and favor strategies that favor preemptive or even surprise attack. In the Indo-Pakistani case, arms acquisitions on both sides since the late 1970s have included high-performance strike aircraft capable of delivering nu-clear weapons. In addition, as noted earlier, both are close to indigenous or purchased missile capability.[57] Finally, both sides have moved toward "offensive defensive" strategic postures that include capabilities for preemptive attacks with armor and air power.[58] Military exercises by both sides in the past five years have focused on deep penetration, the coordi-nation of air power and highly mobile ground forces, and the use of increasingly sophisticated electronic "eyes" and communication.[59] Neither army envisions fighting stodgy, gritty, and stationary defensive battles.

From New Delhi's view, the situation with China may be less unstable, though not without dangers. On the one hand, while Chinese military power is fearsome, New Delhi perceives three constraints: logistical diffi-culties along the mountainous border terrain limit Chinese offensive power; Chinese conventional forces have not modernized as fast as India's (or Pakistan's), although this is changing; and China's strategic environ-ment is more complicated that Pakistan's or India's, because Beijing must contend not only with India but with numerous economic and military powers—Central Asian republics, South Korea, Taiwan, Vietnam, and above all, Japan, Russia, and the United States.

On the other hand, Beijing has ICBMs and IRBMs that could reach Indian territory. While these have for the most part been deployed against the former Soviet Union, India has accused China of placing IRBMs in Tibet and aiming them at India.[60] Moreover, with the improvements in China's relations with the former Soviet republics, New Delhi fears that Chinese weapons have been freed for other deployments. India's 1962 experience, as well as its reading of Chinese choices in other conflicts (Korea in 1950, Vietnam in 1979), suggest that Beijing likes to strike first, strike hard, and strike fast. These factors make for instability. Chinese missiles are not defendable, and Chinese defensive strategy stresses surprise, preemption, and the staging of engagements at a time and place of Beijing's choosing.[61]

4. The Costs of War

New Delhi better appreciates that a future war fought with new conventional weaponry, and perhaps even with nuclear weapons, will be far more costly than earlier wars, which were relatively tame in terms of military or civilian costs.[62] In the Indo-Pakistani case, although neither side has thus far targeted civilian facilities or populations, neither government can count on this norm prevailing in a future war. Punjab and Kashmir are symbolically very important to India, and Punjab is materially very important too. But given the potential for escalation and the likelihood that the costs of war would far outweigh any rational goals, New Delhi increasingly understands the need for dealing with Pakistani involvement without provoking full-scale hostilities.

With China, too, New Delhi appreciates that war will be costly and disproportionate to any rational goals. China has logistical terrain advantages over India and enormous conventional strength. It has been estimated that Beijing can deploy up to twenty divisions on the border with India, a number New Delhi cannot match. Moreover, China has the capacity to devastate any part of India with nuclear weapons; the Chinese heartland is largely beyond the range of Indian aircraft. Although the state of Indian nuclear weaponry is unknown, the asymmetry in capabilities is evident. India may not be advanced enough to mount a weapon on a missile, and in any case, its missiles are still under development. Beijing has of course declared it would not use nuclear weapons against non-nuclear states and that its stands by a no-first-use policy, but New Delhi is not reassured; Beijing may not count India as a non-nuclear state given the speculation, fueled in part by Indian statements, that India has bombs in the basement; and New Delhi cannot rely on Chinese nuclear scruples in a crisis.

5. Miscommunication, Misperception, and Misinterpretation

Given the increasing inability to defend against certain weapon systems and the destruction they can wreak, New Delhi is worried about the role of miscommunication, misperception, and misinterpretation in leading to inadvertent war.

The military exercises crises of 1986–87 may have been a watershed. Explanations for holding the massive Indian exercise Operation Brasstacks, which was the catalyst of the crisis, range from the ostensive (military training and modernization) to the Machiavellian (a cover for invading Pakistan). Between those is the view that Brasstacks was training/modernization plus coercive diplomacy—swaggering and flexing in front of Pakistan to show Islamabad what it could expect if it did not curb its involvement in Punjab.[63] Whatever the intent, Pakistan's reactions and Indian counter-reactions seemed to threaten war.

In 1990, the two sides seemed poised to replay the earlier crisis. Indian Prime Minister V. P. Singh's warning in Parliament of war over Kashmir and the build up of Indian troops along the border led to tensions. U.S. intelligence reported Pakistani actions consistent with preparing F-16s for nuclear weapons. Indian troop movements in and around the border may have been defensive moves to harden the border against infiltration by Sikh and Kashmiri militants, but Pakistani reactions suggested that they saw offensive rather than defensive moves. In the light of U.S. information on the extent of Pakistani preparations, India apparently allowed the American military attaché in New Delhi to confirm that Indian forces were in a defensive mode; this was communicated to Pakistan and may have played a role in defusing tensions.

These episodes showed three things. First, Indian moves to deal with Punjab and Kashmir could be misread and thus lead to an escalatory spiral. Second, New Delhi did not have technical or diplomatic systems that could rapidly clarify misperceptions and defuse a crisis. Third, Indian and Pakistani militaries have put in place 1914-type action-reaction plans to deal with each other's offensive defensive postures. These plans, once triggered, have their own momentum. Internal misperceptions, miscommunications, and misinterpretations probably also contributed to the crises.[64] Thus, New Delhi is conscious that the two sides need better high-level political communication to stop the drift to war.

The 1986–87 crisis with Pakistan was paralleled by tensions with China. In 1986–87, there were the Sumdurong Chu confrontations, and, in the spring of 1987, Operation Checkerboard raised temperatures along the India-China border, resulting in Chinese redeployments and reinforcements.

Once again, let us note certain lessons from the experience. First, whatever Indian intent—whether the exercise was purely an exercise, or a probing of Chinese preparedness and reactions, or even a testing of third-party reactions—what was worrisome was that, at the very moment relations were improving, and in the midst of the border talks, misjudgments and the responses to them, as well as the unpredictability of local military dynamics, produced a dangerous slide. Second, the Sumdurong Chu tensions revealed communications problems. Beijing and New Delhi exchanged accusations and counteraccusations but apparently did not enter into serious communications over the affair. Among the public charges and countercharges, there seemed to be no high-level private contact.[65] It is clear from these two episodes that India had no reliable and quick means of serious communication at the high or local level. Finally, New Delhi has noted that both sides have moved toward quick-response military postures with an accent on offensive capabilities and that this hair-trigger position is dangerous.

6. Between War and Peace

Finally, New Delhi realizes that the threat or use of force is less and less plausible and that various modes of peacemaking are either ineffective or insufficient in regulating relations with Pakistan and China.

The history of Indo-Pakistani conflict and cooperation in particular shows the threat or use of force is implausible, not just for reasons of cost. After three wars with Pakistan, New Delhi sees that the threat or use of force as a means of dispute resolution has accomplished little for either side. The 1948, 1965, and 1971 wars only brought about temporary peace. None of the wars solved the primary Indo-Pakistani conflict, i.e., Kashmir. Attempts at coercive diplomacy have had little impact on problems such as Pakistani aid to Sikh and especially Kashmiri militants.[66]

On the other hand, the record of multilateral peace-making on the scale of earlier efforts—summitry, official talks, and extra-regional efforts involving the UN or great powers—is equally dismal. New Delhi understands that it is unlikely that internal challenges to weak governments and the preoccupations of outside agencies and powers will permit either a thoroughgoing bilateral or a multilateral peace effort to be mounted, let alone carried through to a successful conclusion. The early negotiations on functional and economic issues fared better—the post-partition agreements on sharing assets, refugee compensation, and the Indus Rivers Treaty are the most positive episodes in Indo-Pakistani relations. Yet after these initial successes, there have been limits. In spite of several agreements to resume trade, communications, and travel, the two countries have not normalized transnational interactions. From New Delhi's point of view, Islamabad is at fault.[67]

With China, there is little prospect that India would choose war on the border issue except in a defensive sense. India's attempt at compellent behavior from 1960 onward—the "forward policy"—was certainly a factor in the disaster of 1962. Depending on the perspective, either the forward policy was the fateful catalyst of war or it served conveniently as a *casus belli* for a Chinese leadership intent on teaching India a lesson. More recently, it is unclear what Operation Checkerboard accomplished politically (as against militarily). The display of muscle-flexing may have been intended to strengthen India's position at the border talks by reminding China of Indian commitment and power, but there is little evidence that it did so.[68] Beyond the experience of the 1960s and 1987, there are structural constraints on the use of force against Beijing. Perhaps the most important constraints are terrain, climate, and logistical impediments to any substantial fighting.

If force and coercive diplomacy are not serious options against China, peace-making efforts have not been particularly salutary either. A Tibet agreement did not assuage Chinese suspicions of India's role in fomenting rebellion, and the pre-1962 correspondence, official talks, and summits failed to resolve the border issue or the drift to war. Since 1981, although there has been a more or less continuous process of talks, the two sides are not conspicuously close to a border settlement. The only real agreements have been to separate the border issue from trading, cultural, and scientific interactions, and to proceed on a sector-by-sector basis. At the October meeting of the Joint Working Group, the Chinese once again offered a swap: Indian concessions in the west for Chinese concessions in the east.[69] India has neither agreed to nor rejected the idea, which probably reflects the divisions on this issue between "non-settlers" and "settlers" (the latter favoring some sort of swap), as well as nervousness over public reaction.[70] India's internal distractions and the fragility of present and foreseeable governments make it unlikely that New Delhi will shake hands on any kind of deal for some time to come.

In this liminal period between war and peace, conditions seem ripe for CSBMs. From New Delhi's point of view, the Indo-Pakistani and Sino-Indian relationships appear to meet the six-point CSBM test outlined above. This is not to suggest that other options, such as negotiations and functional and economic cooperation, can or should be ignored. But it does suggest that CSBMs may be singularly apt for the present. The threat and use of force may be too costly. Peacemaking may be too ambitious and too slow. In the meantime, relations must be stabilized.

Conclusion

India's view of conflict and cooperation with Pakistan and China led it to propose CSBMs beginning in the 1990s. New Delhi senses that relations with both have come full circle since the early days of their relationships:

with Pakistan, Kashmir is once again the central conflict; with China, Tibet and the border issue are once again the core concerns. In addition to these pivotal matters, there are now various other conflicts, incipient as well as more advanced: the nuclear and conventional arms race with Pakistan, and long-term competition with China for influence in Southeast Asia and the Indian Ocean.

Theoretically, India has three options in regulating relations with Pakistan and China: force, peacemaking, and confidence-building. India's experience with the threat or use of force has not been particularly encouraging. The wars with Pakistan and China have only postponed the reckoning on issues such as the future of Kashmir and the border with China. Moreover, New Delhi increasingly appreciates that the costs of future wars could be enormous and disproportionate to any rational goals. It understands that all three states have moved toward military strategies that privilege speed, offensive capability, and preemption and also that misperception, miscommunication, and misinterpretation could trigger inadvertent war.

New Delhi has engaged in various forms of peacemaking with both Pakistan and China, sometimes successfully, often not. Comprehensive peace negotiations—bilateral or multilateral—as a way of dealing with present tensions may be overly ambitious. Functional and economic cooperation will likely be too slow to develop and too slow, if at all, to ameliorate conflict. No-war, no-first-use, and common defense agreements are of little advantage: those in the first two categories risk formalism if they are not accompanied by far-reaching changes in military deployments and practices; those in the last category seem irrelevant, even utopian, in the present global and internal political environment.

Confidence- and security-building charts a middle course between force and peacemaking; it does not attempt to solve conflict either through violence or through comprehensive dispute settlement. Rather, it attempts to prevent, regulate, and terminate violence and thus give peacemaking a chance. India recognizes that CSBMs may be a middle way, appropriate to the challenges of the 1990s.

Notes

1. For the notion of a "security complex," see Barry Buzan, *People, States, and Fear,* 2nd ed. (Boulder, Co: Lynne Rienner, 1991), pp. 186–229; and Barry Buzan, Gowher Rizvi, Rosemary Foot, and Nancy Jetly, *South Asian Insecurity and the Great Powers* (London: Macmillan, 1986), for its application to South Asia. Buzan would not agree that India, China, and Pakistan constitute a security complex, but rather that the two South Asian states alone do and that China is an intrusive and influential outsider.

2. I have borrowed the term "brother enemies" from Nayan Chanda's fine book on the relationships between the communist-controlled states in Indochina. See Chanda, *Brother Enemy: The War after the War* (New York: Harcourt Brace Jovanovich, 1986).

3. Douglas Makeig, "War, No War, and the India-Pakistan Negotiating Process," *Pacific Affairs* 60 (summer 1987), pp. 271–94, has a useful summary of the "operational codes" of India and Pakistan in their mutual disputes.

4. I mean peace partly in a negative sense, i.e., the absence of war, but also partly in a positive sense, i.e., as cooperative endeavor. Clearly though, this was not a time of more thoroughgoing peace. The phrase "the long peace" is from John Lewis Gaddis and his work on the post–World War II international system. See Gaddis, *The Long Peace: Inquiries into the History of the Cold War* (New York: Oxford University Press, 1987), especially chapter 8.

5. For a systematic and detailed account of these conflicts and the agreements associated with them, see Charles Heimsath and Surjit Mansingh, *A Diplomatic History of Modern India* (New Delhi: Allied, 1971), pp. 121–83.

6. W. Norman Brown, *The United States and India and Pakistan*, rev. ed. (Cambridge, Mass.: Harvard University Press, 1963), pp. 188–203.

7. On the three wars between India and Pakistan, see Sumit Ganguly, *The Origins of War in South Asia*, 2nd ed. (Boulder, Co.: Westview, 1986); for the role of the Rann of Kutch episode on the way to the 1965 war, see esp. pp. 70–72.

8. This duet is nicely covered in Sisir Gupta, *India and Regional Integration in Asia* (Bombay: Asia Publishing House, 1964).

9. Heimsath and Mansingh, *Diplomatic History of Modern India*, pp. 141–42.

10. For discussion, see Robert Jackson, *South Asian Crisis: India-Pakistan-Bangladesh* (London: Chatto Windus, 1975).

11. New Delhi was also aware that, potentially, the creation of Bangladesh had negative implications for India. On February 12, 1972, two months after the victory in Bangladesh, there was already uneasiness in India. The *Far Eastern Economic Review* reported Indian interest in regional "confederation" and noted, "From the Indian point of view a confederation is welcome not only because it would ensure lasting peace in the area but because it would give an opportunity to consolidate the federal structure in India itself—signaling an end to fears that secessionist movements might someday grow."

12. For an analysis of Indo-Pakistani negotiations leading to the accord, see Imtiaz H. Bokhari and Thomas Perry Thornton, *The 1972 Simla Agreement: An Asymmetrical Negotiation*, FPI Case Studies no. 11, Johns Hopkins Foreign Policy Institute, Washington, D.C., 1988.

13. By now this position is familiar enough, but see Susan Burns, "Arms Limitation," in Stephen P. Cohen, ed., *Nuclear Proliferation in South Asia: The Prospects for Arms Control* (Boulder, Co.: Westview, 1994), pp. 146–47.

14. For a variety of approaches to nuclear cooperation in South Asia, see Cohen, ed., *Nuclear Proliferation in South Asia*. On the various Pakistani proposals, see Akhtar Ali, "A Framework for Nuclear Agreement and Verification," in the Cohen volume, pp. 265–97.

15. For an excellent and subtle account of India's travails over Afghanistan and its attempts to distance itself from the Soviet Union, see Robert Horn, *Soviet-Indian Relations: Issues and Influence* (New York: Praeger, 1982), pp. 180–212.

16. Indian arms purchases from the Soviets were being negotiated by the Janata government in 1977–79, and Pakistan had begun talks with the United States in 1978.

17. Bokhari and Thornton, *The 1972 Simla Agreement*, p. 39, refers to Pakistan's different interpretation of bilateralism.

18. For accounts of the latest round of the Kashmir problem and the consequences for the Indo-Pakistani relationship, see Sumit Ganguly, "Avoiding War in Kashmir," *Foreign Affairs* (winter 1990/91), pp. 57–73; and various essays in Raju G. C. Thomas, ed., *Perspectives on Kashmir: The Roots of Conflict in South Asia* (Boulder, Co.: Westview, 1992), including Ganguly's chapter, "The Politics of War and Peace in Kashmir."

19. A point made, somewhat differently, by Neil Joeck, "Tacit Bargaining and Stable Proliferation in South Asia," in Benjamin Frankel, ed., *Opaque Nuclear Proliferation: Methodological and Policy Implications* (London: Frank Cass, 1991), pp. 77–91.

20. "Pakistan, India Exchange Lists of Nuclear Facilities," *Washington Post*, January 2, 1992.

21. Steve Coll, "India Rejects Pakistani Bid for Talks on Nuclear Ban," *Washington Post*, June 9, 1991.

22. Seymour Hersh, "On the Nuclear Edge," *New Yorker*, March 29, 1993, suggests that the events of 1990 were more serious than is generally appreciated. Hersh's contentions are controversial, however. See Douglas Jehl, "Assertion India and Pakistan Faced Nuclear War is Doubted," *New York Times*, March 23, 1993; and Aziz Haniffa, "Threat of '90 Atom War Doubted," *India Abroad*, April 2, 1993.

23. On Indo-Pakistani CSBMs, see Moonis Ahmar, "Indo-Pak Relations: Confidence-Building Measures and the Normalization Process," *Globe* (February 1993), pp. 47–59. For a listing of Indo-Pakistani as well as Sino-Indian CSBMs, see Michael Krepon, Dominique McCoy, and Matthew Rudolph, eds., *A Handbook of Confidence-Building Measures for Regional Security*, Handbook no. 1, Henry L. Stimson Center, Washington, D.C., September 1993.

24. Thus Indians argue that New Delhi was one of the first states to recognize Communist China; it fought vigorously for Chinese membership in the UN; in the 1950s, it helped ease China's relations with a suspicious Third World by championing China's membership in the UN and by insisting that China be at the Afro-Asian conference in Bandung in 1955; and it warned the United States of Chinese intervention during the Korean War.

25. It is of course true that until about 1952 Beijing was suspicious and contemptuous of India's "bourgeois" leadership and of notions such as nonalignment. New Delhi ignored the ideological barrage, for the most part. By 1952, at least in part because of India's mediation in the Korean dispute, China came around to a more friendly view.

26. The following account of conflict and cooperation draws on Kanti P. Bajpai and Bonnie L. Coe, "Confidence-Building Measures between India and China," in Michael Krepon and Amit Sevak, eds., Crisis Prevention, Confidence-Building, and Reconciliation (Washington, D.C.: Henry L. Stimson Center, 1995), pp. 199-226.

27. India continued to play an intermediary role on the Korean issue as a way of ending the war. See Heimsath and Mansingh, *Diplomatic History of Modern India*, pp. 66–74.

28. Timothy George, "Sino-Indian Relations: Opportunities and Limitations," in Zalmay Khalilzad, Timothy George, Robert Litwak, and Shahram Chubin, eds., *Security in Southern Asia* (New York: St. Martin's, 1984), p. 5.

29. The Chinese had proposed something similar in Zhou Enlai's letter to Nehru on January 23, 1959. See Dorothy Woodman, *Himalayan Frontiers: A Political Review of British, Chinese, India, and Russian Rivalries* (New York: Praeger, 1969), pp. 236, 241; and Maxwell, *India's China War*, p. 122.

30. Woodman, *Himalayan Frontiers*, p. 248.

31. Maxwell, *India's China War*, p. 135.

32. Maxwell, *India's China War*, p. 137; and Woodman, *Himalayan Frontiers*, p. 251.

33. Woodman, *Himalayan Frontiers*, p. 251; and Maxwell, *India's China War*, pp. 141–43.

34. Steven Hoffman, *India and the China Crisis* (Berkeley: University of California Press, 1990), pp. 88–89.

35. Hoffman, *India and the China Crisis*, pp. 92–114.

36. See Woodman, *Himalayan Frontiers*, pp. 285–95 and Maxwell, *India's China War*, pp. 417–20.

37. See Maxwell, *India's China War*, pp. 428–33; and Woodman, *Himalayan Frontiers*, pp. 295–301, for an account of the Colombo Conference and its proposals.

38. George, "Sino-Indian Relations," pp. 9–10.

39. S. Nihal Singh, *Yogi and the Bear: The Story of Indo-Soviet Relations* (New Delhi: Allied Publishers, 1986), pp. 76–79.

40. Šumit Ganguly, "The Sino-Indian Border Talks, 1981–1989," *Asian Survey* 29 (December 1989), p. 1124.

41. One of the sharper episodes was over India's integration of Sikkim into the Union in 1975.

42. Ganguly, "The Sino-Indian Border Talks," p. 1125.

43. See, for instance, the discussion in Manoranjan Mohanty, "India-China Relations on the Eve of the Asian Century," in Ramakant, ed., *China and South Asian Relations*, pp. 78–80.

44. George, "Sino-Indian Relations," p. 13. Surjit Mansingh and Steven I. Levine, "China and India: Moving Beyond Confrontation," *Problems of Communism* 38 (March–June 1989), p. 36, notes that sections of Indian opinion saw the invasion of Vietnam during Vajpayee's visit as deliberately aimed at India.

45. Ganguly, "The Sino-Indian Border Talks," p. 1126.

46. There has been no serious and extended analysis of Operation Checkerboard. The best dissection of this episode is Mansingh and Levine, "China and India: Moving Beyond Confrontation," pp. 41–44. Also see Mohanty, "India and China Relations," pp. 77–78, which suggests that China brought its strength in Tibet up to twenty divisions during this period. On China's reactions to the 1986–87 episodes, see Gary Klintworth, "Chinese Perspectives on India as a Great Power," in Ross Babbage and Sandy Gordon, eds., *India's Strategic Future: Regional State or Global Power* (New York: St. Martin's, 1992), pp. 103–4. Klintworth claims that China calculated it could not take on the modernized Indian army.

47. These concerns and views come through clearly in Guang, "A Chinese Perspective," in Mendis, ed., *India's Role in South Asia* and in Klintworth, "Chinese Perspectives on India."

48. For details on the various rounds of talks, see Ganguly, "The Sino-Indian Border Talks," pp. 1126–32.

49. Aung San Suu Kyi, it should be remembered, lived in India for many years.

50. David I. Steinberg, *The Future of Burma: Crisis and Choice in Myanmar* (New York: University Press of America, 1990), pp. 86–88.

51. For many of these details, see Tai Mai Cheung, "Smoke Signals: China, India Tentatively Increase Military Ties," *Far Eastern Economic Review*, November 12, 1992. Chinese road building activity in Burma was brought to my attention by Prof. George Yu of the Department of Political Science, University of Illinois, Urbana-Champaign.

52. See the Joint Press Release issued at the end of the fourth meeting of the Joint Working Group, New Delhi, February 20–21, 1992. These measures are also reported in K. K. Katyal, "India, China Resolve to Keep Peace on the Border," *The Hindu* (International Edition), February 29, 1991, p. 12.

53. While the two sides are working on greater transparency toward each other, they have evidently chosen not to be more transparent toward their own publics. This would seem to be a mistake. If there are misconceptions, doubts, and fears about CSBMs among certain domestic constituencies, the two governments have done little to assuage them.

54. See "Text of India-China Agreements," *Times* of India, September 9, 1993.

55. W. P. S. Sidhu, "Siachen: The Forgotten War," *India Today*, May 31, 1992.

56. These worries were signaled in a talk by K. Subrahmanyam entitled "Peace and Security in the 1990s: A Perspective from India," given at the Program in Arms Control, Disarmament, and International Security, University of Illinois, Urbana-Champaign, November 30, 1992. See also Subrahmanyam, "The Challenge of China," *Economic Times*, October 20, 1993.

57. On Indian missiles, see Amit Gupta, "Fire in the Sky: The Indian Missile Program," *Defense and Diplomacy* 8 (October 1990); and Janne Nolan, *Trappings of Power: Ballistic Missiles in the Third World* (Washington, D. C.: Brookings, 1991), esp. pp. 40–48 and 86–91 (the latter pages also include some comments on Pakistani missiles).

58. On Pakistan's decision to move toward "offensive defense" notions, see Stephen P. Cohen, *The Pakistan Army* (Berkeley: University of California Press, 1984), pp. 144–47 and similarly on Indian moves, see George Tanham, "Indian Strategic Culture," *Washington Quarterly* 15 (winter 1992), pp. 129–42.

59. See Jasjit Singh, "The Air-Land Battle Doctrine: Implication and Application," *Indian Defence Review, January 1988* (New Delhi: Lancers International, 1988), pp. 42–54, for a discussion of U.S. air-land battle ideas and their applicability to South Asia.

60. There is no confirmation of Chinese missile placements in Tibet. However, it is widely believed in India. For instance, Mohanty, "India-China Relations" cites U.S. journalist Richard Avedon as reporting 90 nuclear missiles—70 medium range and 20 intermediate range—in Tibet and targeted on India. Mohanty reports China's denial of July 22, 1987.

61. Klintworth, "Chinese Perspectives on India" pp. 100–102, is suggestive.

62. Ganguly, *Origins of War in South Asia,* cites figures on the costs of the various Indo-Pakistani wars. See also S. Rashid Naim, *"Aadhi Raat Ke Baad* (After Midnight)," in Cohen, ed., *Nuclear Proliferation in South Asia,* pp. 23–61, for estimates of civilian casualties and other costs of nuclear war in South Asia.

63. For the Machiavellian view, see Ravi Rikhye, *The War that Never Was* (New Delhi: Prism India, 1989). For the view that it was an attempt at coercive diplomacy related to Pakistani involvement in Punjab, see the letter by Ishwar Singh, "General Sundarji: Media Myth or Military Hero," *Indian Defence Review,* July 1988 (New Delhi: Lancers International, 1988), p. 162.

64. See Kanti Bajpai, P. R. Chari, Pervaiz Cheema, Stephen Cohen, and Šumit Ganguly, *Brasstacks and Beyond: Perception and Management of Crisis in South Asia* (New Delhi: Manohar, 1995).

65. Mansingh and Levine, "China and India: Moving Beyond Confrontation," pp. 41–42, reports that the Chinese used U.S. Secretary of Defense Caspar Weinberger and Secretary of State George Schulz, both of whom were visiting Beijing, to convey warnings to New Delhi in October 1986 and March 1987. This is an indication, I would suggest, of the lack of serious communication between the two countries.

66. At least one reason this may be so is that, whatever Pakistan's actions, the flow of guns and money, even people, is in substantial measure beyond the government's control. In the aftermath of the Afghan war, Pakistan is awash in guns. Money from expatriate Kashmiris and various Muslim states is also difficult to control.

67. India and Pakistan are among those who have signed the South Asian Preferential Tariff Agreement (SAPTA). This should help normalize Indo-Pakistani trade. However, New Delhi feels that Islamabad remains hesitant about trade and will continue to slow down moves toward a regional trade regime.

68. Ganguly, "The Sino-Indian Border Talks," makes no reference to any great change between the seventh and eighth border talks that bracketed Operation Checkerboard. K. Subrahmanyam, though, suggest that the Chinese evidently respected General K. Sundarji: soon after his retirement, they invited him to visit China.

69. "Ties With PRC, Border Situation Viewed," Foreign Broadcast Information Service, *Daily Report: Near East and South Asia,* November 9, 1992, pp. 50–51.

70. See Ganguly, "The Sino-Indian Border Talks," p. 1127.

2

Conflict between Pakistan and India: A View from Islamabad

Shireen M. Mazari

The conflict between India and Pakistan continues to dominate the strategic disunity of South Asia, despite global and regional structural changes over the decades. After the 1971 crisis and the signing of the Simla Agreement in 1972, Pakistan finally gave de facto recognition to India's dominant status in the subcontinent. The Simla Agreement laid the framework for future India-Pakistan relations; Pakistan agreed to a longstanding Indian demand by consenting to deal with all bilateral issues (except Kashmir, which was already on the UN agenda) on a bilateral basis. However, that framework has been subject to differing interpretations on both sides.

According to Indian analysts such as K. P. Misra, "never before in the history of the two countries [had] an agreement of such far-reaching consequences . . . been concluded."[1] Despite the significance of Simla, the conflictual relationship between Pakistan and India persists and continues to influence intra-regional relations.

Historical Overview

Even after nearly fifty years of independence, relations between Pakistan and India remain in a state of flux. The historical origins of this conflict are well known. The two states have fought three wars against each other and have engaged in numerous border skirmishes. In addition to their long-standing territorial dispute over Kashmir, the two states have accused each other of aiding various other ethnic conflicts in each other's territory. A new territorial dispute arose between the two states in 1982, after Indian forces occupied the Siachen Glacier.[2]

For a variety of reasons, including the mind-set of the decision-making elite, Pakistan has been unable to develop a regional answer to the security threat it perceives from India. Pakistan has therefore looked outside its immediate region to bolster its security. Until the mid-1960s, Pakistan relied upon an alliance with the United States to counterbalance the Indian threat. In fact, Pakistan's whole approach to international relations was defined by the western-oriented cold war framework—despite the strength of the non-aligned movement and the rising tide of Third World solidarity against the superpowers.

The failure of this U.S.-oriented security policy became all too clear after the Sino-Indian war in 1962, during which the United States provided military assistance to India. Ties with the United States frayed further when Washington penalized Pakistan for its rapprochement with China in the border agreement of 1964, first by suspending a $4.3 million loan, then by pressuring other industrialized states to postpone the 1965 meeting of the Aid to Pakistan Consortium. Finally, the United States suspended arms supplies to both India and Pakistan during their 1965 war. For Pakistan, this cutoff was a crucial blow, for unlike India, Pakistan was totally dependent upon the United States for its military supplies.

Although these moves strained U.S.-Pakistan ties somewhat after 1965, Pakistan maintained its links with the United States through military alliances and bilateral agreements, as well as through Pakistan's increasing interaction with the Gulf states and Iran. Not until the creation of Bangladesh was Pakistan finally shown the futility of its alliance with the United States. The so-called U.S. tilt toward Pakistan was not perceived as such by Pakistan, especially since the U.S. Naval Task Force did not enter the Bay of Bengal until after the fall of Dacca.

After 1971, Pakistan attempted to view its security concerns within a more indigenous framework of analysis, based upon lessons learned from recent experiences. The reality of the threat from India and the reluctance of the United States and other allies to provide the necessary support compelled Pakistan to completely restructure its defense potential. This restructuring included the development of an indigenous arms industry and an expansion of Pakistan's nascent nuclear program.

At the level of foreign policy, Pakistan's civilian government moved the country toward nonalignment and away from the United States. Prime Minister Z. A. Bhutto attempted to deal with the new realities in South Asia following the creation of Bangladesh by increasing Pakistan's involvement in the Middle East and decreasing it in South Asia. His goal was to develop a West Asian identity for Pakistan, drawing on its links with the Muslim states of the Middle East.

India's nuclear explosion in 1974 compelled Pakistan to deal once again with the threat posed by India. This time, however, the threat was from a potential nuclear power. This fact brought home to Pakistan yet again the necessity of acknowledging South Asia as the location of its primary external security concern, and therefore as the determinant of its strategic parameters.

Pakistan's security environment became critical with the 1979 Soviet invasion of Afghanistan and the Iranian revolution, both of which altered the region's geopolitical environment. Pakistan's ruling elite immediately shifted its attention to the northwestern and western borders. This dramatic shift was partly a product of the cold war psyche that still predominated among the decision-making elite; the influx of Afghan refugees provided the symbolic reality on which this psyche could thrive. Moreover, Pakistani elites realized that the Afghan crisis provided an ideal opportunity to reestablish links with the United States.

By playing an active role in the Afghan insurgency and willingly accommodating the surge of refugees pouring into the Northwest Frontier Province and Baluchistan, Pakistan's military dictatorship ensured a steady flow of military and economic assistance from the United States and its allies. Thus, the Afghan crisis forged an economic and military alliance between the United States, Pakistan, and Saudi Arabia that continues to shape Pakistan's security perceptions.

But by focusing almost single-mindedly on its border with Afghanistan, Pakistan neglected the security on its eastern front. In the next decade, Pakistan was confronted with India's incursions into Siachen and a brazen display of military might through Operation Brasstacks. Both of these incidents reiterated for Pakistan the continuing threat to its security from India.

Siachen and Brasstacks revealed clearly not only India's hostility toward Pakistan, but also the imbalance in conventional forces that continued to put Pakistan at a strategic disadvantage, despite the modernization of Pakistani weapons systems during the course of the Afghan crisis. This realization led the Zia regime to keep open Pakistan's nuclear option—an option that had gained credence since the Indian nuclear explosion of 1974. It was also this adamant defense of Pakistan's nuclear policy that made clear to Pakistani decision-makers the limitations of any alliance with the United States.

With the reestablishment of civilian rule in Pakistan in 1988, attempts were made at launching diplomatic overtures toward India and the U.S., but these also failed to resolve Pakistan's security problems. Although the U.S. initially seemed to be altering its biased approach to the issue of nuclear proliferation by calling for a regional solution, it nonetheless reverted to applying unilateral pressure upon Pakistan. Likewise, despite efforts at rapprochement with India, it became obvious that until basic conflictual issues were resolved there could be no long-lasting easing of tensions. The renewed movement for freedom in Kashmir made it clear that this issue, above all others, defines the parameters of the Pakistan-India relationship.

This historical overview shows that Pakistan's external security problems remain focused upon South Asia, and specifically upon India. Despite scholarly talk about the changing international environment, for Pakistan the regional socio-psychological milieu and the conflict with India remain essentially unchanged.

Prevailing Perspective

Two critical dimensions define the Pakistani-India conflict today: the psychological dimension and the structural dimension.

Psychological Dimension

From the Pakistani perspective, the Indian leadership continues to be perceived as one that persistently refuses to accept the finality of the creation of the state of Pakistan.[3] Although the manner in which they express it may have altered, Indian leaders have consistently reiterated the central belief of the Indian political psyche in relation to Pakistan: that inherently there is no difference "religiously, culturally, and otherwise" between the two nations. For instance, in an interview in November 1991, the then-foreign secretary of India, Muchkund Dubey, referred to the "psychological syndrome and barrier that was built by the two-nation theory,"[4] and in the process himself echoed the deeply ingrained psychological barrier that has prevented the Indian leadership from accepting the legitimacy of the creation of Pakistan since 1947.

At the same time, the Pakistani psyche has undergone subtle shifts in its perception of India as a result of its experiences in the three Indo-Pakistani wars, the last of which led to the break-up of Pakistan and the creation of Bangladesh. As Lawrence Ziring puts it, "the trauma associated with the 1971 dismemberment is not necessarily visible but it permeates the attentive public's psyche."[5] Pakistan increasingly viewed its strength negatively in relation to India, abandoning the psychological ascendancy that was propagated in the early years of independence through popularization of the "martial races" theory, whereby one Muslim soldier was equivalent to at least four Hindus.

This lowered self-image has tremendously affected Pakistan's security perceptions, especially within the subjective context of the notion of security as the "absence of fear" of an attack on "acquired values."[6] A subjective assessment of security threats is as important as objective factors in evaluating long-term security needs for any state, since the future cannot really be measured objectively. This subjective assessment is influenced, however, by perceptions of a state's own power and the frequency of past conflicts.

So, noticeably, Pakistan perceives itself as having recognized the new power imbalance on the subcontinent and as having made concessions on a number of issues in relation to India since the Afghan crisis. Furthermore, these concessions are perceived as having gained little substantive response from India. For instance, compare General Zia's no-war-pact offer to India with Indian incursions into Siachen; Benazir's conciliatory policies toward India (where the agreement not to attack each other's nuclear facilities means that either Pakistan will have to reveal its entire nuclear program [which unlike India's is not public] or the nondeclared facilities will continue to be under threat of attack) with India's response to the Kashmiri insurgency; the Sharif government's overall low profile on Kashmir with India's continuing intransigence on this conflict; or the continuing issue of sectarianism in India, and India's increasing externalization of the issue by attempting to cite Pakistan's involvement.

This psychological dimension becomes critical, since it plays upon and aggravates the structural dimension of Pakistan's relationship with India.

Structural Dimension

One major source of instability in the region remains the prevalence of internal subnational conflicts that spill over into neighboring states—e.g., the Tamil and Sikh conflicts and the revival of Hindu militancy in India. From Pakistan's perspective, India has attempted to capitalize on its domestic ethnic and sectarian conflicts by linking them with the Kashmiri struggle in an effort to incriminate Pakistan in all these conflicts, especially at the level of global projection. U.S. threats to label Pakistan a terrorist state have only encouraged India to capitalize upon this and accuse Pakistan of aiding "terrorism" in India.

Of course, Pakistan has a commitment to provide assistance against Indian repression in what it calls Occupied Kashmir, which has been recognized as disputed territory within the UN itself and therefore is not an integral part of India. This commitment, however, has been used by India to show that Pakistan is in fact abetting ethnic and religious violence across India wherever it happens to erupt. These charges in turn put pressure on the U.S. to declare Pakistan a terrorist state, which increases fears in the Pakistani psyche that this is about to happen and thereby compels the latter to accommodate the demands of the new U.S. regional agenda in South Asia. This agenda includes accommodation with India, especially over the nuclear and Kashmir issues, on terms not necessarily consonant with Pakistan's perception of its security interests.

Given Pakistan's perception of its disadvantaged position in relation to its regional security at the structural level, Pakistan has abandoned efforts to equate its military strength and status in the region with that of India, and instead attempts to define its military needs in terms of maintaining a minimum level of a credible deterrence as defense against what is perceived as a very real threat from India. Thus Pakistan's approach to arms control has been dominated by its regional defense and security concerns in relation to India, particularly given Pakistan's disadvantage in terms of conventional military strength. Conventional defense has not only proved inadequate for Pakistan, it has also proved to be a heavy financial burden. Given India's qualitative and quantitative advantages in this area, Pakistan's conventional military doctrines cannot provide either a viable deterrence or defense capability.

The Nuclear Rationale

Within the framework of this Indo-Pakistan relationship, the nuclear factor has tended to promote stability in the region, in that Pakistan is no longer driven to establish conventional arms equality with India, since it no longer suffers from heightened insecurity in the face of India's preponderant conventional military advantage. Pakistan's nuclear capability and limited missile-delivery system have provided the opportunity to rationalize its strategic doctrines within a mix of counter-force and counter-value options.[7]

It is believed that in the summer of 1990, at the height of the Kashmir insurgency, war between India and Pakistan was averted after Pakistan informed India of its nuclear capability. This implies that the nuclear factor has and will continue to limit local conflicts.

Since the development of missiles by these two states seems rational primarily within a nuclear context, these technologically advanced means of delivery can only lend stability to the threat environment within the region. Any arms reduction efforts in the region, therefore, can arise only out of regional initiatives, which in turn are only feasible when the states concerned feel their security is not being undermined.

Meanwhile, the acquisition and production of missiles, when combined with nuclear capability, also allow India and Pakistan to reduce their huge conventional force budgets and divert scarce resources into the development sector—thereby easing some internal problems—despite the continuance of a mutual threat perception. The case of South Asia, in fact, shows that, far from creating instability in the region, missile development has stabilized conflictual relationships by preventing limited military confrontations from escalating into all-out wars.

Now the relevant issue is the development of confidence- and security-building mechanisms and structures for the peaceful resolution of conflicts.

As Janne Nolan has pointed out, the advantage of confidence- and security-building measures (CSBMs) is that they allow the issue of relative military capabilities to be bypassed, since the purpose of CSBMs is to assess intent rather than actual capability.[8] Given that numerous efforts for confidence-building and détente between India and Pakistan have collapsed in the face of the resurgent issues such as Kashmir, the importance of creating structures for the peaceful resolution of conflicts is critical to the implementation of CSBMs.

Additionally, what is perceived as a highly discriminatory approach by the United States and its allies toward Pakistan's nuclear program has not only hindered regional nonproliferation, it has also politicized the issue. This negative political interventionism, whether in the form of isolation or deprivation of technology and aid, has made it difficult for the government in Pakistan to renounce the acquisition of nuclear weapons, because of anticipated domestic fallout.[9] By its almost exclusive focus on the Nuclear Nonproliferation Treaty (NPT), the United States has excluded the evolution of other, more viable regional nonproliferation options.

From the nuclear proliferation perspective, Pakistan has three options:

1. To succumb to international pressure and sign the NPT unilaterally;
2. To arrive at a regional nonproliferation arrangement; and
3. To declare its weapons capability.

The NPT in its present form is not an option; apart from the treaty's inherent inequalities, it offers no concrete security guarantees against nuclear attack for non-nuclear-weapons parties to the treaty. For practical purposes, from the Pakistani perspective, the NPT is a dead treaty and outdated in its very definition of a nuclear-weapons state.[10] This fact became even more relevant when the breakup of the Soviet Union suddenly produced four new nuclear weapons states.

The ruling elite in Pakistan tends to favor the second option listed above, while domestic opinion increasingly leans toward the third option. One major factor in the public popularity of a nuclear declaration is the belief by a number of Pakistani analysts that a nuclear weapons capability is the country's only viable long-term defense policy option. The history of Pakistan's attempts to provide for its security and to preserve its territorial integrity through conventional military means, alliances, UN diplomacy, and friendship with China and the Arab world is a history of failure. With international sanctions having been imposed in what is seen as a highly discriminatory fashion, there is a growing belief in Pakistan that the time is at hand to declare the country's weapons capability. Furthermore, even if Pakistan opts for nonproliferation in the long term, acquiring a weapons capability will offer it a bargaining chip in seeking a suitable nonproliferation arrangement with India.

Rational Options to Improve the Indo-Pakistani Relationship

Within the overall prevailing regional scenario, then, Pakistan presently sees its relationship with India as a major security concern, in which the U.S. has created an increasing disadvantage for Pakistan. Any long-term improvements in the relationship must address the security concerns of Pakistan. They would also have to resolve the dispute over Kashmir in accordance with the wishes of the Kashmiris. Since the Indo-Pakistani problem is primarily one of security and defense, dialogues and efforts to develop regional integration frameworks like the South Asian Association for Regional Cooperation (SAARC) will not get very far unless these two basic issues are dealt with.

Regional economic and social integration will come about only as a result of political motivation, as has been the case in the development of most other organizations for regional cooperation and integration, such as the European Union (EU) or the Association of Southeast Asian Nations (ASEAN). Unless it develops mechanisms for dealing with the political conflicts dominating the region, SAARC can only work on the fringes of regional integration and cannot have any impact upon conflict resolution. The focus for conflict resolution, therefore, needs to center on the issue of security, and therefore on CSBMs in the field of arms control.

Advanced Weaponry Nonproliferation

A more equitable approach toward India and Pakistan is a prerequisite for any meaningful progress toward the nonproliferation of advanced weaponry in the region. Specifically, discriminatory policies aimed only at Pakistan will continue to hinder any real progress in this area. A rational starting point would be to acknowledge the nuclear weapons capability of both India and Pakistan and, if a need is felt by the two states to renounce their nuclear capability, to seek to develop a regional nonproliferation regime based upon this premise. Currently, Pakistan perceives a need to maintain a nuclear deterrent, regardless of what India decides, as long as conflictual issues remain unresolved.

Within a nonproliferation framework, however, the more feasible policy options include

1. a regional framework for nonproliferation in South Asia;
2. confidence- and security-building measures, especially those intended to increase transparency; and

3. multinational cooperation in the nuclear energy field.

The first of these options offers a more viable option than the NPT. The Tlatelolco Treaty, which established a nuclear-weapons-free zone in Latin America, offers a viable model. Yet India has consistently objected to Pakistan's various proposals for a nonproliferation arrangement for South Asia, on the grounds that the issue extends beyond the region. This position reflects both India's desire to play the role of a regional power and its reluctance to join a regional nonproliferation arrangement in the face of China's nuclear weapons status. India has denied its regional power ambitions, but the second consideration has been voiced clearly on a number of occasions. Pakistan's narrow, bilateral focus has prevented any attempt to deal with India's concerns vis-á-vis China in its various proposals.

Again, the Tlatelolco Treaty model can give Pakistan the initiative on the nonproliferation issue in South Asia and at the same time, would allow both India and Pakistan to explore beyond their original, stalemated positions. First of all, unlike the NPT, the Tlatelolco Treaty places no time limit on its definition of a nuclear weapons state. It also distinguishes between military and peaceful uses of nuclear technology, thereby allowing states the economic benefits of the latter.[11] Furthermore, Protocol I of the Tlatelolco Treaty requires, through signatures and ratification, a commitment by external states with territorial interests in the region "to undertake to apply the statute of denuclearization in respect of warlike purposes" in these territories. This protocol has been ratified by all the concerned states (Britain, the United States, the Netherlands) except France, which has signed but not yet ratified the protocol. Protocol II of the Tlatelolco Treaty commits nuclear-weapons states to respect fully the "denuclearization of Latin America in respect of warlike purposes" and also to "undertake not to use or threaten to use nuclear weapons" against parties to the treaty. This protocol has been signed and ratified by all five nuclear-weapon states.

With protocols like these in a similar treaty for South Asia, India's concerns relating to China and other nuclear-weapons states would hold little validity. China, by signing a Protocol II–like model for South Asia, would be making an international treaty commitment to desist not only from using or threatening to use nuclear weapons against India (if the latter was party to such a treaty), but also from introducing nuclear weapons within the area covered by the treaty. The Chinese have already signed and ratified similar protocols that are part of other NWFZ treaties.[12]

With regard to the second policy option, confidence- and security-building measures between Pakistan and India, especially transparency measures, can reduce the likelihood of preemption. Indeed, some have already been initiated, although so far they have proven to be of limited value. The Pakistan-India accord on non-attack on each other's nuclear facilities will ease to some degree Pakistan's fears regarding its nuclear facilities, once both sides declare their nuclear capabilities. The military hotline and the sharing of advance information regarding military exercises are developments that enhance stability in the region.[13]

As to the third option, multinational nuclear fuel centers and other nuclear cooperation in the energy field need to be developed. Pakistan has very limited conventional energy sources; access to a secure source of nuclear energy has played a critical role in Pakistan's nuclear policy formulation. Multinational nuclear fuel centers, in which the technology would be controlled jointly by India and Pakistan, would allow both states to utilize nuclear energy for peaceful purposes without any suspicions being cast on this use—since neither state would allow the other to divert resources from such centers for military purposes.

As for the overall issue of technology denial, as long as regional conflicts persist in the absence of any mechanism to resolve them peacefully, the option of war and appropriate weapons capability will always be present. Given the excessive technical information available in the open literature, as well as the availability of a skilled labor force to both India and Pakistan, technology denial can at best delay the acquisition of advanced weapons capability—especially since arms control and disarmament in this region are premised almost entirely on politico-military rationales; economic and technical factors are at best secondary.

Conventional Force Reductions

From Pakistan's perspective, conventional force reductions in South Asia would greatly enhance Pakistan's security perceptions, since it is in this field that it finds itself unable to sustain either a qualitative or a quantitative balance with India. One viable example of a conventional force reduction agreement for South Asia could be based on the 1990 Paris Treaty, which laid the ground for force reductions in Europe (CFE Treaty). In the case of India and Pakistan, a similar treaty could also require both India and Pakistan to thin out troop deployments along the borders as well as to carry out overall troop and weapons reductions within measures instituted to achieve military transparency.

Conclusion

Of course, any conventional force reductions would have to be preceded by positive steps toward the resolution of the Kashmir dispute. For Pakistan, the issue is not one of Kashmir acceding to Pakistan or becoming independent. Instead, Pakistan has consistently maintained that it seeks the implementation of the UN resolutions on the issue, which require the holding of a plebiscite.[14] The uprising in Kashmir is indigenous and cannot be controlled or manipulated by external forces. That India has lost Kashmir politically is obvious. The Indian argument that, if it lets go of Kashmir, it will be under increasing pressure from internal "fissiparous" forces does not hold much weight, since Kashmir was never an integral part of the Indian state. The UN and therefore the international community as a whole, has acknowledged the disputed status of Kashmir. The UN needs to fulfill its obligations in relation to this dispute. Unless the Kashmir issue is resolved, taking into account the wishes of the Kashmiri people, there can be no long-term easing of tensions between India and Pakistan and therefore no reduction of military buildups in South Asia.

Apart from Kashmir, the most pressing need is for India to tone down its rhetoric against Pakistan every time it is faced with domestic political violence, especially sectarian violence. The Indian polity must accept the changing and eroding national consensus that was premised on secularism. Merely blaming Pakistan only results in an equally hostile response within Pakistan's domestic polity. Given the very real conflicts that exist between the two states, such efforts to build up hostile nationalist swells against each other only increase the chances of an unwanted military conflict. With increasingly dissipated domestic political structures in both India and Pakistan, neither side has much to gain from entering into a military conflict.

In the prevailing environment in South Asia, there is not only an increasing linkage between the psychological and structural dimensions of the conflictual Pakistan-India relationship, the former is increasingly aggravating the latter. This means that unless the psychological dimension is dealt with, the structural dimension of the conflict will remain inaccessible to resolution by peaceful means.

Notes

1. K. P. Misra, "Regional Peace and Security: Coalescence and Clash in Indo-Pakistan Relations," *India Quarterly* 40, nos. 3 and 4 (July–December 1984), p. 270.

2. Col. Edgar O'Ballance, "India's South Asian Doctrine," *Armed Forces* 8, no. 5 (May 1989), p. 228. After the 1949 cease-fire in Jammu and Kashmir, a cease-fire line was demarcated. This became the line of control in 1972 as a result of the Simla Agreement. The northern part of this line runs into the Himalayas and stops just short of the Siachen Glacier. At the time it was considered unnecessary to demarcate the line further as the terrain ahead was impassable. Pakistan has claimed the glacier as part of its territory.

3. These suspicions regarding Indian objectives vis-à-vis Pakistan are brought out consistently in off-the-record conversations with Pakistani civil and military decision-makers. Indian decision-makers' statements in times of heightened tension between the two states tend to substantiate the credibility of this theme.

4. *The News* (Rawalpindi/Islamabad), November 2, 1991.

5. Lawrence Ziring, ed., *Pakistan: The Long View* (Durham, N.C.: Duke University Press, 1977), p. 6.

6. Arnold Wolfers, *Discord and Collaboration* (Baltimore, MD.: Johns Hopkins University Press, 1962), p. 150.

7. A feasible scenario for Pakistan, initially, would be a counter-value doctrine at the strategic level focusing on three to five of the population-industrial centers of India within medium-range striking distance—such as Bombay and Delhi. Within this overall nuclear framework, Pakistan would have the ability to utilize conventional state-of-the-art weaponry within a tactical counter-force doctrine focusing on the main battlefront, which will be the southeast border with India—given the focus of India's Operation Brasstacks and Pakistan's Zarb-i-Momin. This doctrine will allow Pakistan to trim its vast conventional forces yet retain a highly professional and technologically sophisticated armed force.

8. Janne Nolan, *Trappings of Power* (Washington D.C.: Brookings, 1991).

9. Komal Anwar, "Pakistani Nuclear Policy: Domestic Perspective," unpublished monograph written under the aegis of the Department of Defence and Strategic Studies, Quaid-i-Azam University, Islamabad, June 1993. In this paper, a sample survey was conducted in Islamabad of a cross-section of educated public opinion. The findings indicated an overwhelming majority of those questioned favored the nuclear option for Pakistan.

10. It has a static definition whereby nuclear-weapons states are those that had exploded a nuclear device before January 1, 1967. See Article IX:3.

11. Although there has been little discussion of the civilian aspect of nuclear capability within Pakistan, India has always maintained that its 1974 nuclear explosion was a peaceful nuclear explosion (PNE). Since the Tlatelolco Treaty allows for PNEs, keeping the option open while committing to nuclear weapons nonproliferation would answer detractors in both states who use the PNE argument against making a nonproliferation commitment within the NPT framework.

12. Although any state can renege on its treaty commitments, international censure must be considered. There is no rational reason to assume that the Chinese are less likely to keep their international treaty obligations than are the United States and other major powers.

13. Although a state determined to carry out a preemptive attack can always ignore these agreements, the very fact that states enter into such agreements shows a willingness to create a stable security environment. Nor will states give up their own national intelligence surveillance means, so using the CSBMs for purposes of deception would not be feasible. In any event, if deception were the policy objective, then CSBMs would hardly be a priority for the states concerned.

14. The sticking point over one component of the 1949 resolutions has been over the withdrawal of forces. Pakistan was required to withdraw its forces from Kashmir while India was to withdraw the bulk of its forces. The problem arose because there was no agreement over what constituted the "bulk." But, in principle, Pakistan has officially maintained its adherence to the UN resolutions as a framework for resolving the Kashmir conflict.

3

Sources of Conflict between China and India as Seen from Beijing

Rosemary Foot

In a recent semi-official Chinese study of the diplomacy of modern China that was prepared for publication in the late 1980s, the start of the chapter on India emphasized the similarities between these two great Asian powers and notes with appreciation India's support for China during the difficult decade of the 1950s. Both countries, the study argues, had "suffered deeply from colonial aggression and oppression" and shared similar or identical views on many international issues. The study also recalls that India had given early recognition to the People's Republic of China (PRC); had steadfastly supported the PRC's assumption of the UN seat and the return of Taiwan to the mainland; had been helpful to China's position during the Korean War; and had worked with China to make a success of the Bandung Conference in 1955. In 1954, Premier Zhou Enlai and Prime Minister Nehru had signed an agreement based on the newly formulated five principles of peaceful coexistence, principles that are deemed to be of crucial significance in determining the basis of China's foreign relations to this day.[1]

Yet differences developed between these two neighbors. The study mentioned above highlights Tibet as an early trouble spot; India in 1950 and 1951 attempted to maintain a "special status and influence in that area," and interfered during the 1959 rebellion there. The boundary dispute—"the biggest problem left over from history"—was also a source of tension. The first armed conflict on the border in 1959 has been linked to developments in Sino-Soviet and Soviet-American relations; according to the Chinese, Soviet Communist Party Chairman Nikita Khrushchev believed that the armed conflict between China and India might undermine the success of his upcoming summit in the United States and thus issued a statement that

Beijing perceived as being partial to India. In Beijing's view, this made Sino-Soviet differences "public to the world."[2]

These three issues—Tibet, the boundary demarcation, and the Sino-Soviet-Indian relationship—have been the explicit focus of the dispute with India as far as the Chinese are concerned, and two of them still have salience in the post–cold war era. The first chapter in this book examines these matters from the Indian point of view. This chapter will outline the Chinese perspective on these issues over the three main phases of the Sino-Indian relationship: the era of friendship in the 1950s; the period of intense hostility and conflict from the late 1950s to the early 1970s; and the movement toward normalized relations from the late 1970s to the current day.

The Era of Friendship

Points of contention arose between China and India even during the 1950s. Although New Delhi and Beijing initialed a trade agreement in April 1954 that regulated commerce between Tibet and India, three years earlier India had expressed concerns about China's assertion of control over Tibet. In February 1952, New Delhi had presented China with a memorandum outlining India's interests in the region, which included the rights to trade, to pilgrimage, and to maintain military escorts in the area. During the negotiations over these issues, Zhou had referred to the boundary as an outstanding question whose settlement could be left to some future date.[3]

In a broader sense, it was clear that these two nations had competing visions of their roles in Asia and beyond. Although both sides tried to stress their common experiences and hopes for the future, as Mansingh and Levine have argued, "Maoist China saw itself as a revolutionary socialist great power providing symbolic leadership to all oppressed peoples against the dominant powers," whereas "India's self-image in Nehru's time was that of a major power pioneering new principles of peaceful international relations through the concepts of nonalignment and evolutionary change."[4] The superpowers were to reinforce these perceptions of competing images. From the Truman through the Kennedy administrations, for example, U.S. officials posed India as the democratic alternative to China, and argued that if China advanced while India failed then the totalitarian model would influence all of Asia.[5] Soviet courting of India from the mid-1950s owed much to Moscow's positive reappraisal of the role of the nonaligned in the struggle between the socialist and capitalist blocs and to its assumption that a peaceful transition to socialism was both possible and to be encouraged.

Finally, although both China and India shared the language of anti-imperialism, the corollary of this for each country was a fierce commitment to the protection of its own national sovereignty and territorial integrity, commitments that were likely to raise the sensitivity of issues such as Tibet and the boundary.

Without the unrest that emerged in Tibet, this underlying rivalry might not have deepened into the outright hostility of the 1960s. The Chinese army's entry into Tibet in 1950 had dissolved a useful buffer zone between the two states. It was the continuing unrest in Tibet, however, that highlighted the border issue. Because a large section of the disputed boundary runs along Tibet's southern frontier, the tension over conflicting claims is exacerbated by the sensitive issue of the status of Tibet as a signatory to the McMahon agreement. This agreement was negotiated between the Tibetans and the British in Delhi in March 1914, after London had failed at Simla to secure the formal adherence of China to a trilateral agreement. Acceptance of the McMahon agreement could imply that, in the earlier part of this century, Tibetans had the recognized right to negotiate and sign treaties with foreign powers, an implication to which the Chinese do not want to give added currency.[6]

In order to be in a better position to quell disturbances in Tibet, the Chinese Army in 1956 began the construction of a road, some 750 miles in length, joining Xinjiang and Tibet. The road followed a traditional caravan route through the Aksai Chin plateau. At the time, it provided the only modern means of transporting troops between potentially rebellious regions. In October 1957, the New China News Agency announced the road's completion. Indian patrols were then dispatched to investigate the accuracy of the announcement. By October 1958, New Delhi was formally protesting that the road cut across Indian territory and the boundary dispute was set to enter a more acute phase.[7]

The Period of Hostility

The revolt in Lhasa in March 1959, which led to the flight of the Dalai Lama and about 100,000 of his followers to India, enhanced the strategic significance of the Xinjiang-Tibet road. These developments led to an outburst of hostile polemics between China and India and a buildup of Chinese troops in the Tibet-India border area. Minor skirmishes took place between July and October 1959; the most serious, in October, led to the death of nine Indian policemen and one Chinese soldier.[8] China's distrust of Indian sympathy for the Dalai Lama was compounded by Beijing's realization that his flight to India had been a U.S. CIA operation. For years, in fact, Chinese leaders had been accumulating evidence that linked Tibetan insurgents with Chinese Nationalist agents and the CIA operating from bases in Southeast Asia.[9] Thus, the Tibetan rebellion, in which India had now become directly involved, always had for China a broader security context.

As relations with India deteriorated and it proved impossible to find a means of delineating the border, the movement toward the 1962 war quickened. From China's perspective, fears about India's "aggressive patrolling" in 1962 came at a time of internal disarray in China, brought about by the failure of the Great Leap Forward. Chinese Nationalist leader Chiang Kai-shek's bold words about using the opportunity provided by these calamities to launch an attack on the mainland heightened Beijing's siege mentality and its sense of India as a strategic enemy. Furthering this sense of vulnerability was Chinese leaders' apparent belief that Chiang's plan had U.S. backing and that Beijing could not count on Moscow's support. As China's foreign minister, Chen Yi, told a group of Japanese journalists in May 1962, "Pentagon generals . . . may support Chiang Kai-shek in starting a 'counter-offensive on the mainland' . . . . Or they may be planning to raise trouble in the western border area of China by utilizing the China-India border dispute. . . . On the one hand we must overcome the economic difficulties due to the three years of natural calamities and, on the other, provide against the provocations of a Chiang Kai-shek supported by America . . . [and] against incidents that may occur on other borders."[10]

This reference to other borders referred not only to the Sino-Indian but also to the Sino-Soviet boundary in the area of Xinjiang, which had become tense during this period. The Chinese had been attempting to settle large numbers of Han people in this region and measures to Sinicize the area had been stepped up, particularly during the Great Leap Forward. Local resistance to the policies associated with the Great Leap and their subsequent disastrous economic effects led dissidents to flee north into Soviet Central Asia, a migration that both Moscow and Beijing acknowledged took place in 1960 and again more seriously in 1962. That year, China linked these border incidents and the general deterioration in its relationship with Moscow with its vulnerability on other fronts: "In 1962, when China was faced with temporary economic difficulties and when the Taiwan authorities who had the backing of the United States were clamoring for a 'counterattack on the mainland,' the Soviet Union instigated and coerced more than 60,000 Chinese citizens in the Ili and Tacheng areas of China's Xinjiang to cross the border into the Soviet Union and even stirred up the Yining Rebellion in May the same year, causing increasing unrest along the Sino-Soviet border."[11] According to Ambassador Wang Bingnan's memoirs, it was also in May that he was called to see Premier Zhou and told that Chiang thought it a good time to attack the mainland because "externally the CPC was on bad terms with the Soviet Union, and at home on the mainland there were serious natural disasters."[12] Although shortly after this the Chinese government received assurances that the Kennedy administration would not support a Chinese Nationalist invasion of the

PRC, the combination of these threats powerfully influenced China's beliefs about its security environment.

The Sino-Soviet alliance was collapsing at the same moment that Soviet-Indian ties were tangibly strengthening. As Soviet technicians were being withdrawn abruptly from China, Moscow was signing new military and economic aid agreements with New Delhi. Some $500 million was offered in mid-1960 in support of India's third five-year plan. Military credits were granted in the autumn of 1960, and in April 1961 Moscow sold India eight Antonov-12 four-engine turboprop transport planes and agreed that forty Russian pilots, navigators, and mechanics would accompany them. This was followed by twenty-four Ilyushin-14 transports and ten Mil-4 helicopters capable of lifting troops and supplies to altitudes of 17,000 feet. In addition, New Delhi purchased six Soviet-made jet engines for indigenously manufactured aircraft and in 1962 acquired a further sixteen Mil-4s and eight An-12s. In August 1962 an agreement was reached for the purchase of twelve MiG-21s and the provision of Soviet technical assistance for the manufacture of these aircraft under license in India.[13] The juxtaposition of Soviet statements of neutrality over the Sino-Indian border dispute with these military agreements and deliveries gave strong support to the argument that India had replaced China as Moscow's major partner in Asia. Even after the war with China had broken out and as India turned to Washington for military assistance at a time when it feared a wholesale Chinese invasion, Nehru took the step of informing Soviet leaders of his request to the United States and was allegedly reassured that "Moscow understood both the request and the need for it."[14]

In light of these developments, China moved swiftly to enhance its ties with Pakistan, the one state that could form a breach in the arc of hostile powers that seemed to surround the PRC. In 1963, the two governments signed border, trade, and air agreements, the border being that along the disputed territory of Kashmir. In 1964, China gave its support for the Pakistani position on Kashmir; previously it had tried to steer clear of the issue. Also that year, China offered its first interest-free loan to Pakistan and began high-level military contacts. Chinese military assistance started in 1966 and, as a result of the U.S. embargo introduced in 1965, Beijing quickly became Islamabad's main arms supplier.[15]

The Pakistan-China axis was never a match for the Soviet-Indian relationship, which was based on a consistency of approach from the mid-1950s and a wide range of military, political, and economic resources that Moscow put at New Delhi's disposal. Moscow, for example, could veto resolutions in the UN Security Council unfavorable to India's positions, could offer oil and economic assistance on generous terms, and could provide some of its most sophisticated military hardware. Between 1954 and 1975, India was the largest recipient of Soviet economic aid—some $1.26 billion in grants and credits, representing 18 percent of all Soviet assistance provided to the non-communist world. By 1965, India had become Moscow's largest non-communist trading partner. The military hardware transferred between 1965 and 1974 has been valued at over $1.37 billion, and, according to SIPRI calculations, $1.1 billion of that came between 1970 and 1976, a time when the Soviet Union was China's primary enemy. The signature in 1980 of a military credit worth $1.63 billion was intended to provide India with the ability to purchase Soviet weaponry, including the MiG-29, over the following ten to fifteen years.[16]

During the 1965 Indo-Pakistani war, China had tried to convince Islamabad of the value of the Sino-Pakistani relationship. Beijing publicly supported "Pakistan's counterattack in self-defense against India's armed provocations" and attempted to raise fears that India faced a two-front war when it demanded that New Delhi "dismantle all aggressive military structures on the China-Sikkim border, withdraw its aggressive armed forces and stop all its acts of aggression and provocation against China in the Western, Middle, and Eastern sections of the Sino-Indian border."[17] But it was Moscow that hosted the subsequent peace conference at Tashkent later in the year and followed it with improved ties with Pakistan—temporarily at least.

China was not as forthcoming in its support in the 1971 war that dismembered Pakistan, partly because of the terms of the Soviet-Indian Treaty of Friendship signed in August that year, which had a defense clause pledging "appropriate effective measures to ensure peace and security for their countries" should either be attacked by a third party. Allegedly, the Soviet Union also issued explicit threats against China, warning it of a Soviet reaction if Beijing intervened in the conflict between India and Pakistan. It has also been suggested that Moscow moved ground and air forces into position along what was already a heavily armed border in Xinjiang and that it trained missiles on Chinese targets.[18]

As relations with the Soviet Union deteriorated to the point where the Soviets came to be viewed as China's main strategic enemy, relations with India became hostage to the state of Sino-Soviet relations. For several years, therefore, China tried to undermine Soviet schemes to encircle China by undermining the strength of India, either by offering support to the weaker regional states such as Pakistan, Bangladesh (after Mujib's overthrow in 1975), and Nepal, or by offering support to insurgent groups such as the Nagas and Mizos. In the latter half of the 1970s, however, new developments in China's internal and external policies began to push Beijing toward a reappraisal of its relationship with India. Chinese leaders decided that relations should be normalized—a process that has been slow and halting[19] but which nevertheless has witnessed progress, even as the border issue has proved stubbornly resistant to resolution.

Movement toward Normalization

The Chinese approach to and perception of India changed for two main reasons. In the post-Mao era, Chinese leaders reassessed many of their past foreign and domestic policies and reflected on the mixed results of those policies. It was doubtful whether by 1976 the Beijing regime had managed to provide its people with the national wealth and security that supposedly had been its prime goals since 1949. The "Four Modernizations Program," implemented energetically once Vice Premier Deng Xiaoping had consolidated his grip on power, was designed to address these economic and security failures. Deng understood that, apart from the obvious desirability of raising the standard of living, an economically strong and developed China would be better able to guarantee the country's safety. Furthermore, Deng argued that, in order to concentrate primary attention on economic advancement, a peaceful international environment was essential. Obviously, a normalization of relations with India would contribute to that need. Given the signs that India also desired a more productive relationship with its Asian neighbor—not least in order to provide greater political distance between itself and Moscow—the prospects for normalization seemed promising.

The other major impetus for change related to the nature of the Indo-Soviet and Sino-Soviet relationships in the late 1970s and early 1980s. The Chinese leadership interpreted the Soviet intervention in Afghanistan as part of a move to secure warm-water ports on the Indian Ocean that could then be used to control sea lanes carrying vital materials to Western Europe and Japan. Locally, it meant that Afghanistan no longer operated as a buffer between western China and the USSR and that Pakistan itself had come under a renewed threat. In these circumstances, China was anxious to chart the Indian reaction to this alteration in the geostrategic environment of South Asia. Beijing was reasonably reassured by the outcome and took note of India's refusal to identify itself closely with the Russian position. An authoritative article in *Renmin Ribao* in February 1980, for example, stated that the "Indian prime minister has said that the situation in Afghanistan has brought danger closer to India." The New Delhi government "would not support any country sending troops into another country." The article went on: "These propositions and views are very conducive to the strengthening of relations among the countries of South Asia, to opposing hegemonism, and to maintaining peace in Asia."[20] The inability of Moscow or New Delhi to mention the Afghan issue directly in any of the joint communiques produced after official visits in the early 1980s led Beijing to conclude that the two allies had "agreed to disagree" on this key issue.[21]

These positive appraisals of India and the apparent resentment felt in New Delhi at heavy-handed Soviet attempts to impede the normalization of relations between China and India led swiftly to two specific policy changes in Beijing. First, China shifted its position on Kashmir; in June 1980 Deng Xiaoping described the issue as a bilateral problem between India and Pakistan that they should settle peacefully. Second, China expressed a willingness to discuss the border issue, which it previously had argued should not be tackled before progress had been made in other areas. Official talks on the boundary were held in December 1981 and seven more rounds of talks were arranged between then and 1988. The first four concerned "basic principles" and the last four the "situation on the ground."[22] The fourth round was the most significant of the eight, in that the Chinese dropped their insistence on an all-encompassing proposal and substituted a sector-by-sector approach, and both sides agreed to the improvement of relations in other areas.

Despite this joint desire to be more accommodating and despite foreign minister–level meetings in New York and an invitation in 1985 to Prime Minister Rajiv Gandhi to visit Beijing, the boundary question was not resolved. Nor did these developments prevent a serious flare-up of tension on the border in 1986 and 1987. But the period between the seventh round of talks in July 1986 and the eighth round in November 1987 appears to have been an important learning exercise for both sides. Increased border patrolling in the summer of 1986 had brought Chinese and Indian troops into close and more frequent contact. Charge and countercharge raised tension to a pitch so high that the Chinese used U.S. Defense Secretary Caspar Weinberger—during his visit to the subcontinent—to pass on a message to New Delhi's leaders that Beijing would have to "teach India a lesson" if it did not stop "nibbling" at Chinese territory.[23] The Indian decision in December 1986 to raise Arunachal Pradesh, which was disputed territory, to the level of a state further increased Chinese irritation. The PRC described it as an "illegal act . . . on a part of Chinese territory it has illegally occupied, an act that grossly violates China's sovereignty and territorial integrity and hurts the national feelings of the Chinese people."[24] When Indian forces launched Operation Checkerboard in the spring of 1987, the Chinese foreign ministry issued a statement urging India to withdraw its troops along the border, and "avoid a possible unpleasant event."[25] Later in the year, the delicate issue of Tibet's status was raised when Chinese sources noted that Indian newspapers were urging Rajiv Gandhi to insist that China honor the McMahon agreement of 1914.[26]

Unlike in 1962, however, neither side allowed these border disturbances to get out of hand. In their explanation of this greater restraint in 1986–87, Mansingh and Levine point to a variety of changes that had occurred in both countries' external and internal policy environments. On the Chinese side, Beijing did not feel as vulnerable in 1987 as it had in 1962; its economy was much stronger, its relations with both superpowers had been improved in the intervening twenty-five years, and, despite unrest in Tibet, India offered reassurances that it regarded upheavals in this area as China's internal affair. Perhaps there was a recognition, too, that any war this time would be a more bloody and costly business given India's increased conventional strength. Thus in 1987 the outcome was not war but Rajiv Gandhi's decision to go to Beijing the following year.

Beijing's adoption of its "independent foreign policy" in 1982 and the "independent foreign policy of peace" in 1985 led to a steady improvement in its relations with the Soviet Union

and a greater emphasis on developing good relations with all countries regardless of their political systems. The advances in relations with Moscow, in turn, had a positive influence on Sino-Indian relations. During the border crisis of 1986 and 1987, India looked to its Soviet ally for support. In India to celebrate the fifteenth anniversary of the Soviet-Indian treaty of friendship, Moscow's chief representative was dogged by reporters in vain search of some statement of support for the Indian position. The Soviet leader, Mikhail Gorbachev, felt similar pressure during his visit to India in November 1986, but "typically refused to take India's side in its conflict with China," pleading "ignorance regarding the Sumdorong Chu incident" and calling for better relations among all three parties so that "no one will have to choose sides."[27] China was swift in pointing out the significance of this change in the Soviet-Indian relationship. Beijing also suggested in a report of Gorbachev's second visit to New Delhi in November 1988 that, with greater closeness between Moscow and the Asian-Pacific nations, "New Delhi [had] increasingly felt its importance reduced in Soviet diplomacy." To underline the triangular diplomacy then taking place, it was also noted that Gorbachev's visit had come on the eve of Rajiv Gandhi's trip to China and of the Chinese foreign minister's departure for Moscow. The Soviet leader, moreover, had stated his pleasure at the improvement in Indo-Chinese relations.[28]

There were many significant aspects to the Gandhi visit, not least the symbolic. The first visit by an Indian prime minister since 1954, it was depicted by the Chinese as ushering in a new era in relations. Tibet featured prominently in the talks and communiqué; Li Peng expressed "admiration for the Indian government's principled position on the Tibet issue," and for its agreement not to "allow Tibetan separatists in India to conduct political activities aimed at splitting up China."[29] Gandhi proposed the setting up of a Joint Working Group (JWG) of survey personnel to review the geographical features of the border areas, and suggested that military experts devise measures to ensure "peace and tranquillity" along the boundary, the first step in the establishment of a confidence-building regime. In addition, China and India agreed to develop relations in trade, science, technology, and culture, measures that the Chinese see as an important part of the psychological process of transforming the Sino-Indian relationship from one of conflict and suspicion to one based on confidence and trust.

Perhaps the most significant result of the summit was the decision that, in the absence of a final resolution of the border dispute, confidence- and security-building measures (CSBMs) should be introduced. The restraint exercised over the tensions in 1986-87 demonstrated that neither side wanted a war, the costs of which would be wholly disproportionate to any benefit that might ensue. That understanding, combined with China's primary objective (then and now)—achieving what it terms "comprehensive national strength"—has led it to seek peaceful relations with its neighbors. Beijing believes that the development of economic ties in border areas—whether between Xinjiang and Central Asia in the northwest, or Heilongjiang and Korea in the northeast, or Tibet and India in the southwest—is essential to the promotion of border tranquillity. It also perceives the need to combine such economic contacts with technical and military measures. In the Indian case this has meant reducing the prospects for misunderstanding between border forces and ensuring that Beijing would never again have to use a high official from a major power to communicate with New Delhi.

At the second meeting of the JWG in September 1990 it was agreed that military personnel would meet from time to time to maintain "peace and tranquillity" on the border.[30] At the fourth meeting in February 1992 this decision became more concrete when China and India decided to hold regular meetings between military border personnel each year in June and October at Bumla Pass in the eastern sector and Spanggur Gap in the western area; to establish telephone links; and to exchange views on confidence-building measures in areas of the actual line of control, including prior notification of military exercises.[31]

The sixth meeting of the JWG held in June 1993 led to a decision to enhance the transparency aspects of the CSBM regime by exchanging information about the location of military positions and about activities along the actual line of control. It was also agreed that the JWG should meet more frequently, presumably to hasten the creation and implementation of such measures.[32] Contacts at the highest military levels were initiated with the visit to Beijing in July 1992 by the Indian defense minister, accompanied by border experts. This visit produced a decision in principle to allow a Chinese warship into an Indian port, and agreements to develop military academic, scientific, and technological exchanges.[33]

Most significant of all was the visit of Prime Minister P. V. Narasimha Rao to Beijing in September 1993, during which it was agreed that, pending a final resolution of the border issue, the two sides would agree to "strictly respect and abide by the lines of actual control, and undertake no military maneuvers of specified sizes in special areas recognized by both sides."

This does not represent a final solution, but as one of Rao's aides is alleged to have said, "once a line is drawn and stabilized, it naturally etches itself into people's minds with time."

Also during the summit, it was decided to seek troop reductions along the border, to examine means for avoiding airspace violations, and to set up a task force of diplomatic and military experts to assist the JWG in devising effective verification measures.[34] Such progress owed much to the breakthrough that had come at the fourth meeting of the JWG shortly after Li Peng's December 1991 visit to New Delhi. That visit demonstrated the importance to China of high-level declarations in a CSBM regime. During Li's trip, both sides stated that the border issue would only be solved by peaceful means, a point that was reiterated during Rao's visit to Beijing.[35] Furthermore, events in 1991 gave India the opportunity to demonstrate the credibility of its pledge that it would give no support to Tibetan separatists. Tibetan groups demonstrated throughout Li's visit, which led the Chinese to include in the joint communiqué an expression of "concern about continued activities in India by some Tibetans against their motherland." The Indian side firmly reiterated its longstanding pro-Chinese position on Tibet; more particularly, Indian police were reported to have beaten up and arrested many of the demonstrators.[36]

There are broader issues at stake for China than the defusion of the border dispute, however, issues that relate to the fundamental changes that have occurred in international relations with the advent of the post–cold war era. These changes also spur China to improve ties with India and to work with New Delhi to deal with the problems these "two largest developing countries" face in this "complex and volatile world."[37] China's concern about the rise of Muslim fundamentalism, and what this might mean for Xinjiang province, has led it to reverse its previous support for self-determination for Kashmir.[38] Thus interests have become complementary over this matter of religious unrest. The constant requirement for India to reiterate its position on Tibet is designed not only to send a signal to the exiles and to tie India unequivocally to a particular legal position, but also to elicit New Delhi's support for China's position on human rights questions. Other occasions have been used to show such support on the general position: during General Secretary of the Indian National Congress G. N. Azad's meeting with President Jiang Zemin in Beijing in July 1989 (a month after Tiananmen)—the Chinese leader noted that this was his "first meeting with foreign visitors since China won a decisive victory in putting down the recent counter-revolutionary rebellion in Beijing." The Chinese "appreciated," he said, the Indian government's position of noninterference in the matter. Azad made a gratifying reply, describing the issue as the PRC's "internal affair" and adding that "it was up to the Chinese people to choose their own road and future."[39]

High-level meetings over the next several years were accompanied by similar supportive pronouncements. During Li Peng's visit in December 1991, Rao underscored mutual interest by stating that it was difficult for India to "copy the Western way of human rights." The joint communiqué on that occasion claimed that "for the vast number of developing countries the right to subsistence and development is a basic human right."[40] The following May, during the Indian president's visit to China, Beijing applauded his statement that for developing countries the first requirement was the provision of employment and basic needs for their people, and his remark that no country or group had "the right to lay groundless charges against another country." China was also gratified by Indian support during the forty-eighth meeting of the UN Human Rights Committee.[41] Clearly, in the post–cold war era, China has chosen to stress the similarities in the international positions of the two great nations of Asia and thus to emphasize the need for a new international political and economic order based on the five principles of peaceful coexistence first elaborated in the 1950s, which in themselves make a point of non-interference, territorial integrity, and sovereign equality.

China and India have come to share a concern over Western efforts to forge a more interventionist world order (although Beijing might be exaggerating the degree of closeness in their positions). With Russia no longer a significant player and Sino-American relations under strain, China's foreign policy is currently dominated by a desire to find common cause with states similarly concerned about the latitude that the end of the cold war has given to Western countries in their dealings with the developing world.[42]

The Future

The international environment of the 1990s—as each perceives it—is therefore conducive to a further improvement in bilateral relations. Such an improvement is reinforced by changes in the way in which Beijing tackles foreign policy issues. China for some years has sought not to reinforce the polarization of relations within South Asia, but to encourage bilateral negotiations between Islamabad and New Delhi. India's dominant position in the subcontinent is recognized, even as China remains wedded to the maintenance of an independent Pakistan.

However, the comfort derived from political support in the global and local arenas does not mean that India is no longer seen in terms of the generalized rivalry of the 1950s era of friendship. Although with China's adoption of market-led economic reform and India's more recent attempts to reduce the state role in its economy the two can no longer be seen as alternative models of economic development, they can still be considered as competitors politically and in terms of economic resources. Moreover, China is clearly concerned over India's developments in the fields of civilian and military technology. The Indian test firings of the Agni missile in 1989 and 1992 confirmed that New Delhi now has IRBM capability with a range of 950 miles. The range of this missile probably will be extended to the point where it could reach Beijing from Arunachal Pradesh.[43]

Indian advances in the naval field are also of concern to the Chinese. In mid-1987, India acquired a second aircraft carrier and, in early 1988, leased a Charlie-class nuclear attack submarine from the former Soviet Union—a development that probably triggered Pakistani interest in acquiring the same from China. According to one Japanese source, China interpreted these developments as an indication that India was determined to become a major military power, complete with an ocean fleet.[44] China, whose burgeoning foreign trade has increased its need to defend vital sea lanes, seems to fear the Indian Ocean becoming an Indian lake.[45] China intends to develop a blue-water navy in part to protect its seaborne freight and to prevent encroachment in its territorial waters, two-thirds of which are subject to dispute.[46] Beijing's determination to support its claims over island groupings in the South China Sea has led it to enhance its ties with Myanmar (Burma), a state where India traditionally has had more influence. China's widely reported arms sales to Myanmar, together with suggestions that China is building and upgrading naval port facilities in that country, including those at Hanggyi island at the mouth of the Bassein river and at Great Coco Island near India's Andaman Islands, were topics raised during Rao's visit in September 1993.[47]

Such areas of tension suggest that one of the most important CSBMs that the two states could adopt in the future would be to institutionalize regular contacts between defense ministries, in order better to understand each country's strategic doctrine and perceived security environment. Practical measures designed to reduce the fear of surprise attack and to codify procedures for dealing with incidents at sea could form a part of a dialogue on security concerns that go well beyond the border issue.

If each country's forward defense policies currently cause a general concern about medium- and long-term intentions, domestic political change in both China and India could also lead to tension. Communal violence and weak central governments have been a part of the Indian political landscape for some years and undermine the country's ability to devote resources and attention to issues outside of the subcontinent. In China itself, few commentators would be willing to forecast a wholly predictable or stable China once Deng Xiaoping dies. Tibet remains an area of serious concern to the Beijing leadership, as the Dalai Lama seems to grow in international status. An unstable, post-Deng China could give added impetus to those seeking greater autonomy or independence for

Tibet. As noted earlier, and whether it likes it or not, India is embroiled in the Tibetan issue as long as it provides sanctuary and assistance to the Dalai Lama and his followers.[48] The modern-day insistence on the concept of the sovereign equality of independent nations means that we rarely contemplate other, more relaxed arrangements for managing the coexistence of diverse human communities.[49] That insistence on sovereign independence—so much a part of Chinese thinking about its foreign relations—suggests that the related issues of Tibet and the Sino-Indian border retain the potential to take center stage at some point in an uncertain future.

Notes

1. Xue Mouhong and Pei Jianzhang, eds., *Diplomacy of Contemporary China* (Hong Kong: New Horizon Press, 1990), pp. 213–14. The five principles are mutual respect for sovereignty and territorial integrity; mutual non-aggression; non-interference in each other's internal affairs; equality and mutual benefit; and peaceful coexistence.

2. Xue and Pei, eds., *Diplomacy*, pp. 215 and 144. We have known about the Indian factor in the deepening of the Sino-Soviet polemics for three decades or more. However, it is interesting that in today's more pragmatic era of China's foreign policy, events of 1959 are still interpreted in the same way.

3. Xue and Pei, eds., *Diplomacy*, p. 218.

4. Surjit Mansingh and Steven I. Levine, "China and India: Moving Beyond Confrontation," *Problems of Communism* 38, nos. 2–3 (March–June 1989), p. 32.

5. Dennis Merrill, *Bread and the Ballot: The United States and India's Economic Development, 1947–1963* (Chapel Hill: University of North Carolina Press, 1990).

6. Mansingh and Levine, "China and India," pp. 31–32.

7. Allen S. Whiting, *The Chinese Calculus of Deterrence: India and Indochina* (Ann Arbor: University of Michigan Press, 1975), pp. 8–9.

8. John Gittings, *Survey of the Sino-Soviet Dispute, 1963–1967* (London: Oxford University Press, 1968), pp. 110–11.

9. Whiting, *Chinese Calculus*, esp. pp. 12–19.

10. Whiting, *Chinese Calculus*, pp. 63–64.

11. Xue and Pei, eds., *Diplomacy*, p. 151.

12. Wang Bingnan, "Nine Years of Sino-U.S. Talks in Retrospect" (memoirs), *Shijie Zhishi* [World Knowledge], reprinted in Joint Publications Research Service, *China Report*, 85-079 (August 7, 1985). Wang was the Chinese representative at the Sino-American ambassadorial talks, held first in Geneva, then in Warsaw.

13. Whiting, *Chinese Calculus*, p. 73; P. R. Chari, "Indo-Soviet Military Cooperation: A Review," *Asian Survey* 19 (March 1979); Robert C. Horn, *Soviet-Indian Relations: Issues and Influence* (New York: Praeger, 1982), p. 8.

14. Neville Maxwell, *India's China War* (London: Jonathan Cape, 1970), p. 434.

15. Rosemary Foot, "The Sino-Soviet Complex and South Asia," in Barry Buzan and Gowher Rizvi, eds., *South Asian Insecurity and the Great Powers* (London: Macmillan, 1986), p. 190.

16. Rosemary Foot, "Arms Control and Sino-Indian Relations," in Gerald Segal, ed., *Arms Control in Asia* (London: Macmillian, 1987), p. 105.

17. United States Department of State, *Survey of the China Mainland Press (SCMP)*, nos. 3535 and 3536 (September 5 and 8, 1965), U.S. Consulate General, Hong Kong.

18. Foot, "The Sino-Soviet Complex," p. 192. Henry Kissinger, national security adviser to Nixon, has reported that the Soviets were informed that the United States "would not stand idly by" if Moscow attacked China. See Kissinger, *White House Years* (Boston: Little, Brown, 1979), p. 910.

19. For example, relations with India were set back in 1979 when promising developments during Foreign Minister Vajpayee's visit to Beijing were undermined by its coincidence with the Chinese attack on Vietnam, and in 1980 when India recognized the Heng Samrin government in Cambodia. The attack on Vietnam inevitably evoked memories in India of the 1962 war with China.

20. Quoted in John W. Garver, "The Indian Factor in Recent Sino-Soviet Relations," *China Quarterly* 125 (March 1991), pp. 64–65.

21. *Beijing Review* 22 (June 3, 1985).

22. Sumit Ganguly, "The Sino-Indian Border talks, 1981–1989: A View from New Delhi," *Asian Survey* 29, no. 12 (December 1989), p. 1126.

23. Mansingh and Levine, "China and India," pp. 41–42; Garver, "The Indian Factor," pp. 79–80.

24. *Beijing Review* 9 (March 2, 1987), p. 9. The state of Arunachel Pradesh, formerly the Indian North East Frontier Agency, abuts eastern Tibet along the McMahon boundary line.

25. *Beijing Review* 20 (May 18, 1987), p. 7.

26. *Beijing Review* 32 (August 10, 1987).

27. Garver, "The Indian Factor," pp. 79–80.

28. *Beijing Review* 49 (December 5–11, 1988), p. 12.

29. *Beijing Review* 1 (January 2–8, 1989). Indian officials are required to make similar statements at the conclusion of every high-level visit—for example, in February 1991 during the Indian Foreign Minister's visit to China, and in December 1991 during Li Peng's visit to India.

30. Foreign Broadcast Information Service, *Daily Report China* (hereafter cited as FBIS-CHI) 90-172, September 5, 1990. This agreement had been preceded by the visit of a high-level Indian defense team from the National Defense College. FBIS-CHI-90-131 (July 9, 1990).

31. FBIS-CHI-92-036 (February 24, 1992).

32. FBIS-CHI-93-124 (June 30, 1993).

33. FBIS-CHI-92-143 (July 24, 1992); *Far Eastern Economic Review*, November 12, 1992.

34. *Beijing Review* 38 (September 20–26, 1993); *Far Eastern Economic Review*, (September 16, 1993); Ganguly, "Slouching Towards a Settlement: Sino-Indian Relations 1962–1993," Occasional Paper no. 60, Asia Program, Woodrow Wilson International Center for Scholars, Washington, D.C., May 1994, p. 21.

35. See for example Li Peng's interview with the *Hindustan Times*, reprinted in FBIS-CHI-91-243 (December 18, 1991), and Narasimha Rao's interview with *Blitz*, reprinted in FBIS-CHI-92-015 (January 23, 1992. See also *Beijing Review* 51 (December 23–29, 1991) and 38 (September 20–26, 1993).

36. *Far Eastern Economic Review*, December 26, 1991.

37. Said by Li Peng during his banquet speech, as cited in FBIS-CHI-91-243 (December 18, 1991).

38. *Far Eastern Economic Review*, January 13, 1994.

39. *Beijing Review* 29 (July 17–23, 1989).

40. *Beijing Review* 51 (December 23–29, 1991) and 52 (December 30, 1991–January 5, 1992).

41. FBIS-CHI-92-098 (May 20, 1992).

42. China obtained observer status at the Bali meeting of the Nonaligned Movement (NAM) in June 1992. In an article on that meeting it pointed to the NAM agreement that the promotion of human rights could not take place through "confrontation or imposing one's own values upon others." It also noted the meeting's concern about some countries' attempts to link the political rights of citizens to the provision of economic aid. See *Beijing Review* 23 (June 8–14, 1992).

43. For further discussion of the nuclear issue in the Indian subcontinent see Brahma Chellaney, "South Asia's Passage to Nuclear Power," *International Security* 16, no. 1 (summer 1991).

44. FBIS-CHI-92-159 (August 17, 1992).

45. Tai Ming Cheung, "The Growth of Chinese Naval Power," Pacific Strategy Papers, Institute of Southeast Asian Studies, Singapore, 1990, esp. pp. 11–16.

46. You Ji and You Xu, "In Search of Blue Water Power: The PLA Navy's Maritime Strategy in the 1990s," *Pacific Review* 4, no. 2 (1991), p. 137.

47. *Far Eastern Economic Review*, November 12, 1992, and September 16, 1993; Andrew Mack and Desmond Ball, "The Military Build-up in Asia-Pacific," *Pacific Review* 5, no. 3 (1992), p. 200.

48. Mansingh and Levine, "China and India," p. 47, provides a valuable commentary on the Tibet issue in Sino-Indian relations in the late 1980s.

49. This point is suggested in Adam Watson's stimulating study, *The Evolution of International Society: A Comparative Historical Analysis* (London: Routledge, 1992).

4

Past Attempts at Mediation and Conflict Prevention in South Asia: Would CSBMs Have Made a Difference?

Šumit Ganguly

CSBMs long worked in the European theater between the nations of NATO and the Warsaw Pact because these countries had no unresolved territorial disputes that could have resulted in war. But what of other areas of the world, where borders are still disputed and where CSBMs have not yet been instituted? Specifically, would the existence of confidence and security-building measures (CSBMs) between India and Pakistan and India and China have prevented the outbreak of the four wars that have taken place on the subcontinent since 1947?

The evidence about the historical utility of CSBMs in the region is ambiguous. Certain CSBM-like agreements did have salutary effects in both the 1965 and 1971 wars. But whether the existence of explicit CSBMs would have made some difference in the outcomes of the 1962, 1965, and 1971 wars, depended upon the politico-military conditions prevailing before the three Indo-Pakistani wars and the Sino-Indian war.

What are CSBMs and what utility do they possess? CSBMs fall into four general categories: mutual security pledges, transparency measures, managing dangerous and potentially dangerous military activities, and crisis-management measures. Transparency measures include the monitoring of military exercises, the stationing of observers at military bases, and the exchange of military data and information about a country's military doctrines. The range of crisis-management devices and techniques includes hotlines between central military commands and direct contacts between local military authorities. CSBMs may also involve the prohibition or limitation of certain activities that are deemed to be provocative or dangerous. These can include restrictions on overflights of territory, the creation of demilitarized zones, and the prior notification of military exercises.

CSBMs serve three basic purposes: preventing inadvertent conflicts between adversaries, providing warnings about an impending attack and enabling response through diplomacy or deterrence to fend off an attack, and providing avenues of communication even after war has broken out. Thus although CSBMs can help terminate a war by providing means of signalling and communication, they cannot always or perhaps even usually substitute for diplomacy and negotiation. Nor are they meant as a panacea for underlying political disputes. CSBMs simply help create a climate of trust which may then enable adversaries to tackle the central sources of conflict.

The First Kashmir War

Much that has been written about the 1947–48 Kashmir war is composed of military memoirs from the two sides of the border.[1] From these various accounts it is possible to reconstruct a narrative of the events that led to the war.

With British withdrawal from the subcontinent the status of Kashmir became a source of contention between the two nascent states of India and Pakistan. While the ruler of Kashmir, Maharaja Hari Singh, toyed with notions of independence, he was subjected to considerable pressure from both sides to accede to them.[2] In December 1947, as the Maharaja vacillated on the question of accession, a tribal rebellion broke out along the western reaches of the state, near the Kashmir-Pakistan border. The Maharaja's troops proved incapable of suppressing the rebellion and it continued to gather force.

The Pakistani leadership saw this as an opportunity to forcibly seize the state by supporting the tribal rebellion. Though no precise accounts are available, it is widely believed that soldiers from the regular Pakistani military joined the rebels and started to approach the capital of Kashmir, Srinagar. In a panic, Maharaja Hari Singh sought Indian assistance. After consultations with Sheikh Mohammed Abdullah, the leader of the Kashmiri National Conference, Prime Minister Nehru obtained the Instrument of Accession from the maharaja and authorized the dispatch of Indian troops to Kashmir. In the absence of a referendum Sheikh Abdullah's imprimatur on the Instrument of Accession was of enormous significance. At this time Abdullah was the leader of the largest secular and popular organization within the state.

Following the arrival of the Indian army, the Pakistani army entered the fray in regular formations. The war lasted till January 1, 1948, when India referred the case to the Security Council of the United Nations. The Security

Council promptly called for a cease-fire, which both sides accepted. At the time of the cease-fire, two-thirds of the state remained under Indian control; one-third had fallen to Pakistan.

Could the existence of CSBMs have made a difference in preventing the first Kashmir war? The available evidence suggests otherwise. First, there had been little or no possibility of establishing any CSBMs. The British Indian army had just been divided between the two new states, and the political leaderships of the two sides were engaged in a furious debate over the division of military assets.[3] Under these conditions, marked with acrimony and mutual recriminations, it was virtually impossible to even contemplate CSBMs. Furthermore, as the Kashmir war itself demonstrates, neither state had firmly established its territorial limits, and both sides were determined to incorporate Kashmir into their newly created states. Most importantly, Pakistan, with a quickly fashioned politico-military strategy, seized upon the first opportunity to annex the state. This involved a deliberate decision to resort to war. Simultaneously, once the maharaja appealed to India for assistance, its leadership was equally determined to integrate Kashmir into the Indian Union. The question of conflict through inadvertence or misperception was simply irrelevant to the situation. Consequently, even in the unlikely event the two sides had instituted minimal CSBMs, they would have served little purpose.

The Second Kashmir War

In 1965, India and Pakistan went to war a second time over the state of Kashmir. The origins of this war are more complex. By the early 1960s, both multilateral and bilateral negotiations over Kashmir had accomplished little. Furthermore, since 1948, both India and Pakistan had steadily integrated their respective portions of Kashmir. The Pakistani irredentist claim on Indian-held Kashmir nevertheless remained alive and powerful.

A series of developments on the subcontinent prompted Pakistani decision makers to use force to wrest Kashmir from India. First, with the death of Prime Minister Nehru in November 1964, questions were raised in India and abroad not only about his successor, Lal Bahadur Shastri, but about the viability of India's multiethnic and democratic polity. Second, it appeared that there was widespread unhappiness with Indian rule in Kashmir. The spate of riots that broke out in Srinagar following the theft of a sacred heirloom (a hair of the Prophet Mohammed, from the Hazaratbal mosque in Srinagar) was only the most violent manifestation of the population's growing disaffection with Indian rule. Third, Indian defense spending had increased substantially in the wake of the Sino-Indian border war of 1962. A continuation of this level of defense spending would have upset the military balance on the subcontinent and have placed Pakistan at a substantial strategic disadvantage in any future conflict over Kashmir. Fourth and finally, international interest in the Kashmir dispute was steadily declining following the failure of both multilateral and bilateral efforts to find a resolution.[4]

In an attempt to test India's defense preparedness, the Pakistanis conducted a "limited probe" in January 1965 in the Rann of Kutch, a tract of land in the western Indian state of Gujarat. This involved engaging in a small, reversible intrusion designed to clarify a defender's commitments.[5] The immediate problem in the Rann of Kutch was the poorly delineated Indo-Pakistani border, another legacy of hasty British decolonization policies. As part of their "probe," Pakistani patrols had repeatedly entered what India deemed to be its territory in the early part of January 1965. Subsequently Indian border forces challenged the Pakistani patrols, evicted them, and set up a series of outposts of their own to demarcate their claims. In April of the same year, the Indians sought to dislodge a Pakistani force from an outpost near Kanjarkot. The Pakistanis retaliated and the fighting quickly escalated. Under pressure from the British at the Commonwealth Prime Ministers' Conference, both sides agreed to bring the conflict to a close and revert to the status quo ante. Furthermore, they also agreed to refer the case to the International Court of Justice (ICJ) for arbitration.

Unfortunately this attempt at a settlement did not end the crisis, for Pakistani decision makers had fundamentally misinterpreted two Indian decisions. First, even after the Pakistanis brought in heavy armor, the Indians refused to respond in kind. Second, they quickly agreed to refer the case to the ICJ. The Pakistanis saw these decisions as evidence that the Indians lacked the stomach for battle. (Actually the Indians had chosen not to bring in tanks because the terrain favored the aggressor and because of the impending monsoonal rains; they were willing to refer the case to the ICJ because the Rann of Kutch was of little or no strategic value.) Their erroneous inferences emboldened the Pakistani leaders and in August 1965 they launched a strategy to infiltrate the state of Kashmir using regular forces disguised as local tribesmen. The goal was for the infiltrators to mingle with the local population and foment a rebellion in the state.

The strategy went awry from the start. Unhappiness with Indian rule on the part of the Kashmiri populace did not necessarily translate into support for Pakistan. As the infiltrators crossed the border, the Kashmiri inhabitants promptly turned them over to the local authorities. Despite this setback the Pakistani leadership continued its plans for wresting Kashmir from India, and a number of clashes ensued between Indian forces and the Pakistani infiltrators. On September 1 Pakistan launched a major offensive in the southern sector of Kashmir. In response, the Indians launched an air strike against the invading Pakistani forces and, to relieve pressure on Kashmir, the Indian forces crossed the border near Lahore in Punjab and counterattacked. By mid-September the war had reached a stalemate and international (particularly U.S. and British) pressure to terminate the conflict grew on both sides. On September 20 the United Nations Security Council called for a cease-fire, which was instituted on September 22. Subsequent Soviet-mediated negotiations at Tashkent enabled India and Pakistan to return once again to the status quo ante.

Would CSBMs have prevented an outbreak of war in this crisis? Certainly the case for greater transparency does not stand up under scrutiny. Pakistani analysts had reasonably good estimates of the growth of Indian forces in the wake of the Sino-Indian border war of 1962.[6] Pakistan did not attack India because it feared India's military buildup after the Sino-Indian border war, but because its leaders believed that Indian military preponderance would make it significantly more difficult to seize Kashmir in the longer run. Consequently, even if greater transparency in the form of better knowledge of military doctrines had existed, it is doubtful that the outcome would have been significantly different.

Would other forms of CSBMs, such as the existence of a demilitarized zone (DMZ) along the cease-fire line (CFL), have made a difference?[7] A DMZ might have hobbled the Pakistani strategy by making infiltration rather difficult. However, it would have had little effect on the Pakistani decision to launch a full-scale attack across the CFL on September 1, 1965.[8]

Would the existence of routinized crisis-management procedures have made any difference? Had a hotline existed between the directors-general of military operations (DGMOs) and if weekly conversations were the norm, India may have been able to obtain some advance warning (though admittedly, the Pakistani DGMO would not have revealed war plans to his Indian counterpart). But if an existing hotline had not been activated at the agreed-upon hour or if Indian questions about recent Pakistani troop movements had been answered in a prevaricative fashion, the Indians may have acted with greater alacrity toward mobilization. Furthermore, India may have been able to use the hotline to issue an explicit deterrence signal to Pakistan. Consequently, it is possible that the existence of a hotline may have made some difference in enhancing Indian alertness and also in deterring Pakistan.

The 1971 War and the Creation of Bangladesh

The last Indo-Pakistani conflict took place in December 1971. The causes of this war are well known.[9] In 1970 Pakistan held the first democratic election in its independent history. The overwhelming victory of the Awami League surprised both the military regime of General Yahya Khan and the Pakistan People's Party (PPP), the principal West Pakistani political party led by Zulfiqar Ali Bhutto. In East Pakistan, Sheikh Mujibur Rehman's Awami

League swept the polls, winning 160 out of 162 seats and obtaining 75 percent of the popular vote.[10] The stunning performance of the Awami League in East Pakistan necessarily meant some form of power-sharing with the PPP in the overall governance of Pakistan. Negotiations on this point broke down, however, leading to a brutal military crackdown in East Pakistan against the Bengali intelligentsia and the leadership of the Awami League on March 25, 1971. In the aftermath of the military crackdown millions of Bengalis fled across a porous border into the neighboring Indian state of West Bengal. By June 1971 the refugees who had fled into India numbered nearly ten million. Faced with this extraordinary refugee burden, some Indian government officials started to argue that short of a political solution that would ensure a safe return of the refugees, India should be prepared to go to war with Pakistan.[11] The Indian leadership under Indira Gandhi tried to move the international community to put pressure on Pakistan to create conditions conducive for a return of the refugees. Meeting with little international support, and unwilling to absorb the refugees on a permanent basis, the Indian leadership decided to fashion an appropriate politico-military strategy not only to force the return of the refugees but also to promote the breakup of Pakistan.[12] Accordingly, in a move to protect India's northern flank from a potential Chinese attack and to obtain the support of a veto-wielding power in the United Nations, India signed a twenty-year pact of "peace and cooperation" with the Soviet Union in August 1971. One clause in this treaty effectively bound the two parties to come to each other's assistance in the event of war.

By September 1971 India was actively engaged in supporting, arming, and providing sanctuary for an East Pakistani insurgent group, the Mukti Bahini (literally, "liberation group"). Indian support for the Mukti Bahini continued in the face of repeated Pakistani protests, warnings, and threats throughout October and November of 1971. On December 3, Pakistani aircraft attacked a series of northern Indian air bases, leading to a prompt Indian retaliation. Pakistan had clearly misjudged its ability to cripple Indian air bases in this preemptive strike. Less than two weeks later, on December 16, the Indian forces accepted the Instrument of Surrender from the Pakistanis in Dacca, the capital of East Pakistan.

Would the existence of CSBMs have made any difference to the outcome of the East Pakistan crisis which led to this war? There is little reason to believe that it would have. In 1965 Pakistan found India's expanding military capabilities and their potential for foreclosing Pakistan's military option sufficiently compelling to go to war. Similarly, in 1971 India was faced with both a compelling problem—the refugee burden—and a dramatic opportunity—the political disarray in East Pakistan and the consequentially fragile unity of the Pakistani state. After discovering that no easy solution to the refugee crisis was in sight, Indian decision makers realized that the two problems could be simultaneously solved; the refugees could be made to return and India's principal adversary could be dealt a severe blow. Under these circumstances CSBMs could not have provided an effective barrier to war.

Furthermore, there is little evidence to suggest that greater knowledge of Indian military plans or doctrine would have enabled Pakistan to resort to diplomatic or military means to ward off the impending conflict. Pakistani decision makers were well aware of the evolving Indian war plans,[13] and they undertook all reasonable efforts to warn India of their willingness to fight. These deterrent warnings did not sway Indian decision makers, however; for them, the costs of not resorting to war were intolerable and the potential benefits far too great.

Would a prior agreement on the limitation of dangerous military activities have made any difference? Probably not, since such prohibitions are not usually regarded as relevant to preventing purposeful belligerent actions. Instead they are designed to avoid inadvertent harm or contain the consequences of such harm, should it occur.

But would the existence of any crisis-management arrangements have changed the course of the conflict? The available evidence suggests otherwise. The massive influx of refugees into India and Pakistan's unwillingness to undertake any meaningful efforts to deal with the problem had thoroughly frustrated the Indian leadership. Discussions between military commanders about troop movements and force levels would have accomplished pitifully little. The problem that India and Pakistan faced demanded high-level political decisions. Under these conditions, crisis-management measures would have been largely irrelevant.

The Sino-Indian Border War

This brief survey of the three Indo-Pakistani conflicts reveals that the existence of CSBMs would have made little difference in terms of shaping the outcomes of the crises. The Sino-Indian border war, however, which had markedly different roots, may well have been avoided had a CSBM regime been in place.

The origins of the border dispute between India and China are complex.[14] Although its roots can be traced to British colonial border policies, the more proximate origins of the border dispute lie in the immediate postwar era. In 1950 the Chinese invaded Tibet and quickly incorporated the country into China.[15] The Indian reaction to the Chinese invasion and occupation of Tibet was equivocal: although Prime Minister Nehru expressed concern for the Tibetans, he carefully avoided condemning the Chinese.[16] Nehru's unwillingness to condemn the Chinese must be seen in the context of a larger strategy to prevent tensions from developing with a large, potentially hostile state on India's borders. If anything, Nehru's strategy appeared to be one of containing China through various acts of appeasement—in the pristine sense of the term.[17] Accordingly, India vigorously supported China's entry into the United Nations, sought to play a mediatory role in the Korean War, and attempted to promote "peaceful coexistence" with the Chinese at a bilateral level. Furthermore, in pursuit of this end Prime Minister Nehru conceded to the Chinese in 1952 the extraterritorial rights in Tibet that India had inherited from the British.

These efforts at conciliating the Chinese did not succeed. In 1951, India discovered that Chinese troops had built a road through territory that India deemed to be its own, in the Aksai Chin region near Tibet. The Indians, realizing their own limited military capabilities and desiring to avoid conflict with the Chinese, did not raise the issue. Only when the Chinese premier, Zhou Enlai, visited New Delhi in 1956 did Nehru ask him about depictions of Indian territory on Chinese maps. Zhou responded that these were Kuomintang maps and the new Chinese regime had not had the opportunity to examine them closely. The Indians contented themselves with Zhou's answer. The problem lay dormant until 1957, when the Chinese published new maps that showed portions of Aksai Chin as Chinese territory.[18] The formal publication of these maps made it impossible for India to continue to overlook this issue. Ultimately, in December 1958 Prime Minister Nehru wrote directly to Zhou Enlai about these maps. Zhou's response indicated a willingness to negotiate but was nevertheless prevaricative. At this point, at Nehru's behest, the Historical Division of the Ministry of External Affairs (MEA) decided to gather legal and historical evidence to buttress India's case on the boundary question. In turn, another letter was sent to the Chinese in late 1959 spelling out the evidence that the MEA had gathered from colonial records.

From 1959 onward, relations with the Chinese deteriorated sharply. First, the Chinese suppressed the Khampa revolt in Tibet. Although there is some debate about the extent of Indian involvement in and support for the Khampas, there is little question that segments of the Indian army and the Intelligence Bureau (IB) collaborated with the American Central Intelligence Agency (CIA) in organizing, training, and arming the Khampas. After several Chinese protests, Nehru personally intervened to close down some of the camps that the IB and the CIA had been operating in the northern reaches of West Bengal (the home of a sizeable Tibetan exile community). From the vituperative accounts against India in general and Nehru in particular that appeared in the Chinese media in 1959 it is reasonable to surmise that the Chinese perceived the Indian leadership to be actively conniving against them. Chinese perceptions of Indian perfidy were probably reinforced when the principal Tibetan temporal and spiritual leader, the Dalai Lama, sought refuge in India in late 1959.

Two border incidents underscored the growing tensions. The first was at Longju in August 1959, when a Chinese patrol occupied an Indian post. Then in October 1959, the Chinese ambushed an Indian patrol at Kongka Pass near the Kashmiri-Tibetan border.

Following the publication of the Chinese maps in 1957 Nehru had been publicly attacked in Parliament for having failed to apprise that body of the existence of a border problem. In the wake of the Longju and Kongka Pass incidents, both parliamentary and informed public opinion toward the Chinese hardened. Consequently, Nehru's room for maneuver on the border dispute rapidly shrank. Despite the shifting mood in India, Nehru invited Zhou Enlai for a state visit between April 20 and 25, 1960, to discuss the border question. The meeting accomplished little. The Chinese side sought to use the meetings to legitimize the gains that they had made through cartographic claims and physical intrusions. The Indian side asserted that the acceptance of the Chinese position would be tantamount to legitimizing territory acquired through subtle aggression. Following these inconclusive talks, the two sides instructed their respective diplomatic communities to amass the available historical and legal evidence to support their border claims. The compilation of evidence demonstrated that India had a better case, both legally and historically, at least along the Aksai Chin section of the border. The government of India published this agglomeration of both Indian and Chinese evidence, known as the Officials' Report, in February 1961. Although Chinese and Indian officials met between June and December 1960, both sides refused to budge from their stated positions, and no further discussions with the Chinese took place.

In the face of this deadlock the Indian politico-military leadership decided to embark on a strategy that was to ultimately prove disastrous: the "forward policy." This entailed sending small contingents of lightly armed troops into Chinese-claimed areas. This policy was a recipe for disaster as, in the words of a senior retired Indian general, "it had neither teeth nor tail."[19] The Indian troops lacked adequate firepower and logistical support to offset a more serious Chinese attack. In effect, the forward policy was an attempt at a form of compellence—getting an aggressor to undo its hostile act—without the requisite capabilities.[20] When the Chinese attacked in force in October 1962, the Indian forces were completely routed.

Is it possible that a CSBM regime may have led to a different outcome in this situation? The evidence is somewhat ambiguous. It can be argued that the Indian side made a number of unilateral efforts to demonstrate its benign intentions towards the Chinese regime. Indian support for the Chinese case at the United Nations, its efforts to negotiate an end to the Korean War, and its willingness to cede the British privileges in Tibet in 1954 all point in the direction of conciliation. The one area where India did not seem to make an effort to reassure the Chinese was in its response to the Khampa rebellion.

Furthermore, the forward policy was clearly maladroit from a military standpoint. Contrary to the claims of certain scholars, however, one can argue that it was not especially threatening or provocative to the Chinese.[21] Without access to Chinese accounts of the conflict, this argument has to be made on the basis of inference and attribution. In October 1962 the Chinese attack was carefully calibrated to take advantage of the most ill-defended Indian positions, particularly along the eastern sector in the North-East Frontier Agency; this suggests that Chinese intelligence about Indian border deployments was far from unsound. Consequently, there is little reason to believe that the Chinese found India's forward policy especially threatening, and it is therefore possible to argue that the lack of Indian reassurances alone was not the principal cause of the Chinese attack.

Despite this historical record it is worthwhile to explore a counterfactual possibility: What if exchanges of information *had* been possible between the Chinese and the Indian armies? Had the Indian army had a better appreciation of Chinese capabilities, it may have been able to make a more compelling case to Nehru and his defense minister for larger defense expenditures to counter the Chinese military threat. Greater preparedness based on a more accurate assessment of Chinese military capabilities may have staved off the military debacle of 1962. Finally, better Indian knowledge of Chinese capabilities may also have deterred India from adopting the forward policy in the first place.

Would an agreement on the limitation of dangerous military activities have made any difference to the outcome of the conflict? Probably not. CSBMs relating to the limitation of dangerous military activities are not useful in stopping purposeful military aggression. Maoist China was intent on asserting its claim on every parcel of "lost" territory that China's imperial rulers may have once controlled. It is therefore unlikely that the Chinese would have been willing to abide by an agreement that limited their ability to advance a territorial claim.

From the Chinese standpoint, the development of India's forward policy probably amounted to dangerous military activity. Had an explicit prohibition existed against such activity India may have been loath to carry out the forward policy, and instead, as a status quo power, would have contented itself with verbal remonstrations against the Chinese.

Would events have taken a different turn had certain crisis-management measures been in place? It is extremely doubtful that they would have changed the course of the conflict. The extensive discussions conducted between June and December 1960 failed to resolve the deadlock on the border question. In effect, these meetings served as an institutional mechanism for preempting the oncoming crisis. Given the failure of these talks to produce any form of accommodation, it is difficult to see how other explicit crisis-management arrangements would have been effectively utilized as politico-military relations worsened between 1960 and 1962.

Conclusions

This examination of the four major conflicts on the subcontinent since 1947 suggests that CSBM regimes would not have made a significant contribution to the prevention of war. Each of the four wars was the result of deliberate design and not of accident. Consequently, better understanding, better crisis communication, or more information would not have restrained the losing side. The only possible exception in the Indo-Pakistani context would have been the 1965 war. If Pakistan had had a better appreciation of Indian military capabilities it may have acted with greater restraint. Similarly, in the Sino-Indian context, India may not have adopted the forward policy.

The same reason made the limitation of dangerous military activities, of the kind that are amenable to CSBMs, largely irrelevant. Finally, it is equally unclear that timely warning would have made much difference in any of the four cases, except perhaps marginally. Nor is it clear that the requisite conditions existed for the pursuit of CSBM regimes.

Given this dismal assessment of the likely utility of CSBMs in the region, is there any reason to believe that the future will be different from the past? There is indeed room for guarded optimism, particularly on the Sino-Indian border.

Four issues are significant in any discussion of the future of a CSBM regime in South Asia. First, Indian military preponderance has played a significant role in preventing war from breaking out since 1971. Pakistan can ill afford to start another war with India; the political and economic costs would be prohibitive. Furthermore, despite inflammatory rhetoric from certain quarters in India, its leadership has no territorial ambitions on Pakistan. Moreover, as India's military advantage precludes a full-scale Pakistani attack under most circumstances, it would be possible to begin moving toward the installation of various CSBMs. Despite the avoidance of full-scale conflict, the extant danger of inadvertent conflict underscores the need for CSBMs. For example, there have been at least two "war scares," one in 1987 and the other in 1990.[22]

Second, paradoxically enough, the difficulty of resorting to full-scale war seems to have made the region safe for low-intensity conflict. There is ample evidence that Pakistan is involved in supporting the Sikh and Kashmiri insurgencies.[23] Allegations have often been made in the Pakistani media that Indian intelligence agencies are involved in inciting ethnic violence in Sind. Such mutual support for low-intensity conflicts in India and Pakistan poses a barrier to the discussion of CSBMs. As a senior Indian diplomat stated in the course of an interview, "It is difficult to discuss CSBMs with an adversary that is engaged in providing assistance to terrorists in your country."[24] His Pakistani counterparts would, no doubt, make similar assertions.

A third factor that has inhibited a resort to full-scale war is the advanced level of weapons technology in the region. Although both sides continue to deny possession of nuclear weapons, there is little question that they possess crude nuclear forces.[25] The danger of nuclear escalation from a conventional conflict has no doubt inhibited both sides from undertaking a large conventional conflict. Perhaps in recognition of these dangers, the two sides signed an agreement in December 1988 not to attack each other's nuclear facilities. Furthermore, a conventional war in the region would be cost-prohibitive, because of the expensive, high-technology weaponry that would be expended by both sides.[26]

Fourth, the Sino-Indian case demonstrates that it may well be easier to discuss the creation of a CSBM regime once a disputed border has taken on the status of a de facto border. India still has a formal claim to some 14,000 square miles of territory that has been under Chinese control since 1962. Yet there is no reason to believe that any rational Indian regime seriously contemplates the recovery of that territory. Consequently, a range of CSBMs can now be negotiated with the Chinese. The Indian side sees significant advantages in pursuing a CSBM regime with the Chinese. It would enable India to thin out forces along the Sino-Indian border at a time when they are needed elsewhere (in Kashmir, for example). It would enable India to reduce the costs of defense preparations at a time of significant budgetary constraints. And lastly, it would help create a climate of expectations among India's "attentive public" for an eventual settlement of the border dispute with China.[27]

The Chinese, in turn, have their own incentives for pursuing a CSBM regime with India. Such measures would ensure that India will not strike them at their Achilles heel—Tibet. This is not an insignificant concern for the Chinese; given the increasing restiveness of the Tibetans after years of highly repressive Chinese rule, the Chinese are acutely concerned about obtaining Indian neutrality, if not outright support, on this issue. To mollify China, India has sharply and demonstrably constrained the activities of the expatriate Tibetan community.[28] CSBMs along the Sino-Indian border would also enable the Chinese to devote more resources to their substantial economic modernization program, and would allow their mountainous communities to pursue cross-border trade with India.

Thus, despite the persistence of two major unresolved conflicts in South Asia, it is now possible to gradually construct CSBM regimes. These would greatly reduce the likelihood of war and also reduce the costs of preparing for war. The pursuit of a CSBM regime between India and China is likely to prove more fructuous in the foreseeable future, as the Sino-Indian border dispute lacks the same visceral quality as the Indo-Pakistani dispute over Kashmir. Moreover, the Sino-Indian border question does not have the same resonance in Indian or Chinese domestic politics. The Kashmir dispute, which involves ethnic and irredentist claims, has considerable significance in the domestic politics of both adversaries. The complexity of this problem and its potential for domestic political exploitation in both states set distinct political limits on the pursuit of CSBMs between India and Pakistan. Nevertheless, given both nations' interest in avoiding another full-scale conflict, CSBMs can play a useful role to that important end.

Notes

I wish to thank Ted Greenwood of the Sloan Foundation and Kanti Bajpai of the Jawaharlal Nehru University for useful comments on an earlier draft. The usual qualifications apply.

1. On the Indian side see Brig. Gen. L. P. Sen's *Slender Was the Thread* (New Delhi: Orient Longman, 1988) and on the Pakistani side see Lt. Gen. Akbar Khan's *Raiders in Kashmir* (Rawalpindi: Pak Publishers, 1970). The only comparative study of all three Indo-Pakistani conflicts is Šumit Ganguly, *The Origins of War in South Asia*, 2nd ed. (Boulder, Co.: Westview, 1994). A somewhat idiosyncratic account of the war can be found in Alistair Lamb, *Kashmir: A Disputed Legacy* (Karachi: Oxford University Press, 1992).

2. Kashmir was one of some 565 so-called princely states, which were nominally independent as long as they recognized the British Crown as the "paramount" power in India. With the end of colonial rule, the doctrine of paramountcy lapsed. Lord Mountbatten, the last viceroy, informed the rulers of the princely states that they had to join either India or Pakistan on the basis of two principles—demographic composition and geographic location. Kashmir posed a problem because it shared borders with both India and Pakistan, and had a Hindu monarch and a Muslim-majority population. For a detailed discussion of this issue, see Šumit Ganguly, "Avoiding War in Kashmir," *Foreign Affairs* 69, no. 5 (winter 1990/91).

3. On this point see Ayesha Jalal, *The State of Martial Rule* (Cambridge, U.K.: Cambridge University Press, 1989).

4. For a detailed account of the forces that led to the second Indo-Pakistani war over Kashmir see Šumit Ganguly, "Deterrence Failure Revisited: The Indo-Pakistani Conflict of 1965," *Journal of Strategic Studies* 13, no. 4 (December 1990).

5. For a more detailed discussion of this concept see Alexander George and Richard Smoke, *Deterrence in American Foreign Policy* (New York: Columbia University Press, 1974).

6. See "Extinction or Survival?" *Dawn* (Pakistan), November 28–December 2, 1964.

7. The CFL refers to the cease-fire line in Kashmir. It reflected the troop dispositions of the two sides when the U.N. Security Council resolutions brought the first

Kashmir war to a close in 1948. The CFL was subsequently changed to the line of actual control (LOAC) following the 1971 war and the Simla Agreement of 1972.

8. It may be pertinent to mention that two "CSBM-like" measures operated throughout the 1965 border war. Owing to an early and direct conversation between Air Marshal Arjan Singh of India and his Pakistani counterpart, Air Marshal Asghar Khan, the two sides agreed not to use their air forces in the Rann of Kutch. Using their respective air forces against the infantry in the open terrain of the Rann of Kutch would have resulted in substantial casualties for both sides. Subsequently, even after full-scale hostilities ensued in September 1965 the two sides again agreed to avoid bombing population centers and irrigation facilities. For a discussion of these and other instances of Indo-Pakistani cooperation see Šumit Ganguly, "Discord and Collaboration in Indo-Pakistani Relations," in Kanti Bajpai and H. C. Shukul, eds., *After the Cold War: International Politics and International Society: Essays in Honor of A. P. Rana* (New Delhi: Sage Publications, 1994).

9. Two of the best analyses of this war are Robert Jackson, *South Asian Crisis* (New York: Prager, 1975), and Richard Sisson and Leo Rose, *War and Secession* (Berkeley: University of California Press, 1990).

10. Sisson and Rose, *War and Secession*, p. 32.

11. On this point see Sisson and Rose, *War and Secession*, pp. 149–50.

12. Two factors contributed significantly to the Indian decision to promote the break-up of Pakistan. At one level the Indian leadership became convinced that the international community would do little to ensure the return of the refugees to East Pakistan. At another level Indian decision makers also realized that they could accomplish the first goal and permanently weaken Pakistan by creating an independent state of Bangladesh. For an excellent discussion of Indian motivations and plans see Pran Chopra, *India's Second Liberation* (Delhi: Vikas, 1973).

13. On this point see Sisson and Rose, *War and Secession*, pp. 225–26.

14. The best work on this subject is Steven Hoffmann, *India and the China Crisis* (Berkeley: University of California Press, 1990).

15. Tibet's legal personality as an independent state is the subject of some dispute. The best case for Tibet's status as a sovereign state has been made by Michael C. van Walt van Praag, *The Status of Tibet: History, Rights, and Prospects in International Law* (Boulder, Co.: Westview, 1987). See also Tsepon W. D. Shakabpa, *Tibet: A Political History* (New Haven, Ct.: Yale University Press, 1967). For an alternative formulation see A. Tom Grunfeld, *The Making of Modern Tibet* (London: Zed Books, 1987).

16. For a description and analysis of the Indian reaction see Subimal Dutt, *With Nehru in the Foreign Office* (Calcutta: Minerva, 1977), pp. 81–82.

17. This term, prior to Munich and Neville Chamberlain's attempt to conciliate Hitler, had a honorable meaning. It meant the avoidance of conflict through the accommodation of legitimate differences of interest in the realm of foreign policy. On this issue see Paul Kennedy, "The Tradition of Appeasement in British Foreign Policy, 1865–1939," in Paul Kennedy, ed., *Strategy and Diplomacy* (London: Allen and Unwin, 1983).

18. Hoffmann, *India and the China Crisis*, p. 35.

19. Personal interview, New Delhi, July 1988.

20. The best discussion of a compellent strategy can be found in Thomas Schelling, *Arms and Influence* (New Haven, Ct.: Yale University Press, 1968).

21. This argument has been advanced by Allen Whiting in *The Chinese Calculus of Deterrence: India and Indochina* (Ann Arbor: University of Michigan Press, 1975). The central problem with Whiting's otherwise excellent analysis is that it relies uncritically on the polemical work of Neville Maxwell: Neville Maxwell, *India's China War* (New York: Anchor, 1972).

22. The 1987 "war scare" arose from Brasstacks, the largest Indian peacetime military exercise. This exercise provoked Pakistani fears of an impending Indian attack, causing the Pakistanis to extend two of their own milita y exercises, "Flying Horse" and "Sledgehammer." These episodes created a spiral of hostility that seemed to push the two states to the brink of war. Prompt pressure from the United States forced both sides to de-escalate and war was avoided. This incident prompted the first discussions on CSBMs between India and Pakistan.

The second "war scare" developed in August 1990 when the insurgency in Kashmir peaked. Fearing that Pakistani support, particularly the provision of sanctuary for the insurgents, was fueling the uprising, Indian leaders threatened to destroy the sanctuaries in Pakistan. Again, U.S. (and Soviet) pressure proved significant in restraining both sides. Further discussions of CSBMs followed in the wake of this second "war scare." For a controversial discussion of the 1987 incident see Seymour Hersh, "On the Nuclear Edge," *New Yorker*, March 29, 1993, pp. 56–73.

23. On this point see Hormuz Mama, "India and Pakistan retreat from the brink," *International Defense Review* 8 (1990).

24. Interview with senior Indian diplomat, Ministry of External Affairs, New Delhi, January 1993.

25. On this point see the various chapters in Stephen P. Cohen, ed., *Nuclear Proliferation in South Asia* (Boulder, Co.: Westview, 1991).

26. Dilip Bobb and Raj Chengappa, "War Games," *India Today*, February 28, 1990.

27. The term "attentive public" is derived from Gabriel Almond, *The American People and Foreign Policy* (New York: Praeger, 1960), p. 151.

28. On this point see Sumit Ganguly, "Mutual Beneficiaries," *Far Eastern Economic Review*, January 30, 1992, pp. 24–25.

PART TWO

Experience with CSBMs Elsewhere

5

Experience from European and U.S.-Soviet Agreements

Ted Greenwood

There are numerous differences between Europe and South Asia, and between the U.S.-Soviet relationship during the cold war and the Indo-Pakistani or the Sino-Indian relationship today. The historical and cultural setting of international politics in South Asia is more diverse than in the Atlantic community of Europe and North America. Unlike in Europe during the cold war, where there was one dominant security fault line—the boundary between North Atlantic Treaty Organization (NATO) and Warsaw Treaty Organization (WTO) countries, especially the eastern border of the Federal Republic of Germany—in South Asia there are two such lines, the India-Pakistan and the China-India borders. A military stalemate between two roughly equal parties, such as that which existed between the United States and Soviet Union and within Europe at least after the early 1970s, does not exist in South Asia, although the nuclearization of the subcontinent might gradually be achieving this. Furthermore, U.S.-Soviet and European security relations were dominated and complicated by competitive alliances that are absent in South Asia. Perhaps most important, there is not yet in South Asia a willingness to set aside force as an acceptable means to alter the territorial status quo; in Europe, by contrast, such a willingness emerged simultaneously with the creation of the first regional confidence- and security-building measures (CSBMs).

Because of these differences, any drawing of lessons for South Asia from the European or U.S.-Soviet experience must be careful not to go too far or claim too much. Despite this caution, the long European and U.S.-Soviet experience with confidence- and security-building measures is not totally irrelevant to South Asia.

This chapter makes no attempt at a comprehensive description of the many confidence-and security-building agreements that were reached between the United States and the Soviet Union or among the states party to the Conference on Security and Cooperation in Europe (CSCE), or even to mention all the provisions of these agreements. Rather, it draws upon the content and contexts of those agreements to illustrate general themes appropriate to South Asia.

For present purposes, the most useful way to categorize these many agreements is according to their functions (see table 5.1). Doing so not only illustrates their variety but also suggests what functions CSBMs might serve in South Asia, even if their shape and content differ greatly from those of agreements reached in Europe or between the United States and the Soviet Union. The agreements can be classified into four functions: mutual security pledges, transparency, management of dangerous and potentially dangerous military activities, and crisis management. It is more these functions of CSBMs in bilateral and European regional relationships than their detailed provisions that are worth exploring for potential lessons in South Asia.

The following discussion will lead to three results. First, it will suggest several particular CSBM avenues that might fruitfully be explored in South Asia, as well as some that should be avoided. Second and more important, the U.S.-Soviet and European experience suggests that incremental progress toward narrowly focused but meaningful CSBMs can be made between hostile and suspicious states, at least if a mutual deterrence relationship exists that makes revision of the status quo by force seem unattractive. The nuclearization of the three major actors of South Asia is likely to create such a mutual deterrence relationship, making the prospects for CSBMs there more hopeful in the future. Third, the European experience also suggests that CSBMs can not only act to preserve the status quo, but also catalyze peaceful and constructive change in the political and economic spheres.

Mutual Security Pledges

The first function of confidence- and security-building measures is to provide mutual reassurance between or among potentially hostile states through pledges that one of them will not act in a manner that will threaten the security of another. The first example of a mutual security pledge between the United States and the Soviet Union was the Basic Principles of Mutual Relations, signed in Moscow in May 1972. These principles pledged both sides, among other things, to "always exercise restraint in their mutual relations, and . . . be prepared to negotiate and settle differences by peaceful means." Both sides agreed that "the prerequisites for maintaining and

TABLE 5.1 U.S.-Soviet and European CSBMs

	Date Signed	Signatories
Mutual security pledges:		
Basic Principles of Mutual Relations	May 1972	U.S.-Soviet
Prevention of Nuclear War	June 1973	U.S.-Soviet
Helsinki Final Act, document on confidence-building measures and certain aspects of security and disarmament	November 1975	CSCE members
Stockholm Agreement on Confidence- and Security-Building Measures	September 1986	CSCE members
Joint Declaration of Twenty-Two States	November 1990	CSCE members
Transparency measures:		
Measures to Reduce the Risk of Outbreak of Nuclear War (Accidents Measures)	September 1971	U.S.-Soviet
Incidents at Sea	May 1972	U.S.-Soviet
Ballistic Missile Launch Notification	May 1988	U.S.-Soviet
Helsinki Final Act, Document on confidence-building Measures and certain aspects of security and disarmament	November 1975	CSCE members
Stockholm Agreement on Confidence- and Security-Building Measures	September 1986	CSCE members
Vienna Agreement on Confidence- and Security-Building Measures	November 1990	CSCE members
Open Skies agreement	March 1992	CSCE members
Managing dangerous and potentially dangerous military activities and accidents:		
Direct Communication Link (Hotline)	June 1963	U.S.-Soviet
Modernization	September 1971	
Expansion	July 1984	
Measures to Reduce the Risk of Outbreak of Nuclear War (Accidents Measures)	September 1971	U.S.-Soviet
Incidents at Sea	May 1972	U.S.-Soviet
Prevention of Dangerous Military Activities	June 1989	U.S.-Soviet
Crisis management:		
Direct Communication Link (Hotline)	June 1963	U.S.-Soviet
Modernization	September 1971	
Expansion	July 1984	
Prevention of Nuclear War	June 1973	U.S.-Soviet

strengthening peaceful relations between the U.S.A. and the U.S.S.R. are the recognition of the security interests of the parties, based on the principle of equality and the renunciation of the use or threat of force." Although an important document in the evolution of relations between the two super-powers, and referred to subsequently in the preambles of the Agreement on the Prevention of Nuclear War and SALT II, this statement of principles did not carry the same legal force as a formal agreement.

The first formal agreement to include a mutual security pledge was the Agreement on the Prevention of Nuclear War. Here, each side pledged to act "in such a manner as to prevent the development of situations capable of causing a dangerous exacerbation of their relations, as to avoid military confrontations, and as to exclude the outbreak of nuclear war between them and between either of the Parties and other countries" (Article I). Moreover, each party agreed "to proceed from the premise that each Party will refrain from the threat or use of force against the other Party, against the allies of the other Party and against other countries, in circumstances which may endanger international peace and security. The Parties agree that they will be guided by these consid-erations in the formulation of their foreign policies and in their actions in the field of international relations" (Article II).

Two even more significant mutual security pledges were signed by the members of the CSCE. The first was the Helsinki Final Act of 1975, which ratified the borders of post-World War II Europe, including the division of Germany, the Oder-Neisse border between the German Democratic Repub-lic and Poland, and the incorporation into the Soviet Union of territory that before the war had been Polish, Czechoslovak, Hungarian, Romanian, and Bulgarian. It also stated the principles of inviolability of borders, territorial integrity, refraining from the threat or use of force, and nonintervention in internal affairs. The Helsinki Final Act was a watershed agreement in the evolution of postwar Europe because it indicated for the first time that both the winners and losers of World War II were willing at least to acquiesce in the de facto borders that resulted and would seek to settle differences without recourse to force. These principles were restated in the Stockholm Agreement. In both cases, they set the context within which other confi-dence- and security-building measures were constructed.

The second European mutual security pledge was the Joint Declaration of Twenty-Two States, signed by the states of NATO and the dying WTO in November 1990. It declared, among other things, that these states were "no longer adversaries" and restated again that they would "refrain from the threat or use of force against the territorial integrity or the political inde-pendence of any State."[1] Coming after the collapse of Soviet hegemony in Eastern Europe, but before the disintegration of the Soviet Union itself, this declaration was intended to put an end to the Cold War and give greater credibility to the assurances that the threat and use of force were no longer regarded as legitimate instruments of state policy to settle international disputes among the previously hostile states in Europe.

Such mutual security pledges have been important in Europe as symbols and embodiments of major shifts in attitude. How useful they really are, however, for preventing crisis or war, for managing crises once they develop, or for preventing armed coercion or intimidation of one state by another is uncertain at best. Mutually hostile states are likely to hedge against another's violation of a mutual security pledge and, with or without such agreements, to act in the way that seems best at any moment, taking into account many factors, not only the terms of prior pledges. For example, during the October 1973 Middle East war, shortly after the Agreement on the Prevention of Nuclear War was signed, the United States resupplied Israel, the Soviet Union resupplied Egypt, the Soviet Union threatened to send airborne troops to the region and took actions in preparation for doing so, and the United States put its military forces, including its nuclear forces, on alert worldwide. All of these actions might have been interpreted by some as inconsistent with the provisions of the recently signed agreement. On the other hand, neither the United States nor the Soviet Union made overt nuclear threats against the other after 1973. Whether this was the result of the agreement, contemplation of the potential consequences of the 1973 crisis, the general evolution of thinking about the what kinds of military threats are appropriate and useful, or the absence of any subsequent situation that might have elicited such threats is difficult to tell.

Two mutual security pledges already exist between India and Pakistan: the Simla Accord of 1972 and an agreement not to attack one another's nuclear installations. One such pledge exists between India and China: the declaration of 1991 that the border issue would be resolved only by peaceful means. With India and Pakistan and India and China still in the early stages of managing bilateral nuclear relationships, reaching agreement on a regional or bilateral pledges for no first use or no early first use of nuclear weapons or on pledges not to attack population centers might be worthwhile. Pledges to refrain from the threat or use of force to settle disputes or from interference in the internal affairs of the other would probably be more difficult to achieve, but might be useful to help break the cycle of mistrust and suspicion that poisons bilateral relations, especially between India and Pakistan.

However, as discussed in chapter 7 of this volume, crises between India and Pakistan that occurred after the Simla Accord were resolved more despite this agreement than because of it. Moreover, neither the mutual pledge not to attack nuclear installations nor the pledge to resolve the Sino-Indian border dispute peacefully has yet been put to a test. Unlike the Simla Accord, the other pledges were the results of mutual agreement, not (as interpreted by Pakistan) imposed on a losing side by a winning side and its supporters. They might, therefore, have greater influence on actual behavior. The same would presumably be true of any future mutual security pledges reached between India and Pakistan or India and China.

Some authors in this volume argue that these and additional mutual security pledges are essential before progress can be made on other bilateral or regional CSBMs or on structural arms control. However, there is no evidence from the U.S.-Soviet or European experience to support this contention and no reason, based on that experience, why other CSBMs should be delayed if mutual security pledges turn out to be difficult to achieve.

Transparency

Probably the most useful function of confidence- and security-building measures is to increase the transparency of military activities. With any military forces, nuclear or conventional, there exists a possibility that routine military exercises, movement of forces, or equipment tests detected by another country might be misinterpreted as hostile acts or preparations for hostile acts, resulting in temporary anxiety or, worse, preemptive military action.[2] Transparency measures avoid these possibilities by making military activities of potential adversaries more open to scrutiny and their intentions less ambiguous. Transparency measures also reduce the ability to use exercises, missile tests, or the movement of military forces as a means to coerce or intimidate another state. Of course, any transparency measure that a state agrees to on one occasion can be ignored or disavowed at another. However, noncompliance with or disavowal of an agreed measure signals the likelihood of malevolent intent. Therefore the purpose of transparency measures can be said to be threefold: to increase the confidence of states that the benign military activity of others is indeed benign; to reduce the possibility of intimidation or coercion by military means; and to increase the security of states by providing timely warning of hostile intent to potentially hostile military activity. For example, transparency CSBMs in Europe reduced, if not eliminated, the risk of surprise attack and the associated feeling of insecurity and greatly reduced the risks of conflict resulting from misunderstanding or miscalculation.

Prior Notification

Several types of transparency measures have been embodied in agreements between the United States and the Soviet Union or in European regional agreements. The first is prior notification of military exercises, military tests, and troop movements. In the nuclear arena, the focus has been on missile tests. The Accidents Measures Agreement between the United States and the Soviet Union required that "each Party . . . notify the other Party in advance of any planned missile launches if such launches will extend beyond its national territory in the direction of the other Party" (Article 4). (This agreement had little value because rarely, if ever, did the United States or Soviet Union conduct a test that qualified as notifiable under this provision). The Incidents at Sea Agreement went further, requiring that "parties provide through the established system of radio broadcasts of information and warning to mariners, not less than 3 to 5 days in advance as a rule, notification of actions on the high seas which represent a danger to navigation or to aircraft in flight" (Article VI.1) . This includes all tests of ballistic missiles for which the landing area was on the high seas. The Ballistic Missile Launch Notification Agreement requires that "each Party shall provide the other Party notification . . . no less than twenty-four hours in advance, of the planned date, launch area, and area of impact for any launch of a strategic ballistic missile" (Article I). This provision covers even strategic missile tests for which the intended impact area was within the territory of the testing state.

In the arena of conventional forces, prior notification provisions have been focused mostly on exercises and somewhat on troop movements. The Document on Confidence-Building Measures and Certain Aspects of Security and Disarmament, incorporated into the Helsinki Final Act, required that each party give notice through usual diplomatic channels to all other parties twenty-one days in advance of military maneuvers exceeding a total of 25,000 troops that occur on the territory within Europe, defined to extend 250 kilometers from a frontier facing or shared with another European state, or in the adjoining sea area or airspace.[3] The term "troops" included ground, amphibious, and airborne troops. For a maneuver arranged on shorter notice, notification was to be given "at the earliest possible opportunity prior to its starting date." States were also recommended to provide notification of smaller maneuvers to other states, "with special regard for those near the area of such maneuvers." Lest this nonbinding recommendation be thought to have had no effect on states' behavior, note should be taken of the fact that NATO, Warsaw Pact, and neutral and nonaligned states did provide notice for some, although not all, of their maneuvers involving fewer than 25,000 troops.[4]

The Stockholm Agreement extended the notification requirements of the Helsinki Final Act. It required "notification in writing through diplomatic channels in an agreed form of content, to all other participating states 42 days or more in advance" of a planned military activity, troop transfer from outside the zone of applicability, or concentration involving at least 13,000 ground troops (including ground, airborne, air mobile, amphibious and support troops) or at least 300 tanks if organized into a division structure or at least two brigades/regiments. The participation of air forces in the military activity was to be included in the notification if it was foreseen that 200 or more sorties of fixed-wing aircraft would be flown. Notification was also required of an amphibious landing or a parachute assault involving at least 3,000 troops. These requirements of notification applied to military activity anywhere in Europe, from the Atlantic to the Urals, and the adjoining sea area and airspace and up to 250 kilometers beyond for states whose territory extends beyond Europe, namely the Soviet Union and Turkey. Otherwise notifiable activities, carried out without advance notice to the troops involved, were exempted from the prior notification requirement and were required to be notified when the activity commenced. These same provisions were repeated in the Vienna Confidence- and Security-Building Measures Agreement, which is still in effect.

The Stockholm Agreement also included a new type of notification not mentioned in the Helsinki Final Act. An annual calendar of notifiable activities, including information about dates, types of forces participating, location, and purposes, must be provided to others by November 15 of the preceding year, and by November 15 of the year before that for activities involving more than 40,000 troops. No activity involving more than 40,000 troops could be carried out unless it had been included in the calendar of the previous November, and none with more than 75,000 troops could be carried out unless it had been in the calendar the year before that. The Vienna Agreement made these so-called constraining provisions more onerous by prohibiting the conduct of notifiable military activities involving more than 40,000 troops unless notice is given both two years and one year in advance in the annual calendar. This calendar requirement not only increases the predictability and therefore transparency of military activities in Europe, but also prohibits large exercises not planned long in advance, including those that might be employed to intimidate or coerce others. Thus the detection of any large military activity that was not notified in advance is good grounds for suspicion of malevolent intentions.

Even with such prior notification, governments still must be concerned whether the notifying state's intention is benign or whether hostile or coercive action is being planned or taken under cover of a notified test or exercise. This is even more true for alert activities for which no prior notification need be given and which might be used as cover to prepare an attack. Therefore, CSBMs requiring prior notification do not eliminate the concerns that might exist without them or the requirement for states to reach their own conclusions about others' military activities. However, prior notification requirements do facilitate reaching such conclusions by permitting intelligence assets to be focused more accurately on anticipated activities. The primary value of prior notification requirements is probably to ensure that detection of unnotified military activity, including a large troop activity for which notice was not given on the annual calendar, would trigger suspicion that belligerent action is imminent.

Monitoring of Military Activities

The second type of transparency measures that have been embodied in agreements between the United States and the Soviet Union and in European regional agreements is the monitoring of military activities. Monitoring can provide more information about military activities than does notification alone. By ensuring that the activities are indeed what they were claimed to be, monitoring is even more likely to relieve anxiety that an activity might not be benign. Of course, even monitoring cannot prevent premeditated aggression, but it would provide early warning of such intention either through direct observation of activities that are clearly preparatory for war or because access is denied to observers when it should be allowed. Monitoring requirements, therefore, can reduce or eliminate the risk of and concern about surprise attack. They can also provide considerable intelligence information about the disposition and readiness of forces and tactics.

For nuclear forces, the only monitoring agreements in place apply to certain nuclear tests, portal monitoring of some missile manufacturing facilities, and various types of on-site inspection. In all cases the intention is verification of an arms control agreement, an activity not usually included as a confidence- and security-building measure.

For conventional forces, there are agreements for monitoring of exercises in Europe. The Helsinki Final Act merely asserts that "participating States will invite other participating States, voluntarily and on a bilateral basis, in a spirit of reciprocity and good will towards all participating States, to send observers to attend military maneuvers." Despite the voluntary nature of this provision, many states invited observers both to major military maneuvers (i.e. over 25,000 troops) and to smaller exercises.[5]

The Stockholm Agreement, however, requires that states "invite observers from all other participating States" to notifiable military activities involving more than 17,000 troops, except for amphibious landing or parachute assault for which the threshold number is 5,000, unless the troops have no advanced warning and the notifiable event does not last more than 72 hours. Up to two observers may be sent by each state and what they must be allowed to see and how is specified in considerable detail. These provisions for inviting observers were repeated in the Vienna Agreement. Monitoring, including inspection on demand, is also permitted for purposes of verification of compliance with the terms of these agreements.

Data Exchanges

The third type of transparency measures are data exchanges. These might include data on the order of battle, weapons inventories, procurement, or defense budgets. Such data exchanges have, of course, accompanied all nuclear arms reduction agreements since SALT II and the Treaty of Conventional Forces in Europe. Again, however, such exchanges are for purposes of treaty verification, not confidence- and security-building, although they have that effect as well. As CSBMs, data exchanges increase the knowledge of one country about the military activities and plans of another.

The Vienna Agreement requires extensive exchange of military information annually. Included are detailed information about ground and air forces organization, manpower, and major weapon and equipment systems (including unit designation, subordination, normal peacetime location of headquarters, peacetime authorized personnel strength, and numbers of each type of combat aircraft, helicopters, or major organic weapon and equipment systems of ground and amphibious units down to brigades/regiments); information on plans for the deployment of major weapons and equipment systems (by formation or units, when possible, and whether the deployments is add-on or substitution); and information on the military budget for the forthcoming fiscal year. In the case of budgetary information, the supplying state must be responsive to questions by other states within two months.

Military-to-Military Contacts

The fourth type of transparency measure is military-to-military contacts. The exchange of information and views between military officers of different countries and visits of officers of one country to the schools or bases of another increases understanding of how the others think about their missions, their strategy, and their forces. Among the contacts called for in the Vienna Agreement are reciprocal visits to air bases, exchanges and visits between senior and mid-level officers and defense officials, contacts between relevant military institutions, attendance at courses of instruction of another state, exchanges and contacts between military academies and experts in military studies, and sporting and cultural events between members of their armed forces.

Direct Observation

The final type of transparency measure is one that facilitates the collection of information by direct observation over the territory of another state. The provisions for non-interference with national technical means of verification in the nuclear arms reductions agreements not only facilitate agreement verification but also act as a broader transparency measure. The most elaborate such agreement is the Open Skies Agreement. It opens up the entirety of all signatory countries to aerial surveillance and is therefore the first CSBM agreement of the CSCE countries that applies beyond the confines of Europe. Within the limits of how many inspections per year each country is allowed to make or obligated to accept, the inspections must be on demand, with short waiting time between request and implementation. All the raw data collected must be shared among all participating states.

Although the details of these various agreements are derived from and reflect the unique conditions of U.S.-Soviet relations or of the evolving European security environment, the basic principles they embody and type of transparency measures that they represent are likely to be translatable, perhaps in altered form, to South Asia. In the area of prior notification, for example, with the Indian and Chinese ballistic missile programs remaining active and the Pakistani program becoming more so, bilateral agreements to provide advance notice of test launches might be useful. Agreements exist between India and Pakistan and between India and China for prior notification of military exercises, although the details of these agreements are not publicly known. Such agreements, if they require adequate prior notification of military exercises over an adequately specified size or in specified regions should reduce the likelihood of exercises precipitating crises, as has happened in the past. Advanced publication of an annual calendar of exercises might not be feasible in the near term, but notification weeks to months in advance might be. Even better would be mutual invitations between India and Pakistan and India and China to observe some military exercises of the other. This might start informally, by one country taking the initiative to issue an invitation and the other reciprocating later. Eventually, perhaps a formal arrangement for regular monitoring of military activity could be achieved.

Data exchanges and military-to-military contacts (although fairly extensive now) could certainly be increased. For example, as Jasjit Singh points out elsewhere in this volume, there is need for better mutual understanding of the military doctrines of the countries of South Asia and of their implications for the doctrines and strategies of neighboring states. Here, too, informal initiative might usefully precede formal agreement. Mutual direct observation over the territory of the other state is not likely to occur in the near future, however, except possibly along the India-China border. As in Europe, broad application of this approach is likely to be a late rather than an early step in the evolution of transparency measures.

Managing Dangerous and Potentially Dangerous Military Activities and Accidents

A third function of CSBMs is managing dangerous or potentially dangerous military activities. Although chapter 9 of this volume gives a much broader definition, here "management" is restricted to reducing risks associated with peacetime military activities, preventing accidents, providing warning to another party if a potentially injurious accident is about to occur or has occurred, preventing or limiting unintended injurious effects, and preventing misunderstanding, retaliation, or escalation following an accident, especially one that causes damage to another party.

The Accidents Measures Agreement between the United States and the Soviet Union was intended, in part, to help manage dangers inherent in the routine maintenance of and training with nuclear forces and in false alarms by early warning systems. Each side pledges "to maintain and to improve, as it deems necessary, its existing organizational and technical arrangements to guard against the accidental or unauthorized use of nuclear weapons under its control" (Article 1). Each side agrees "to notify [the other side] immediately in the event of an accidental, unauthorized or any other unexplained incident involving a possible detonation of a nuclear weapon which could create a risk of outbreak of nuclear war. In the event of such an incident, the Party whose nuclear weapon is involved will immediately make every effort to take necessary measures to render harmless or destroy such weapon without causing damage" (Article 2). In addition, "in other situations involving nuclear incidents, [each Party] undertakes to act in such a manner as to reduce the possibility of actions being misinterpreted by the other Party. In any such situation, each Party may inform the other Party or request information when in its view this is warranted by the interests of averting the risk of outbreak of nuclear war" (Article 5). Although it delineates no specific actions to guard against the accidental or unauthorized use of nuclear weapons, this agreement is generally regarded as having significantly encouraged the use of "permissive action links" and other technical devices to prevent the unauthorized use or accidental detonation of nuclear weapons.

To deal with the risk that false alarms from ballistic missile early warning systems might trigger a nuclear exchange, the Agreement commits each Party to notify the other "immediately in the event of detection by missile warning systems of unidentified objects, or in the event of signs of interference with these systems or with related communications facilities, if such occurrences could create a risk of outbreak of nuclear war between the two countries" (Article 3). Of course, there is some danger inherent in this requirement to notify. In the event that the missile warning system were triggered by an actual attack, notifying the other side and waiting for a response might waste precious time that should have been used to take defensive action or initiate retaliation. For the United States and the former Soviet Union this risk is low because any large attack would be identified unambiguously for what it is and a small attack would not carry the same urgency for action. For states with small and perhaps vulnerable nuclear forces, the risk of agreeing to consult before acting might be higher. But so too would be the risk of not consulting, because the fear of losing retaliatory forces before using them might lead to retaliation even when the apparent warning of attack is false.

The communication called for in the U.S.-Soviet Accident Measures agreement could be by means of normal diplomatic channels but, in the event of urgency, would more likely be via the hotline that has existed between Washington and Moscow since 1963. This hotline began as two links, one wire telegraph and the other radio telegraph. By later agreement in 1971, the radio link was replaced by two satellite communications circuits in 1978, with multiple terminals installed in each capital. The system was modernized in 1984 to include facsimile as well as teletype equipment. Such a direct communication system is useful not only for exchanging information related to actual or potential accidents but also for crisis management, as will be discussed below.

Two more specific U.S.-Soviet agreements exist for managing dangerous military activities outside the nuclear arena. The first is an agreement to prevent incidents on or over the high seas. It arose from a realization on both sides that the behavior of their navies when operating in close proximity to each other, especially in the eastern Mediterranean during the 1967 Middle East war, had been provocative and sometimes dangerous. The agreement provides procedures to prevent the collision of ships; prohibits interfering with the evolution of naval formations of the other party (Article III.2); requires surveillance ships to maintain a safe distance from their targets (Article III.4); requires use of accepted international signals when ships maneuver in sight of each other (Article III.5); prohibits one party's ship from simulating attacks at, launching objects toward, or illuminating the bridges of the other party's ships (Article III.6); prohibits aircraft of one party from performing aerobatics over, or dropping objects near, ships of the other party, or simulating attack against its aircraft or ships (Article IV); and requires that both sides observe the letter and the spirit of the International Regulations for Preventing Collisions at Sea (Rules of the Road) (Articles II and III).

Of particular significance in this agreement are the procedures for dealing with incidents that occur despite the agreement's efforts to prevent them (Article VII). These are to be reported by the navy of each country through the Naval Attache of the other in its capital. Similarly, although the agreement does not specify at what level the annual reviews of its implementation should be held, in practice they have been between the two navies at the working level. The purpose of this reliance on working-level officers has been to emphasize the cooperative and technical nature of the agreement, including its implementation and review of failures, and to prevent incidents from escalating into the realm of high politics. This approach has proven highly successful.

The existence of this agreement has not prevented all incidents. However, an analyst who reviewed the relevant history in 1985 concluded that, since the agreement, there have been many fewer incidents and occasions where navies of the two side have risked running into each other, and those that have occurred have been less severe.[6] This includes the period of the October 1973 Middle East war, when close to one hundred Soviet ships were in close proximity to about the same number of U.S. ships in the eastern Mediterranean. Whether this improved record was a direct result of the agreement is, of course, difficult to prove. The U.S. Navy, however, appears to believe that it was.[7] This agreement has also become a model for others. Eight other NATO countries (Canada, France, the Federal Republic of Germany, Italy, the Netherlands, Norway, Spain, and the United Kingdom) signed similar agreements with the then Soviet Union.

The second U.S.-Soviet CSBM agreement for managing peacetime, non-nuclear, dangerous military activities is the Agreement on the Prevention of Dangerous Military Activities. Like the Incidents at Sea Agreement, this one arose from incidents that had occurred between the forces of the two countries. In February 1988, a U.S. ship operating in the Black Sea was purposely bumped by a Soviet ship. The close proximity of U.S. and Soviet ships operating in the Persian Gulf during the Iran-Iraq war gave rise to concern about possible incidents. In addition, instances had occurred in which the United States felt that Soviet forces used lasers in a manner that could harm U.S. personnel.

The Agreement requires that each party "take necessary measures directed toward preventing dangerous military activity" (Article II). Should such activity nonetheless occur, the Agreement established procedures to deal with it by peaceful means. The following categories of "dangerous military activity" are specifically mentioned: "entering by personnel and equipment of the armed forces of one Party into the national territory of the other Party owing to circumstances brought about by *force majeure*, or as a result of unintentional actions by such personnel" (Article II.1.a); "using a laser in such a manner that its radiation could cause harm to personnel or damage to equipment of the armed forces of the other Party" (Article II.1.b); "interfering with command and control networks in a manner which could cause harm to personnel or damage to equipment of the armed forces of the other Party" (Article II.1.d); and "hampering the activities of the personnel and equipment of the armed forces of the other party in a "special caution area" in a manner which could cause harm to personnel or damage to equipment" (Article II.1.c). A special caution area is a region "designated mutually by the parties, in which personnel and equipment of their armed forces are present and, due to circumstances in the region, in which special measures shall be undertaken" (Article I.8). In the event that military personnel of one party enter the territory of another due to unintentional action or force majeure, the Agreement specifies provisions for protecting and assisting them and for ensuring that they can depart at the earliest opportunity (Article III.2 and Annexes 1 and 2).

Perhaps most important, this agreement provides detailed provisions to establish and maintain communication between the armed forces of the parties to prevent dangerous military activities from occurring or to resolve incidents that might occur (Annex 1). This includes communications between the commanders of forces present in a special caution area; between commanders of ships, aircraft, ground vehicles, or ground units of both parties; and between the commander of an aircraft of the armed forces of one party and an air traffic control or monitoring facility of the other party. The provisions include special radio frequencies, visual signals, and the specification of English phrases for use in particular contingencies.

The agreement also creates a Joint Military Commission to meet at least annually to consider implementation and compliance issues and to seek other ways to ensure a higher level of safety for the personnel and equipment of the armed forces of both countries (Article IX). As with the Incidents at Sea Agreement, the locating of this commission at the military level was intended to emphasize the cooperative and technical nature of the agreement and to prevent incidents from escalating into the realm of high politics.

Although, like all CSBM agreements, this one is vague in many respects, it is nonetheless highly significant because it created for the first time a mechanism for direct, immediate communication between the commanders of forces of the two countries when they operate in close proximity. Such arrangements can be useful not only when these forces find themselves in competitive or adversarial proximity, but also when they are working together, as they did in the Persian Gulf during the Iran-Iraq war.

In the context of South Asia, the military forces of India and either Pakistan or China are more likely to be in competitive or adversarial than cooperative proximity, especially at sea and along mutual borders. Agreements that regulate the activities of their forces in order to prevent incidents and that specify how incidents that do occur should be dealt with might prevent misunderstanding and unwanted cycles of retaliation and escalation. The U.S.-Soviet Agreement on the Prevention of Dangerous Military Activities could serve as a useful model. Similarly, as the regional navies, especially India's and China's, continue to expand and extend their operations further from their shores, the U.S.-Soviet Incidents at Sea Agreement might also be taken as a model for bilateral agreements among them.

If, as seems likely, both India and Pakistan possess or could rapidly assemble nuclear weapons, agreements between them and between India and China intended to prevent or limit the consequences of nuclear accidents might be useful. One significant obstacle to such agreements exists, however: Such agreements can only be reached between states that openly acknowledge their possession of nuclear weapons. China does, of course. The public postures of Pakistan and India, however, are more ambiguous.

Crisis Management

The fourth function of CSBMs is crisis management, including crisis prevention. A large element of crisis management between the superpowers during the cold war focused on nuclear weapons. During crises, nuclear forces are likely to be on a higher-than-normal state of alert, which implies that some of the usual safeguards against accidental launch are relaxed. Moreover, people are much more edgy, suspicious, and fearful during a crisis and there is a natural tendency for people under stress to see that which they fear to see. Nuclear accidents, miscalculations about how an adversary will interpret or react to an action, and misperceptions of what an adversary is doing or planning to do are therefore more likely during a crisis.

In time of crisis, especially one with possible nuclear overtones, fast and reliable communication capability between governments — especially between the highest levels of government and perhaps between military authorities as well — could be useful to permit exchange of messages or information. Such channels would avoid the delays and misinterpretations that could result from use of normal, sometimes circuitous channels. This was the primary reason for creating the previously mentioned hotline between Moscow and Washington, and for expanding and upgrading it from time to time. Other states, including France and the former Soviet Union, have copied this example. India and Pakistan have also done so by creating a direct communications link between the military headquarters of each country.

The existence of a hotline does not guarantee that crises can be safely managed, of course. Translation and interpretation of messages received can still be a problem. A hotline can be used purposely to provide misinformation or to deceive and, for that reason, any message would have to be regarded with skepticism if not suspicion. A direct communication link between government or military leaders could even exacerbate this risk because of a tendency to hear what one wants or fears to hear rather than what is being said. Although the speed of transmission is a major advantage of a direct communication link, speed can also be a disadvantage if the result is to invite a spontaneous, emotional, and unthoughtful response rather than a deliberate and carefully considered one. This risk is even greater if the communication link is voice rather than text. Thus U.S.-Soviet crisis management has probably been well served by limiting the hotline to printed text.

The U.S.-Soviet nuclear CSBMs are also intended in part to prevent crises from developing. For example, to manage a crisis once it has emerged, the Agreement on the Prevention of Nuclear War requires that "if at any time relations between the Parties or between either Party and other countries appear to involve risks of a nuclear conflict, or if relations between countries not parties to this Agreement appear to involve the risk of nuclear war between the United States of American and the Union of Soviet Socialist Republics or between either Party and other countries, the United States and the Soviet Union . . . shall immediately enter into urgent consultations with each other and make every effort to avert the risk" (Article IV).

As with mutual security pledges, assessments of the usefulness of agreements for preventing or managing crises are uncertain at best. As already mentioned, with or without such agreements, states are likely to act in the way that seems best at the moment. National decision-makers might take into account the obligations under such agreements, but they are likely to more influenced by other things, including the exigencies of a particular circumstance and perceptions of national interest and of how that interest is best pursued under the circumstances.

A type of confidence- and security-building measure that has been proposed as a means of crisis management, especially crisis prevention, involves restrictions on the conduct of certain military activities. Such restrictions might include zones (perhaps along borders) that are either demilitarized or in which only limited forces may be deployed; zones along coasts from which all or certain kinds of warships of non-littoral states are excluded; limitations on the size, frequency, duration, location, or other characteristics of military exercises;[8] and limitations on missile or nuclear weapons tests. With the exception of certain restrictions on nuclear weapons testing and the prohibition of large military activities unless notified well in advance, no such CSBMs have been adopted in the bilateral U.S.-Soviet or European regional context. This approach, therefore, seems particularly difficult and is not likely to be fruitful in South Asia.

Another type of confidence- and security-building measure that some students of this subject have suggested might be useful for crisis management is the creation of institutions intended to ensure that communication actually occurs and to provide a ready venue for and people trained in crisis management. But either governments have not been persuaded of the utility of such institutions, or agreements to create them are difficult to achieve, because such institutions are not well developed in Europe or between the United States and Soviet Union.

The only specific purpose of the Nuclear Risk Reduction Centers, created under the 1987 U.S.-Soviet Union agreement on this subject (Protocol I), is to transmit notifications of ballistic missile launches, although other communications can also be transmitted at the discretion of each Party. (Thus the agreement to create these centers is closer to a transparency measure than to a crisis management agreement.) This modest institution had much more ambitious beginnings. A Working Group on Nuclear Risk Reduction, convened by Senators Sam Nunn and John Warner in 1982, proposed that Nuclear Risk Reduction Centers might discuss and outline the procedures to be followed in the event of incidents involving the use of nuclear weapons; maintain close contact during incidents precipitated by nuclear terrorists to avoid any possible resulting nuclear confrontation between the United States and the Soviet Union; exchange information on a voluntary basis relevant to nonproliferation policy or about military activities that might be misunderstood during periods of mounting tensions; and establish a dialogue about nuclear doctrines, forces, and activities.[9]

The Vienna-based Conflict Prevention Center (CPC), created by the Charter of Paris for a New Europe and signed by all CSCE states in November 1990, is slightly more ambitious in its mission than the bilateral Nuclear Risk Reduction Centers. Still, it was not initially intended as an institution for crisis management. The CPC's purposes are to support the implementation of CSBMs by serving as a mechanism for consultation and cooperation about unusual military activities, for cooperation regarding hazardous incidents of a military nature, and for the annual exchange of military information as required by other European arms control agreements and CSBMs. It can serve as a venue for CSBM-related meetings, including military doctrine seminars such as those held in January 1990 and October 1991. It is also supposed to maintain files on CSBM-related information and produce a yearly publication based on that information. The CSCE states did not rule out the possibility that the CPC's mandate might be broadened in the future. Indeed, its terms of reference specify that it might assume other functions and perform "tasks concerning a procedure for the conciliation of disputes as well as broader tasks relating to dispute settlement, which may be assigned to it in the future by the Council of the Foreign Ministers."

The reluctance of governments to create real crisis management institutions is perhaps understandable. By their nature, crises engage the attention of the most senior military and political leaders. The likelihood that a crisis management institution would be bypassed when the time actually came to manage a crisis, therefore, seems high. Given that likelihood, if appropriate communications mechanisms exist between the relevant governments, there seems little reason to have created elaborate institutions in Europe or between the United States and the former Soviet Union in the past, or to do so in South Asia in the future.

As previously mentioned, India and Pakistan have already copied the example of the U.S.-Soviet and other hotlines by creating a direct communication system between their respective military headquarters and between adjacent regional commanders. In these cases, however, the communication is through voice, which raises the concerns mentioned above. A similar communication system, preferably based on text, between the political leadership of the two countries would be equally useful. A hotline between political authorities in New Delhi and Beijing has also been created and should be useful in preventing and managing crises.

The lessons from Europe and the U.S.-Soviet relationship for South Asia with respect to other kinds of crisis management CSBMs should temper enthusiasm. Agreements on rules of behavior before and during crises might be symbolically useful, but have limited practical value. Similarly, institutions for crisis management do not seem particularly useful and are probably not worth working for at an early date. Restrictions on the conduct of military activities, such as demilitarized zones along land borders or at sea or limitations on military exercises, although potentially useful, are very difficult to achieve and are not likely to emerge soon in South Asia.

Conclusion

This review of CSBM agreements between the United States and the Soviet Union and among the states of the CSCE does suggest a number of avenues that might be fruitful to explore in South Asia, as well as a few that should be avoided. Perhaps the most significant lesson for South Asia to be drawn from the U.S.-Soviet and European experience with CSBMs, however, is that such agreements can be reached even between hostile and suspicious states.[10] It is true that as relations warmed between the United States and the Soviet Union and between NATO and Warsaw Pact states generally, more numerous and more invasive CSBMs were reached. Nevertheless, the first such agreement dates back to 1963 in the U.S.-Soviet case, a time when the cold war was raging, and to 1975 in the case of CSCE-wide agreements, a full fifteen years before the cold war's end.

Perhaps most significantly for South Asia, some agreements were reached between states that had deep antagonisms and strong ideological differences and that did not fully accept the territorial status quo or each other's legitimacy.[11] Even the Helsinki Final Act and its successor agreements did not indicate an end to these antagonisms or acceptance of the status quo, but rather a commitment not to seek changes by force. The

United States and others continued not to recognize the Soviet Union's annexation of the Baltic states, and certainly hopes were harbored widely in Europe that Germany would one day be unified. Many on both sides of the East-West divide, including national leaders, continued to hope that their own type of political and economic system would eventually encompass all of Europe. What distinguished Europe during the cold war from South Asia today was that, despite the antagonism, ideological differences, and lack of recognition of legitimacy and borders, there existed tacit understanding, especially after 1975, that attempts to effect change by force of arms would be folly. In other words, mutual deterrence existed in Europe, causing all parties to agree that avoiding war should take precedence over changing the political and territorial status quo.

In South Asia such understanding does not yet exist; armed conflict is still widely regarded as an acceptable instrument of state policy to alter the status quo. Under such circumstances, confidence- and security-building measures, intended to discourage changes in the status quo by force, have understandably seemed unattractive. However, as the reality of nuclear possession by all three antagonists in South Asia is gradually internalized in their understanding of their security context, a condition of mutual deterrence is likely to evolve, as it did in Europe, and thus revisionism by force is likely to seem increasingly unattractive. For this reason, the prospects for confidence- and security-building measures in South Asia seem brighter for the future than they have seemed in the past.[12]

There is an understandable tendency for discussions of confidence- and security-building measures in South Asia to take a comprehensive view, seeking broad agreement within the military sphere and encompassing also the economic, social, human rights, and political spheres.[13] The experiences in Europe and between the Soviet Union and the United States, however, suggest the value of resisting this tendency, where possible. Confidence- and security-building measures contributing to military security are best approached incrementally rather than comprehensively. They can also be more readily and more rapidly achieved than measures in other areas, and even more when discussed in relative isolation from other, albeit important, issues. To take the narrow approach might be tantamount to acknowledging the intractability of other matters, at least in the near term. As in other areas, however, in pursuing the security benefits of confidence- and security-building measures, governments might be well served by preventing the best from becoming the enemy of the good.

Once achieved, narrowly drawn confidence- and security-building measures can be expected to have multiple effects in South Asia. In Europe, they reduced not only anxiety about coercion and the risks of war but also the actual risks and the opportunities for coercion. They altered for the better the climate of hostility and suspicion that existed among regional states. They also facilitated the rapprochement that gradually allowed serious attention to be paid to other kinds of discussions and agreements—economic, social, human rights, and political.

There is no doubt that at one level CSBMs are intended to and do have the effect of preserving and stabilizing the status quo. At a deeper level, however, they can also be powerful catalysts of peaceful change.[14] The extent to which they had that effect on the former Soviet Union and in Europe is impossible to distinguish from all the other forces at work over close to fifty years. But they certainly deserve some of the credit for what has been a most remarkable and perhaps unique transformation. It is possible, perhaps even likely, that CSBMs could play a similar role in South Asia.

Notes

1. *Joint Declaration of Twenty-Two States*, paragraph 2, November 20, 1990.

2. Whether or what kinds of exercises, troop movements, or tests really are difficult to identify correctly, given a particular level of sophistication in reconnaissance and surveillance technology, and how much governments actually worry about such activities is never considered in the public debate and is very difficult for outsiders to know.

3. This agreement was politically binding, not a legal obligation.

4. Michael Holmes, "Compliance with Confidence-Building Measures: From Helsinki to Stockholm," Background Paper no. 30, Canadian Institute for International Peace and Security, February 1990.

5. Holmes, "Compliance with Confidence-Building Measures."

6. Sean Lynn-Jones, "A Quiet Success for Arms Control: Preventing Incidents at Sea," *International Security* 9, no. 4 (spring 1985), pp. 154–84.

7. Lynn-Jones, "A Quiet Success."

8. For an examination of restrictions on ground forces exercises in the European context, see Robert D. Blackwill and Jeffrey W. Legro, "Constraining Ground Force Exercises of NATO and the Warsaw Pact," *International Security* 14, no. 3 (winter 1989/90), pp. 68-98. Blackwill and Legro's study concludes that proposals made previously, with the possible exception of a size constraint, would be either unfavorable to NATO or infeasible to implement, or both.

9. "A Nuclear Risk Reduction System," report of the Nunn/Warner Working Group on Nuclear Risk Reduction, November 1983. See also U.S. Department of Defense, *Report to the Congress by Secretary of Defense Caspar W. Weinberger on Direct Communications Links and Other Measures to Enhance Stability*, April 11, 1983.

10. This view contrasts with that of Moonis Ahmar, who says, "The military aspects of CBM's cannot be dealt with in isolation until and unless the political issues are also taken into account." Moonis Ahmar, "Confidence-Building Measures in South Asia," PSIS Occasional Paper no. 3/1991 (Geneva: Graduate Institute of International Studies, Program for Strategic and International Studies, 1991), p. 31.

11. The importance of this point is underlined by the widespread view that acceptance of the status quo is a prerequisite to agreement on meaningful confi-

dence- and security-building measures. For example, the United Nations Institute for Disarmament Research (UNIDR) has claimed that "the negotiations and introduction of confidence-building measures in a given region or situation is predicated upon the recognition and acceptance of the imperative of mutual security and the preservation of the status quo irrespective of the differences which may exist among the parties." UNIDR, *Confidence-Building Measures in Africa* (New York: United Nations, 1987), p. 2.

12. Again, this view contrasts with that of Moonis Ahmar, who says, "The entire task of CBMs would be meaningless without settlement of the nuclear issue in South Asia." Ahmar, 'Confidence-Building Measures in South Asia," p. 18. Another potential advantage of South Asia compared to Europe as a venue for CSBMs is the absence in South Asia of the complications of alliance politics.

13. This tendency to broaden beyond the military sphere was dominant at the United Nations meeting on confidence- and security-building measures in Asia, held in Kathmandu in January 1990. See Yasushi Akashi, "Summary of a Debate," United Nations Department of Disarmament Affairs, *Confidence and Security-Building in Asia* (New York: United Nations, 1990). It is also present in the approach of some of the authors in this volume.

14. A similar view is expressed by Josef Holik, "Underpinnings and Adaptability of European CSBM Concepts," United Nations Department of Disarmament Affairs, *Confidence and Security-Building Measures: From Europe to Other Regions*, Disarmament Topical paper no. 7 (New York: United Nations, 1991), p. 40.

6

Arab-Israeli CSBMs:
Implications for South Asia

Mark A. Heller

The Regional Context of Confidence Building

This analysis examines the Arab-Israeli experience with confidence-and security-building measures (CSBMs) and ventures some preliminary thoughts about the potential applicability of this record to South Asia. Before proceeding, the following point should be borne in mind: This analysis deals almost exclusively with military CSBMs, particularly with technical-military measures (i.e., artificially contrived limitations on the deployment and training of military forces, sometimes referred to as operational arms control) and with political-military measures (i.e., declarations of intent concerning the planned use of force and/or weapons). Little reference is made to the rest of the universe of CSBMs, which includes a variety of diplomatic, economic, cultural, and humanitarian initiatives implied in unilateral concessions and "goodwill" gestures. Such measures (for example, freezing Israeli settlement activity or permitting the emigration of Syrian Jews) are unquestionably important in altering the psychological context of negotiations and conflict resolution, because they consciously encourage the other side to accept a more benign view of one's own long-term intentions. Indeed, some historical studies place conciliatory diplomacy at the very center of the confidence-building process.[1] But while the perception of the adversary's ultimate intentions is a critical element of national security, measures that influence perceptions and affective views have no direct impact on the uses one makes of military forces.[2]

Confidence- and security-building measures play a potentially vital role in shaping attitudes toward a settlement of the Arab-Israeli conflict. This possibility explains the growing interest in applying elements of the Helsinki/Stockholm model of confidence-and security-building to the Arab-Israeli context. Indeed, the elaboration of proposals for Arab-Israeli CSBMs has become something of a cottage industry in recent years. Unfortunately, most efforts in this field have produced little more than annotated laundry lists of measures taken from the East-West record, and many analysts have concluded that it will be exceedingly difficult to adopt and implement any but the most modest CSBMs pending real progress toward resolution of the political conflict between Arabs and Israelis.[3] This difficulty is usually attributed to the structure of the conflict itself, or, more precisely, to the differences between this conflict and that which characterized East-West relations during almost two decades of Conference on Security and Cooperation in Europe (CSCE) and Conventional Forces in Europe (CFE) negotiations.[4]

In the East-West conflict, neither the existential legitimacy nor the existing boundaries of the protagonists were subject to serious challenge, at least in the sense that the parties involved in Europe did not believe that they could reasonably translate revisionist aspirations into a military idiom. Consequently, these governments were willing to maintain diplomatic relations and direct communications even in the darkest days of the cold war. Although opposition to the adversary's policies was persistent and suspicion about its military intentions pervasive, none of the parties concerned insisted that it was in a state of war with the other or reserved the right to use force for other than defensive purposes. In other words, discontent with the status quo, though widespread and sometimes intense, was not incompatible with a principled willingness by governments to adopt measures that inherently favored the political and territorial status quo by constraining offensive military capabilities. As a result, East-West relations increasingly came to focus on an epiphenomenon—the threat-driven military postures of the protagonists—rather than on the essence of conflict, such as ideological or territorial issues. So after the Berlin crises and the Cuban missile crisis, arms control tended to dominate the agenda of the superpowers; indeed, from the 1960s on, Soviet-American relations were increasingly about arms control. This development reflected converging concerns—the mutual fear of the horrifying consequences of misperception, uncertainty, and uncontrolled escalation—and a converging interest in assuaging these concerns. Since declared policy abjured the offensive use of military force, there was no fundamental obstacle to the elaboration of a series of artificially contrived measures intended to enhance confidence that operational intentions really conformed with that policy.

In contrast, Arab-Israeli relations usually lacked most of the enabling conditions of the Helsinki/Stockholm model, especially the fundamental transformation in the focus of relations. Despite the initiation of a peace process and perceptible signs of movement, the Arab-Israeli conflict remained about substantive, even existential issues, rather than about the military postures that are a manifestation of those issues, and the belief persisted that objectives in this conflict could be promoted through the threat or use of military means. In such circumstances, when territorial issues and even basic questions of identity and legitimacy were not fully resolved, the precondition for productive discussions about CSBMs in the European context was absent, and focusing on CSBMs before achieving a transformation in the nature of the political relationship was sometimes likened to putting the cart before (or at least beside) the horse. Syrian President Hafez al-Asad, for example, expressed himself in the following terms:

> Many people say that confidence-building measures can be adopted among different countries and achieve results like what took place between East and West. But, there were no wars between the East and West, neither was there occupation of other countries. . . . In such cases, CSBMs might be useful for proceeding toward a better understanding. In our case . . . one party occupies the land of the other parties. . . . What measure can build confidence among us here in the region other than straightening out matters?[5]

In general, the Arab side was always far less reconciled than Israel to the status quo, and this political asymmetry should logically have produced asymmetrical attitudes toward CSBMs. Thus the Arab approach should have been reserved and unenthusiastic; generally speaking, this was indeed the case. Israel, by contrast, should have been more receptive, not only because CSBMs would reduce the likelihood of an effective Arab military initiative, but also because the very process of negotiation (at least in the case of explicit, formal measures) would entail a degree of Arab legitimation of Israel's existence.

In fact, however, the attitudes of the protagonists cannot be categorized as neatly as this simple taxonomy would suggest. Instead, Arab states assumed a variety of obligations or assented to third-party measures that practically constrained the Arab capability to initiate military operations against Israel. The history of the Arab-Israeli conflict is replete with arrangements, particularly limited-forces and demilitarized zones, that certainly appear to qualify as confidence-building measures.[6] And although Israel sometimes proposed such measures or responded positively to proposals by others, its own approach was often ambivalent and reserved.

Like the Arab-Israeli arena, South Asia—especially the India-Pakistan dyad—is characterized by conflictual relationships. The conflicts involve long-standing disputes over substantive issues, including territory, but also reflect, and therefore perpetuate, deep-seated antipathies and mutual suspicions connected to questions of political and communal identity and images of self and other; the Indo-Pakistani conflict over Kashmir clearly incorporates all these dimensions. Second, the protagonists have frequently resorted to the use of force in the pursuit of their objectives and tend to see deterrence and coercion rather than reassurance and cooperation as the most reliable methods of promoting their security and other interests. As a result, the region is highly militarized, the leading actors have adopted "nervous" military doctrines and force postures, and ongoing arms races are approaching—if they have not already breached—important thresholds with respect to deep-strike delivery systems and weapons of mass destruction. Moreover, as in the Arab-Israeli case, instability in South Asia is exacerbated by the facts that the definition of the theater is ambiguous and states face multiple threats, including domestic security threats with a real or perceived inter-state dimension.

Thus, regardless of conscious policy decisions that may be taken, there is a serious problem of crisis instability in South Asia, with the constant danger that misperception and uncertainty may produce unintended and uncontrolled escalation. The need for CSBMs to minimize this danger is at least as urgent in South Asia as it is in the Middle East. Furthermore, security concerns is South Asia may not be as intimately connected with territorial issues as they are in the Middle East, but to the extent that they affect the willingness of the protagonists to adopt conciliatory positions on substantive disputes, CSBMs can also facilitate conflict resolution in the region.

But in addition to these similarities, South Asia differs from the Arab-Israeli arena in several important respects, and these differences may make the pursuit of CSBMs much easier. First, no matter how intense animosities have been in South Asia, no party denies the very legitimacy of any other. Measures of reassurance, therefore, do not have to contend with inhibitions about indirectly conferring legitimacy on the other side in advance of a comprehensive settlement of all disputes. Second, adversaries maintain normal, if volatile, diplomatic and commercial relations and direct communication between them is routine. There is even a regional institution—the South Asian Association for Regional Cooperation (SAARC)—which, for all its many shortcomings, at least embodies the principle of universality of membership. Channels for communicating and fora for negotiating CSBMs do not have to be invented, nor do tortuous formulae for involving third parties have to be devised (although in some cases third parties can play a constructive role). Finally, and perhaps most important, India and Pakistan have already embarked on the path of formal and explicit CSBMs, in the form of agreements not to attack each other's listed nuclear facilities, to refrain from violating each other's airspace, to provide advance warning of troop maneuvers, and to permit direct communication between their directors-general of military operations (DGMOs).

Thus, if the regional context for confidence- and security-building can be described by a double continuum of urgency and feasibility, then Indo-Pakistani relations constitute an intermediate case, located somewhere between East-West relations, which approximated a best case, and Arab-Israeli relations, which in many ways seem a worst one.

The Need for CSBMs

Analysts have developed a rich menu of ideas and proposals for security arrangements to accompany an Arab-Israeli peace settlement. Most of these incorporate elements of structural arms control—limitations on types and levels of forces and equipment—as well as of operational arms control, especially limitations on the deployment of military forces. But security arrangements incorporated into peace agreements are distinct from CSBMs, which precede peace and are actually intended, at least in part, to facilitate substantive progress toward peace agreements. In the Arab-Israeli context, the role, if not their specific content, of the former is widely assumed; the latter are still seen as very problematic, conceptually as well as operationally.

The immediate purpose of confidence- and security-building measures is to alter the psychological framework of a relationship marked by deep mutual mistrust and suspicion. Psychological change is intended to promote two more concrete objectives: enhancing near-term security by reducing the danger that misperception and miscalculation may lead to uncontrolled escalation in situations of uncertainty or tension, and creating a security environment more conducive to conflict resolution (which is hampered by lack of confidence in the durability of any agreement that might be reached).

The need for CSBMs does not derive from the existence of disputes *per se*; states with a history of routinized peaceful coexistence, such as Canada and the United States, may find themselves involved in conflict, even over fairly serious matters, without doubting the fundamentally pacific intent of the other side. Instead, CSBMs are necessary in a conflictual relationship, that is, a relationship marked by the mutual attribution of underlying hostility to one's own basic values, interests, identity, or very existence (even when no specific dispute is in evidence). Conflictual relationships may be structural (when the power of the adversaries fills all the available space in a given system), they may stem from a protracted dispute over limited resources, or they may reflect primordial or atavistic animosity, for which the "reasons" are lost in the mists of time. Whatever the source, in a conflictual relationship the protagonists ascribe a malevolent frame of mind to each other and put the worst possible construction on the actions and declarations of the other side. In such circumstances, there is a strong belief that security can be assured only through deterrence grounded in the buildup of military strength—of whose existence the enemy should be made aware without revealing information that could help to counter it (hence the obsession with technical and planning secrets)—and a demonstrated willingness to use it. By contrast, a policy of attempting to reassure the other side of one's own benign intentions through openness, accommodation, and conciliation is normally rejected on the grounds that it will be interpreted as weakness and will simply invite more demands and further aggression.

The result is the familiar "security dilemma," in which the competitive search for security through unilateral efforts results in the increased insecurity of both sides.[7] The problem with this conflictual relationship is twofold:

1. It makes the resolution of discrete disputes extremely difficult and a transformation of the relationship virtually impossible, i.e., it is self-perpetuating; and

2. It is highly intolerant of ambiguity, because even if there is no aggressive intent behind any particular action by the adversary, the relationship permits and indeed encourages misperception and miscalculation of the consequences of inaction, i.e., it puts a premium on maximum preparedness, meaning anticipatory or preemptive measures, which further exacerbate tension and may produce inadvertent escalation.

Even in conflictual relationships, therefore, a cooperative search for greater mutual security through acts of reassurance may sometimes be warranted. Unfortunately, these occasions are usually appreciated only in retrospect. There is no proven method for discerning the presence or absence of aggressive intent or of knowing *a priori* which method—reassurance (cooperative search for security) or deterrence (competitive search for security)—is most appropriate to a specific situation, and prudence therefore suggests some combination of both elements.

However, the seeming contradiction between the two methods of reducing the danger of war is almost always spurious. Stabilization actually derives from reassurance of the validity of deterrence, within a specific payoff structure of incentives and disincentives, costs and benefits, and risks and opportunities. It is in this context that CSBMs can play a potentially constructive role, provided that "confidence-building" is understood to mean *both* enhanced trust in the other side's intentions (reassurance) *and* sustained faith in one's own capacity to cope with the consequences, if trust turns out to have been misplaced (deterrence).

To meet this twofold requirement, CSBMs must reduce the amount of ambiguity in a system while enhancing tolerance of the ambiguities that remain by addressing insecurities at both the declaratory and the operational levels of military policy. For our purpose, these insecurities can be collapsed into the general fear of the first use of force by the other side (with the consequent incentive for each side to attack first itself). The task of CSBMs is to reduce this incentive by enhancing confidence that the other side will not attack. In short, destabilizing expectations must be replaced by stabilizing expectations.

Mechanisms for Building Confidence

The major types of measures to promote this objective are described elsewhere in this volume and need only be reviewed briefly here. The most elementary and, in certain circumstances, most effective mechanism for promoting a psychological transformation in conflictual relations is the mutual security pledge. The building of mutual confidence in a relationship marked by pervasive and deeply entrenched suspicions can best be stimulated by a change in declaratory posture regarding *intentions*, especially a declared commitment to pursue the settlement of disputes through peaceful means. It is therefore not coincidental that the major U.S.-Soviet CSBMs in the 1970s—the 1972 Basic Principles Agreement and the 1973 Agreement on Prevention of Nuclear War—included renunciations of the threat or use of force (see chapter 5 of this volume).

Of course, renunciation of the first use of force cannot assuage fears completely, because the very existence of a conflictual relationship causes even the most solemn declarations to be at least partially discounted. Moreover, such pledges normally refer only to direct attack and are necessarily vague about indirect threats to the extended (and often vaguely defined) security interests of a state.

Therefore, trust in the sincerity and credibility of this commitment needs to be strengthened even as the parties retain confidence in their ability to detect and deal with possible defection. Declaratory posture, if sustained and reiterated over time, can certainly contribute to that process. But even the most reassuring statements of intentions need to be reinforced by conscious, voluntary measures to constrain *capabilities* in the military sphere, because only concrete actions of the sort that effectively reduce attack options enhance both types of confidences, namely,

1. trust that the adversary intends to do (or not to do) what he says he intends to do (or not to do)—in this case not to attack; and,

2. belief in the ability to deal with the consequences of failure to conform with declared intentions, normally by ensuring preservation of the means at least to frustrate if not punish any attempted attack.

Such constraints on capabilities, defined as "prohibitions on military activities that are significant, easier to define, and relatively easy to verify,"[8] reduce the fear of surprise attack because they reduce the possibility of such attack, and explicit measures to limit attack options provide a material test by which to evaluate the sincerity of reassuring declarations of non-aggressive intent.

Of course, there are many kinds of CSBMS that can convey the earnestness of one's intention to comply with declared intentions. The most obvious is to provide hostages to good behavior. Long before the term "CSBM" was coined, rulers sent relatives or other high-ranking personages to reside in the courts of potential adversaries; the expectation was that these emissaries would be killed if their master violated an undertaking to refrain from aggressive action.

In one sense, intentionally making Soviet and American cities hostage to good behavior—by limiting defensive capabilities—was the central idea in what arguably was the most important superpower CSBM of all, the 1972 Anti–Ballistic Missile Treaty. However, discussions of CSBMs, especially those inspired by the Helsinki/Stockholm model in Europe, have focused on explicitly offensive capabilities through constraints on the equipment, organization, and preparation of armed forces. Most of the dramatic East-West negotiations, especially in the nuclear sphere—SALT I, SALT II, INF, START—involved structural arms control, i.e., limitations on the material attributes of a military force, especially the number and types of troops and weaponry.

Nevertheless, the first major breakthrough—the Hotline Agreement of 1963—was actually an operational arms control measure.[9] Operational arms control refers to openness in what might be termed the operating systems and software of military forces: deployment, doctrine, planning, procedures, intelligence/operational security, and training. These elements, too, can be intentionally fashioned to discourage worst-case assumptions by providing testable assurances of non-aggressive intent. In this case, the purpose is to reduce ambiguity or broaden the margin of tolerable ambiguity by consciously enhancing the adversary's early warning and increasing the time available for him to prepare, thereby minimizing the prospect that an attack could succeed.

This objective is pursued in a variety of ways.[10] One assumption driving the case for confidence-building through operational arms control is that while camouflage, deception, and artifice are good for war-fighting, they are bad for war-preventing (provided, of course, that what is revealed cannot be exploited by the other side to increase its own offensive capabilities). Many of the practical proposals put forward in this realm therefore relate to transparency, i.e., enhancing each sides's knowledge of what the other is doing or planning to do by disclosing what military forces traditionally try to conceal. Thus transparency CSBMs encourage such things as the publication of data concerning orders of battle and procurement programs and prior notification of the time, scale, nature, and location of planned exercises, troop movements, and weapons tests. Of course, voluntary release of information cannot eliminate suspicions of deception, i.e., the suspicion that only reassuring information is being released while information about retained or improved offensive capabilities continues to be concealed, and transparency also means facilitating the adversary's ability, independently or through credible third parties, to verify the accuracy and comprehensiveness of information through electronic and physical monitoring and on-site inspection. Antecedent or associated measures, such as military-to-military contacts, can have the added benefit of enhancing reassurance presumably because socialization and the resulting de-demonization of the adversary help to diminish insecurities stemming from worst-case assumptions.

Secondly, reassurance can be enhanced through adoption of certain rules or operating norms. The purpose of some of these is crisis avoidance or crisis prevention. These are intended to forestall unwanted escalation into a crisis by constraining routine military activities, thereby ensuring their non-threatening nature; examples include agreements to refrain from certain military activities defined as dangerous and limits on the size of military maneuvers or their proximity to borders and on the trajectories of aircraft training missions and missile tests.[11] One especially noteworthy type of crisis avoidance measure is *physical separation* of opposing forces, which helps reduce the risk of accidents or misunderstandings and increases warning time against possible attack, thereby reducing the incentive to preempt.

Another set of rules or norms focuses more on crisis management, that is, on mechanisms to help contain dangerous situations that may have arisen despite, or in the absence of, any crisis avoidance measures, because of imperfect control of subordinate echelons, the failure to foresee particular circumstances, the actions of third parties, or sheer accidents caused by human failure or technical malfunction. Crisis management CSBMs usually focus on making possible rapid and reliable communication between adversaries. The hotline is the most dramatic example of a high-level crisis management mechanism, but lower-level mechanisms to deal with unintended or accidental breaches of crisis avoidance measures have also been implemented, in the form of institutions such as standing crisis management, conflict prevention, or risk reduction centers.

Arab-Israeli Experience with CSBMs

In contrast to the CSBMs of all types that were adopted at one time or another during the cold war between the Soviet Union and the United States, CSBMs were implemented to a much lesser extent in the Arab-Israeli relationship. Arab reservations about the desirability of CSBMs are readily comprehensible. There is a logical contradiction between the extreme dissatisfaction with the status quo, of most Arabs and acceptance of measures whose express purpose is to reduce the risks of the status quo, i.e., to make it safer, more stable, and, by extension, more difficult to change. Most Arab states were therefore reluctant to endorse military constraints, particularly explicit, directly negotiated, and publicly acknowledged CSBMs, for the same reason that they avoided other forms of direct communication: the implied legitimization of Israel.

Countervailing concerns also affected behavior. At any given time, some Arab actors not only wanted to undo what Israel had done in the past; they were also wary of what Israel might do in the future. Moreover, short-term objectives that required acceptance of CSBMs often prevailed over long-term aims that were inconsistent with the very same measures. Arab decision makers, though reluctant to renounce the war option, could not remain indifferent to the continuing risk that war might break out through misperception and miscalculation, that is, at a time and in circumstances not of their own choosing, and this concern, perhaps reinforced by the more generalized fear of an Israel consistently portrayed as bent on aggression and expansionism, indicated acceptance of some measures that constrained their own offensive capabilities.

These conflicting impulses led the Arab states bordering Israel to implement a variety of military CSBMs, but there was a clear preference for short-term crisis prevention rules and norms, with particular emphasis on physical separation, frequently buttressed by the presence of international "peacekeeping" forces. Indeed, in the record of CSBMs in the Middle East, buffers and demilitarized or limited-forces zones are by far the most prominent. For example, acceptance of both the cease-fire agreements of 1949 (followed by the establishment of UN Truce Supervision Organizations, Mixed Armistice Commissions, and several demilitarized zones and pockets of "no man's land") and the ceasefire in 1956 (followed by the creation of the United Nations Emergency Force in Sinai—UNEF I) were necessitated by Arab fears that continued fighting would result in even more losses, reinforced, at least in the 1956 case, by the understanding that refusal to accept the stabilization and confidence-building implicit in the UN force would prevent retrieval of the territory overrun by Israel. The same considerations came into play in the 1974 Egyptian-Israeli and Syrian-Israeli disengagement of forces agreements.[12]

In addition to these formal agreements on physical separation, there were also several tacit or informal arrangements intended to reduce the risk of unanticipated or unintended confrontations. One example was the pre-1967 Jordanian undertaking not to post armored units to the West Bank. Another was the informal Syrian-Israeli "red-line agreement" of 1976, which established a southern limit to the deployment of Syrian ground forces in Lebanon and excluded the use of Syrian air power following Syria's intervention in the Lebanese civil war.[13] An even less explicit, but perhaps more reassuring and hence conclusive conflict-avoidance measure was Egypt's decision to reopen the Suez Canal and begin reconstruction of canal-side cities after 1973. These actions provided material hostages to Egypt's commitment to pursue its conflict with Israel by nonviolent means, even though no formal commitment was given until 1975.

But while acute need permitted both formal arrangements to terminate active combat and ongoing informal agreements and understandings, political sensitivities made it far more difficult to adopt explicit, longer-term CSBMs expressly intended to provide reassurance. Rules and norms to promote crisis management, for example, were acceptable in the context of ceasefire/crisis avoidance arrangements, such as the military-to-military contacts in the framework of the Mixed Armistice Commissions. Thus, Syrian and Israeli officers established ongoing, direct contacts and even personal friendships. However, this mechanism functioned properly only until the early 1950s and normally dealt only with local, tactical problems with little potential for major crisis; it was ultimately hostage to the political relationship between the two countries and could not fundamentally alleviate their mutual hostility and suspicion.[14] Direct, high-level communication mechanisms were precluded because they implied political legitimization. The same obstacle prevented the adoption of explicit transparency measures, even those to facilitate monitoring of formal physical separation agreements (in some cases, third-party monitoring provided a technically adequate substitute).

Given this political reality, it is not surprising that declaratory measures, especially mutual security pledges, were the rarest of the CSBMs in the Arab-Israeli experience. Apart from the second Egyptian-Israeli disengagement agreement in 1975, there was not a single commitment to refrain from the threat or use of force until the breakthrough Israeli-PLO and Israeli-Jordanian agreements in September 1993. In at least one case, however, public posture was almost equivalent to a formal pledge. Jordan so consistently declared its commitment to a peaceful settlement of the conflict that Israelis came to take Jordan's pacific long-term intentions almost for granted, so much so that when Jordanian statements or actions, such as hostile propaganda, border incidents, and even participation in Arab war coalitions, appeared at variance with that commitment, Israeli analysts were quick to find mitigating circumstances to explain Jordan's "reluctant" or "involuntary" belligerency. This response can be ascribed to the peculiar character and vulnerabilities of the regime, but that does not nullify the basic point the perceptions of the adversary's intentions, even in a continuing state of war, can be influenced significantly by declaratory posture, especially if that posture seems to conform with the declarer's vital interests and is buttressed by informal CSBMs (like the constraint on Jordanian armored forces in the West Bank).

In the end, of course, these measures did not prevent the outbreak of war between Israel and Jordan in 1967, just as the "red-line agreement" did not preclude Syrian-Israeli combat in Lebanon in 1982, although both confrontations stemmed, at least in part, from miscalculation and inadvertent escalation. Nor did these CSBMs produce a psychological environment more conducive to the resolution of conflicts. The same can be said about physical separation arrangements; the Israeli withdrawal from southern Lebanon and the creation of the United Nations Interim Force in Lebanon (UNIFIL) following the Litani Operation in 1978 did not prevent the emergence of conditions that necessitated (at least in the view of the Likud government) a much larger incursion in 1982, and the withdrawal from Sinai following the Sinai Operation and the creation of UNEF in 1956 did not prevent the emergence of conditions that brought about the 1967 war. Thus, if confidence-building measures are defined by their ostensible objectives rather than by their technical specifications, then the limited degree of cooperation/reassurance that emerged in the Arab-Israeli arena has had a very mixed record, at best.

The major exception to this pattern was the second Egyptian-Israeli Disengagement Agreement of 1975 (Sinai II). This agreement was qualitatively different from other CSBMs in several ways. It was the only one that was not implemented simultaneously with or directly after the termination of active fighting for the short-term purpose of stabilizing a military front; instead, it was consciously formulated as part of a political process intended to culminate in long-term resolution of the conflict. As important, it was the only one that explicitly referred to the future intentions of the parties concerning the use of military force. In this sense, Sinai II was not just a military CSBM, but a political-military CSBM, and its significance lay not so much in the operational constraints on offensive options, especially surprise-attack capabilities (though these were far from inconsequential), but rather in the authoritative disavowals of intention to use force, which the operational constraints reinforced. Sinai II did not incorporate renunciations of further Egyptian claims against Israel, but it did constitute a formal security pledge because it codified an Egyptian undertaking (albeit on the basis of mutuality) not to pursue those claims by military means. As explained by Secretary Henry Kissinger, the agreement committed both sides to resolve the conflict by peaceful means and "to refrain from use or threat of force or of military blockade."[15]

Of course, the undertaking itself could not produce total Israeli confidence that the commitment would be honored. Nevertheless, the declaratory dimension seems, in retrospect, to have been indispensable for making possible the ambitious military stabilization measures associated with it, as well as for promoting the other major objective of CSBMs: improving the psychological environment for conflict resolution. The significance of Sinai II was the explicit recognition that "armed conflict was no longer an effective means of achieving political and strategic objectives."[16] This kind of security cooperation/reassurance still falls far short of convergence on political and strategic objectives, but it at least provides the psychological foundation for movement toward conflict resolution, which is something purely military CSBMs, however inventive, could not do.

Extrapolation to South Asia

The Arab-Israeli record in CSBMs is far from a blank slate, but it is not so rich that states elsewhere will be strongly tempted or easily able to borrow from it. Furthermore, even measures recommended by the experience of others must be adapted to local circumstances if they are to have any relevance at all. With this caveat in mind, it may nevertheless be instructive to speculate about the applicability of the Arab-Israeli CSBM record to South Asian security concerns.

The challenge in South Asia, unlike that in the Middle East, is to expand and deepen a process that already exists. Of course, this does not mean that the task is simple. Indeed, the daunting complexities of South Asian regional conflicts suggest that any attempt to extrapolate from the Middle East will be most rewarding if it focuses on guiding principles rather than highly detailed proposals. What follows are several such guidelines, inspired by what has and has not been achieved in the Middle East, that could usefully inform further research and policy analysis.

1. Sinai II demonstrates the critical importance of declaratory policy, especially authoritative, high-level renunciations of the threat or use of force in pursuit of political objectives. Mutual security pledges provide a necessary (though not sufficient) underpinning for truly effective operational confidence-building measures and a more conducive environment for conflict resolution. India and Pakistan have already made such pledges, but it is important to reaffirm them, with maximum publicity, in a form and context that convey conscious reassurance rather than grudging acceptance of necessity. Declaratory CSBMs are also applicable to domestic security concerns, given suspicions about foreign involvement in insurgencies, terrorism, etc., and the danger that these

suspicions can set off an escalatory spiral. Reassurance, in the form of authoritative denials of support for domestic insurgencies and vigorous, prompt, and public denunciations of terrorist actions carried out against persons or property of neighboring states to punish those suspected of being "really" responsible; cooperation in suppressing such actions will add credibility to those denials.

2. If an embryonic CSBM regime already exists, it can be nurtured through modest, incremental progress. India and Pakistan have already moved into the stage of precursor CSBMs (normalized communication and information flows), and a logical next step would be to enhance mutual understanding of the adversary's threat perceptions and security concerns from unmediated sources, perhaps initially through nonbinding exchanges such as visits to war colleges and military academies and seminars on the nature of dangerous military activities. These could create the intellectual basis for more institutionalized crisis-avoidance and crisis-management measures.

3. Further progress on crisis voidance must involve operational arms control, meaning real constraints on dangerous military activities. In the Arab-Israeli experience, the most frequent and useful measure has been physical separation to reduce the fear of surprise attack. A significant pullback of force and especially of heavy weapons from some border areas might also be considered in South Asia. Other possible measures include confining air training exercises and missile test flights to non-threatening trajectories. Such measures can be implemented on a bilateral basis without constraining capabilities in other sectors. Thus, they can ignore the problem of multiple threats faced by both India and, to a lesser extent, Pakistan, a problem that complicates discussions of structural arms control. It is worth noting, moreover, that such measures will be more reassuring, and hence stabilizing, if they are explicit and mutual (though mutuality does not necessarily mean symmetry), but the effect even of unilateral actions should not be underestimated.

4. Any agreed restraints must be verifiable to the satisfaction of all parties. The most ambitious verification regime involves the continuous presence of observers and intrusive on-site inspection—legitimized spying—but until relations permit this sort of regime, aerial overflights and periodic ground surveys provide a partial substitute. Joint verification by the parties themselves is preferable, but if this is politically problematic, third parties can be productively engaged. From the Arab-Israeli experience, the most salient examples are UNEF, the Sinai Field Mission, and the Multi-national Forces and Observers (MFO) for various Israeli-Egyptian disengagement and separation-of-forces agreements; and UNDOF (on the ground) and United States components (in the air) for the Israeli-Syrian disengagement agreement of 1974. Of course, other transparency meas-

ures—prenotifications, information registers, etc.—also help build confidence by enhancing predictability.

5. A low-level crisis-management mechanism already exists between India and Pakistan in the form of the DGMO communications link. It would be useful to extend this link downward, since direct communication between sector commanders could permit some local problems in border areas to be addressed quickly at relatively low levels of command, thereby preempting their politicization and the creation of a crisis atmosphere. Conversely, the top political leaders could establish the practice of routine meetings at regular intervals; this might enable them to deal more effectively with serious problems if and when they do arise.

6. Finally, it should be remembered that there is a limit to what can be reasonably expected or demanded from CSBMs. CSBMs can support the search for political agreements and in some cases they may be necessary, but they cannot be a substitute for political agreements. When security concerns condition positions on territorial or other disputes, credible reassurance can help promote flexibility and compromise. But when positions are determined primarily by factors such as collective rights, national pride, honor, or group solidarity, the burden will be too heavy for CSBMs to bear and solutions to problems will be found, if all, only in other realms.

Notes

1. See, for example, Kevin N. Lewis and Mark A. Lorell, "Confidence-Building Measures and Crisis Resolution: Historical Perspectives," *Orbis* 28, no. 2 (summer 1984), pp. 281–306.

2. Hence, nonmilitary CAMS divorced from constraints on capabilities neither enhance nor diminish confidence in the likelihood of an attack by the adversary. Perhaps the most dramatic such measure in the Arab-Israeli context was the visit to Israel by Egyptian President Anwar Sadat in November 1977. But at least one high-level Israeli official—the IDF chief of staff—suspected that the impending visit was actually a trick aimed at lulling Israel into a false sense of confidence, and he urged a higher state of military alert. Anwar el-Sadat, *In Search of Identity* (New York: Harper and Row, 1978), p. 309.

3. See, for example, Mark A. Heller, "Middle East Security and Arms Control," in Steven L. Spiegel, ed., *The Arab-Israeli Search for Peace* (Boulder, Co.: Lynne Rienner, 1992), p. 134.

4. For example, East-West decision making in the cold war was essentially bilateral, although there was bargaining within the two blocs; the Arab-Israel conflict involves multilateral relationships and decision making centers. Israel has faced multiple serious threats, whereas the United States really only had to deal with one. For more on these differences, see John Marks, "A Helsinki-Type Process in the Middle East," in Spiegel, ed., *The Arab-Israeli Search for Peace*, pp. 71–72.

5. Interview with CNN, rebroadcast by SANA, cited in BBC, *Survey of World Broadcasts* ME/1215 (October 29, 1991), p. A2.

6. This empirical record has led at least one analyst to suggest, perhaps perversely, that there are elements of the Middle East experience from which Europe could learn. David Barton, "The Sinai Peacekeeping Experience: A Verification Paradigm for Europe," *World Armaments and Disarmament: SIPRI Yearbook 1985* (London: Tyler and Francis, 1985), pp. 541–62.

7. For a good elaboration of Israel's version of the security dilemma, see Michael Mandelbaum, *The Fate of Nations* (New York: Cambridge University Press, 1988), pp. 254–66.

8. Richard E. Darilek and Geoffrey Kemp, "Prospects for Confidence- and Security-Building Measures in the Middle East," in Alan Platt, ed., *Arms Control and Confidence Building in the Middle East* (Washington, D.C.: United States Institute of Peace, 1992), p. 22.

9. For an account of the road to the agreement, see William L. Ury, *Beyond the Hotline: How Crisis Control Can Prevent Nuclear War* (New York: Penguin, 1986).

10. The variety of possible measures is described in greater detail in Thomas Hirschfeld, "Mutual Security Short of Arms Control," and Yair Evron, "Confidence Building in the Middle East," in Dore Gold, ed., *Arms Control in the Middle East*, JCSS Study no. 15 (Tel Aviv: Jaffee Center for Strategic Studies, 1990).

11. For some suggested missile-related CAMS, see Mark A. Heller, "Coping with Missile Proliferation in the Middle East," *Orbis* 35, no. 1 (winter 1991), pp. 26–28.

12. These measures are reviewed in Indar Jit Rikhye, "The Future of Peacekeeping," in Gabriel Ben-Dor and David B. Dewitt, eds., *Conflict Management in the Middle East* (Lexington, Mass.: Lexington Books, 1987), pp. 261–68.

13. For more on Syrian-Israeli relations with respect to Lebanon, see Itamar Rabinovich, "Controlled Conflict in the Middle East: The Syrian-Israeli Rivalry in Lebanon," in Ben-Dor and Dewitt, eds., *Conflict Management*, pp. 97–111; and Zvi Lanir, "The Israeli Involvement in Lebanon—Precedent for an 'Open Game' with Syria?" CSS Study no. 10 (Tel Aviv: Center for Strategic Studies, September 1980).

14. Arye Shalev, *Cooperation Under the Shadow of Conflict* (Tel Aviv: Ma'arachot, 1989).

15. *The Quest for Peace: Principal United States Public Statements and Related Documents on the Arab-Israeli Peace Process 1967–1983* (Washington, D.C.: U.S. Department of State, 1984), p. 62.

16. Brian S. Mandell, "Anatomy of a Confidence-Building Regime: Egyptian-Israeli Security Cooperation," *International Journal* 45, no. 2 (spring 1990), p. 203.

PART THREE

CSBMs in South Asia

7

Mutual Security Pledges and Prospects for a Nonproliferation Regime

Neil Joeck

Relations between India and Pakistan have been marked by stops and starts since the two states were created in 1947. Born in conflict, they have never resolved fundamental differences in their views over the status of Kashmir or over a number of lesser issues, and indeed some in India still question the very existence of Muslim Pakistan, disputing the need for "two nations" on the subcontinent. Despite this history of mistrust, however, there is reason to be optimistic that future conflict can be avoided and that these states can work out a *modus vivendi* for resolving their differences.

Perhaps the most important reason for optimism in South Asia today is a sense of confidence on both sides that conflict resolution is now the norm. Disagreements and misunderstandings are still common, but an underlying sense that Indians and Pakistanis can work out their differences without resort to arms seems to mark their interactions. Indeed a certain amount of impatience can be discerned now and then at what is considered hypocritical American enthusiasm for nuclear nonproliferation and arms control in general, and crisis management in South Asia in particular. Seymour Hersh's retelling of the 1990 dispute in the *New Yorker* (wherein India and Pakistan reportedly blundered toward nuclear war, only to be rescued by the timely arrival of American mediators) is cited as an example of this; the publication of *Critical Mass*, an equally dubious account, added fuel to the fire.[1]

With the possible introduction of nuclear weapons to South Asia, however, and with a number of issues still in dispute and not under control, it is certainly appropriate to consider how security perceptions and mutual confidence can be reinforced. This chapter will consider the role of mutual security pledges as confidence-building measures and will evaluate the prospects for a South Asian nonproliferation regime.

Existing Mutual Security Pledges

As defined by Ted Greenwood in chapter 5 of this volume, a mutual security pledge involves reassurance between mutually hostile states "that one of them will not act in a manner that will threaten the security of another." Such reassurances are uncertain at best, as each side in a conflictual relationship will tend to act in its own narrowly defined interest, depending on the circumstances. In other words, in a time of crisis, a state cannot be expected to act against its own national security interests in order to honor a prior pledge not to threaten the security of another state.

The assumption behind a mutual security pledge is that the parties to the agreement could do each other harm, but pledge not to do so. As noted, however, circumstances may alter the willingness of a state to keep a pledge, and national survival may even dictate that it be ignored. If international conflict were so easily avoided that a pledge could provide reassurance, the security dilemma would not operate. Actions taken by each side to ensure its own defense would not be misinterpreted by the other as preparation for aggression.

History is rife with examples of states making security pledges they have every intention of breaking, once time and circumstance suit their grander designs. One egregious example is the Molotov-Ribbentrop pact. Perhaps few outsiders believed in the sincerity of either the German or the Soviet pledges, but the pact served both countries' interests for a time, and both sides understood that they were doing little more than buying time so that other matters could be settled. Thus, as we consider the merits of mutual security pledges in South Asia, it is good to remember that neither side need trust in the other's assurances—each side will continue to take prudent measures to insure against the other's reneging on a pledge—and also that the circumstances that allowed the pledge to be signed in the first place may change.

What can be expected of India and Pakistan, then? Given the history of animosity and mistrust between the two states, it might be argued that little faith can be placed in any mutual security pledge or agreement they might make. But that too-cynical view would overlook areas of compromise that might not strike at fundamental national security interests, and which might well be supported (if not guaranteed) by third parties such as the United States. Such a view would also minimize the importance of agreements already reached and which should be considered by way of background to what further pledges might be reasonable. The two most important agreements already in place are the Agreement on Bilateral Relations between India and Pakistan, signed on July 3, 1972 (commonly referred to as the Simla Accord), and the Agreement on the Prohibition of Attack against Nuclear Installations, signed on December 31, 1988 (commonly referred to as the No-Attack Agreement).[2]

The Simla Accord

Perhaps the best example of a security pledge between India and Pakistan is the Simla Accord of 1972.[3] In that agreement, both sides agreed "to settle their differences by peaceful means through bilateral negotiations or by any other peaceful means mutually agreed upon between them." It is important to consider the conditions prevailing when the agreement was signed, however, for leaders in New Delhi and Islamabad now interpret that provision somewhat differently. India insisted, and continues to insist, that third parties not be brought into negotiations to resolve Indo-Pakistani differences. Pakistan, on the other hand, views the Simla Accord as a pact signed under duress (it had just been defeated by India in the 1971 war when the pact was signed). As the weaker side in any conflict with India, Pakistani is reluctant to forswear any form of international involvement in ongoing South Asian disputes.[4]

The limitations of the Simla Accord were made evident in 1987 and 1990. At the height of the 1987 Brasstacks maneuvers, neither side took comfort that war could be avoided because Simla was in place. The crisis was defused through diplomatic means, including discussions at the already-scheduled meeting of the South Asian Association for Regional Cooperation (SAARC). Of course, it would be expecting too much to suggest that a mutual security pledge would eliminate all disagreements or prevent all crises. What was noteworthy was that neither side appeared to enter the crisis with a sense of detachment or conviction that it would be managed because the Simla Accord was in place. It was more the case that the crisis was resolved despite Simla, not because of it.

The 1990 dispute was less acute than Brasstacks in 1987, but in this case, too, there did not appear to be a sense that the pledges made in 1972 would somehow carry the adversaries through the troubles. Although the 1990 crisis never got to the point that negotiations were required, the contributions by the United States, in the form of a delegation headed by Robert Gates, then–deputy national security adviser, may have played an important part in avoiding conflict. Such intervention was hardly what India envisioned when the Simla Accord was signed, and although Pakistan typically looks to outside actors for some assistance against India, the effect may have been more to discourage Islamabad than to further its interests.

The No-Attack Agreement

The agreement between India and Pakistan not to attack one another's nuclear installations is another, and perhaps better, example of a mutual security pledge. Although Prime Ministers Benazir Bhutto and Rajiv Gandhi reached the accord on December 31, 1988, it was not ratified until the end of 1991, and was then interpreted by Pakistan to call for the release of information only at the end of the first operational year.[5] It was thus January 1, 1992 before the agreement came fully into effect, with each side releasing to the other its list of covered facilities. As soon as the dust settled, however, both sides lodged complaints that the other had failed to produce a complete account. The sites actually specified by the two sides have been kept under fairly tight control, but the Indians complained that a facility at Golra had been left off, while the Pakistanis claimed that a facility at Mysore was omitted.[6]

The text of the agreement itself is short and relatively simple. The specifics of the agreement are contained entirely in a single article.[7] Each side agreed to refrain from undertaking, encouraging or participating in, directly or indirectly, any action aimed at causing the destruction of, or damage to, any nuclear installation or facility in the other country." "Nuclear installation or facility" was defined to include power and research reactors as well as fuel fabrication, uranium enrichment, isotope separation, and reprocessing facilities; installations where fresh or irradiated nuclear fuel and materials or where significant quantities of radioactive materials were stored were also to be included.

The agreement is unique in the world and in South Asia; no other nuclear-capable states have reached such an agreement. If anything, quite the reverse is expected to be the case—i.e., that such facilities *would* be targets in a war.[8] In South Asia, no similar restraint has previously been codified. The continued willingness of both states to honor the requirement for annual notification of covered sites and the general acceptance of this measure as a part of a process suggest that the agreement will not only hold, but may serve as a model for further confidence-building measures between the two sides.

Extending the No-Attack Agreement

Given that the pledge not to attack one another's nuclear facilities has been formalized, it may be possible to extend it by applying it to population centers. This has been proposed by the U.S. government, and then by the Indian government as one of the non-papers it presented to the Pakistani government as part of the January 1994 Foreign Secretaries talks.[9] The non-papers were presented after the talks had concluded, and India thus lost an opportunity to put Pakistan in a more defensive position. The issue is nevertheless on the table, and holds reasonable promise for negotiations.

Indians and Pakistanis sometimes point out that their past wars have been relatively restrained. Civilian loss of life has been minimal, combat has been restricted to the battlefield, and the combat itself, if not polite, was somewhat constrained. (This contrasts with domestic conflicts, such as the

Bangladesh war, and terrorist or communal violence.) That restraint may have been a consequence of the fairly quick settlement of the wars on the battlefields, however, as neither the 1965 nor the 1971 war lasted more than two to three weeks. In neither war was there much possibility for extended and expanded attrition against civilian centers. Nor did India attempt to seize large civilian centers, which might have resulted in massive destruction and civilian casualties, as is so common in urban combat.

Regardless of whether the duration of the wars, Indian and Pakistani restraint, or some other factor spared population centers, this common perception that Indians and Pakistanis are able to limit the intensity of war might support a willingness to pledge not to attack population centers in a conflict. As noted earlier, mutual security pledges are inherently uncertain, but if established on a commonly held perception, they might gain greater weight. It would seem to be the case for both India and Pakistan that, from a national security point of view, neither sees a need to threaten to attack cities, with either conventional or nuclear weapons.

There is also some unique common ground supporting such an approach, in that neither side wants to be in the position of threatening to kill large numbers of Muslims. Pakistan has long since formally acknowledged Indian sovereignty over Indian Muslims, but nonetheless would be reluctant to target cities that have large Muslim populations. For its part, India would not want to risk internal insurrection by its own Muslim minority due to a perception that India, in attacking Pakistani cities, had wantonly killed Muslims. To the extent that the two sides accept a minimal deterrence posture, then, a no-population-centers pledge could reinforce both sides' sense of security during a crisis. This could decrease the likelihood of war, as it could allow more time for negotiations, cooling-off, mediation, and diplomacy.

A No-First-Use Pledge

Pledging not to attack population centers is similar to, but not the same as, a pledge not to be the first to use nuclear weapons. Some Indian scholars have proposed that New Delhi and Islamabad make such an agreement, and this measure was also proposed by the Indian Government in January 1994 in one of the non-papers delivered to Pakistan. Pakistan responded somewhat disingenuously, saying that since Pakistan does not possess any nuclear weapons, a no-first-use pledge is a contradiction.[10] At a more serious level, Islamabad may conclude that such a pledge would fundamentally undermine its national security, especially in the absence of any agreement limiting conventional weaponry.

Nuclear weapons are especially attractive to states that fear they may be eliminated as sovereign nations; Pakistan's nuclear program arose from such concerns following the 1971 war. Fears that another war with India would result in the complete destruction of the Pakistani state drove its leaders to conclude that only the threat of a nuclear response would counter Indian conventional superiority and prevent such an outcome. For Pakistan, a pledge not to be the first to use nuclear weapons would be seen by many as tantamount to agreeing to be overrun by India.[11]

In a particularly candid observation, General K. S. Sundarji suggested that Indians would understand that, in extremis, Pakistan would not be able to abide by such a pledge.[12] If faced with an Indian attack that threatened to destroy Pakistan, Sundarji argued, it would only be natural for Pakistani leaders to use whatever nuclear capability they had at hand, regardless of a no-first-use pledge. Such an outcome would never happen, Sundarji implied, because India would never seek such an objective.

A pledge that amounts to little more than a wink and a nod, however, might do little to reinforce Indian insecurities, especially in a crisis. As is evident from Sundarji's reasoning, many in India dismiss the possibility of any serious threat from Pakistan, even if the latter is armed with nuclear weapons, and assume that India will never put Pakistan in a position where the use of nuclear weapons would be necessary. According to this logic, a no-first-use pledge should be easy, since it would never be challenged.

If Pakistan were willing to rely on Indian confidence about Pakistan's benign intentions, it might never have tried to develop nuclear weapons in the first place. The logic underlying Pakistan's nuclear threat, however, may be consistent with adopting a no-first-use pledge. If another war broke out, few in Pakistan would argue that the use of a few nuclear weapons would prevent India from destroying Pakistan with its conventional forces. The use of nuclear weapons by Pakistan would make the cost of victory for India painfully high, but if the threat of escalation to the nuclear level failed to deter India, the use of nuclear weapons would not prevent the destruction of Pakistan. Thus the primary and almost exclusive utility of nuclear weapons for Pakistan is to deter India from attempting a complete destruction of Pakistan. The possibility that nuclear weapons would be used would still be in the minds of India's defense planners, regardless of a Pakistani no-first-use pledge. Pakistan need rely not on Indian restraint, as Sundarji's argument suggests, but rather on Indian uncertainty about what exactly Pakistan would do if faced with catastrophic defeat. A no-first-use pledge by Pakistan would not remove that uncertainty, as Sundarji's comment makes plain.

Of course, Pakistan may feel that nuclear weapons would serve some purpose in achieving specific military objectives. There may be some in Pakistan decision making circles who would want to use nuclear weapons early in a conflict, and who would therefore argue against a no-first-use pledge. Little doctrinal analysis is evident in current Pakistani academic or military writing, however, and it is difficult to imagine how Pakistan could try to exploit nuclear weapons for offensive purposes. The most creative, but nonetheless dangerous and delusionary, scenario might be for Pakistan to try to seize Kashmir, and then use nuclear weapons either to block Indian access in the narrow corridor to Kashmir, or to threaten some kind of counter value strike if India responded in force. Such reasoning would almost certainly get a cold reception from political and military leaders in Islamabad, given the failure of a similar strategy in 1965 and the unlikely chance that such a "seizure" would succeed. A strictly deterrent use doctrine makes far better sense and could provide Pakistan strategic advantages that would not be compromised by a no-first-use pledge.

The primary strategic advantage of a no-first-use pledge is that it would reinforce Pakistan's underlying need to rely on diplomacy, not arms, for its security. Drawing India into a dialogue, which might also involve outside powers in the outcome, would serve Pakistan's security interests more surely than the threat of nuclear retaliation. Pakistan, of course, developed its nuclear program in the belief that only the threat of nuclear retaliation could prevent India from destroying Pakistan in a future war. India's demonstration of restraint in 1971—its decision not to destroy Pakistan when it could have—ought to give Pakistan some reassurance, but in fact it tends to reinforce the fear in Pakistan. India's decision not to invade is less important than its capability to do so.

Would a no-first-use pledge be in India's interest? India does not feel the same sense of vulnerability toward China that Pakistan does toward India. The 1962 border war with China was humiliating for many in India, but little sentiment within China supports the elimination of the Indian state through military conquest. Furthermore, Indians feel no sense of being marginalized by the community of nations. These facts could allow India to adopt a no-first-use pledge, which would support India's continuing ambiguity with respect to weapons deployment and yet sacrifice little in terms of security.

With respect to Pakistan, a no-first-use pledge by India—perhaps coupled with reassurances about the integrity of the Pakistani state—could reduce risks in a crisis. In diplomatic terms, an Indian counterproposal to Pakistan's numerous arms control proposals would at least make India look less like a constant naysayer and more like a major power capable of constructively linking regional security to arms control on its own initiative.

A No-Early-Use Pledge

Barring a no-first-use pledge, Pakistan might still be prepared to make a unilateral no-early-use commitment, which would have a salutary effect in crises. An important concern in any crisis will be the possibility of either side brandishing nuclear weapons, or threatening to use them out of fear of being preempted. A no-early-use agreement could significantly increase confidence on both sides in time of crisis. Such a pledge would have some of the same limitations as a no-first-use pledge—how long could either state feel safe if national interests were threatened?—and neither side would feel comfortable about what "early" meant during a crisis. Nevertheless, some minimal willingness to commit in advance to seek mediation or to commence negotiations could provide at least a modicum of security beyond what would be felt with no prior restraint agreement at all. Again, India appears prepared to accept the more restrictive no-first-use pledge, so the burden is more clearly on Pakistan.

As Raja Mohan argues in chapter 10 of this volume, crisis management is all-important in a nuclear environment. Extending the time available to resolve or defuse a crisis would significantly help Pakistanis as they seek to avoid a war they cannot win.

An Agreement on Chemical Weapons

India and Pakistan, in their 1992 Joint Declaration against Chemical Weapons, mutually agreed to the "complete prohibition of chemical weapons" and to sign the Chemical Weapons Convention (CWC). India played an important role in the CWC negotiations at the Conference on Disarmament, but neither is committed to ratifying the CWC (although it is expected they will do so). This declaration is, therefore, in effect a pledge not to produce chemical weapons. It is certainly a salutary step, and as with any security pledge, it lacks verification provisions. It may be that this is a pledge both sides can easily make because neither has any plans to develop or field chemical weapons. Even if this agreement fits the common complaint that arms control is possible only where it is unnecessary, and impossible where it is needed, it is precisely the kind of small step that needs to be taken for confidence about the other side's intentions to take hold. Perhaps India and Pakistan had no plans to develop chemical weapons anyway, but saying so makes a difference.

Beyond Security Pledges

As discussed so far, mutual security pledges have proven to be a halfway house in reducing Indian and Pakistani insecurities. The Simla Accord and the No-Attack Agreement have been given lip service by the two sides, but neither agreement prevented or, as near as can be determined, even ameliorated the 1987 Brasstacks crisis or the 1990 near-crisis that arose out of disturbances in Kashmir. Taken in isolation, further security pledges may appear to provide little additional comfort in the future. As part of an overall confidence-building approach, however, they may be more promising. A more difficult next step would be to construct a nuclear nonproliferation regime.

Prospects for Preventing Nuclear Proliferation

Many analysts of South Asia and of nuclear proliferation in general would argue that the nuclear genie is now out of the bottle in India and Pakistan. India's demonstration more than twenty years ago of an ability to design, engineer, and detonate what Dr. Raja Ramanna called a "prototype nuclear weapon,"[13] and Pakistan's repeated hints and claims that it had one or more nuclear weapons at the ready (if not in hand)[14] have convinced many that attention should shift from nonproliferation to arms control. Some analysts speak of managing, rather than preventing, nuclear proliferation, in effect accepting that some states cannot be prevented from acquiring more weapons.

Initiatives by the United States strike a more optimistic note.[15] Enunciated in terms of first capping, then reducing, and finally eliminating the nuclear and ballistic missile capabilities in both countries, the U.S. policy sees nonproliferation almost on a continuum from nonpossession to covert or opaque capability, and back again to overt nonpossession. Bilateral arms control and arms elimination efforts in India and Pakistan would be linked to a multilateral regional effort to achieve the same end, which in turn would be linked to global arms reductions. The two centerpieces of this approach are the cutoff of the production of fissionable material—uranium in Pakistan, plutonium in India—and a comprehensive test ban treaty (CTBT).

Rajiv Gandhi's initiative, referred to as the Delhi Declaration on Principles for a Nuclear-Weapon-Free and Non-Violent World, was signed in New Delhi in November 1986 and included India's longstanding endorsement of a comprehensive test ban as well as a proposal for the elimination of nuclear weapons.[16] India argues that such arms control proposals be pursued on a global, nondiscriminatory basis, but it may become useful for India to push these measures unilaterally with the intent of pressuring China toward arms limitations.

Gandhi's inclusion of provisions for the elimination of nuclear weapons are already contained in Article VI of the NPT, but setting a deadline lent an urgency to the process that the nuclear weapons states found unrealistic and unacceptable. An explicit element of arms control between the United States and the Soviet Union was that arms control would lead to arms reduction, and ultimately to nuclear disarmament. Although the SALT I and SALT II agreements to some degree codified and legitimized further arms acquisitions, the START and INF agreements were more successful in reducing the numbers on both sides. Regardless of U.S. and Soviet promises or hopes, few have held out much optimism that arms control would ever achieve the goal of nuclear disarmament. The Gandhi proposal that all nuclear weapons be eliminated by the year 2010 (reiterated at the Third United Nations Special Session on Disarmament in June 1988) still sounds noble, but even Indians would agree that no monitoring system is available to ensure that cheating would not take place. Given that defect, India itself would never trust that Pakistan and China had given up all their nuclear capability, and willingly give up its own.

Optimism for nuclear control may be well placed in South Asia, given the ongoing reluctance of both India and Pakistan to deploy weapons openly and given the recent development of deterrence concepts that encourage acquiring only a few weapons, or only components for a small number of weapons. These concepts, called "recessed deterrence" by Jasjit Singh and "nonweaponized deterrence" by George Perkovich, might provide reassurance to both India and Pakistan, and yet come close to nuclear disarmament.[17] Discussing nonproliferation in South Asia, therefore, still makes sense as part of the developing post–cold war security environment on the subcontinent.

The Nuclear Nonproliferation Treaty

The most obvious, but least likely nonproliferation measure that India and Pakistan could adopt would be to sign the Nuclear Nonproliferation Treaty (NPT). Indian resistance to the treaty has focused on its discriminatory nature, and many Indians feel that India will not achieve its rightful standing in the world without nuclear weapons. Many strategic analysts also argue that India must have nuclear weapons to deter China, and therefore counsel against agreeing to the NPT. Given these arguments, India has decided not to compromise its independence and status by agreeing to the terms of the treaty.

The discrimination argument has sounded somewhat oversimplified, if not disingenuous, for some years. India and Pakistan are the two principal countries still preoccupied with this issue, while more than 160 countries with equal international standing endorse the NPT. The NPT indeed is inequitable, but it treats the world as it is right now. Certain states have nuclear weapons, but realize, along with the non-weapons states that have signed the NPT, that nuclear war by any set of states could be globally catastrophic. But getting rid of nuclear weapons—honoring the Article VI promise—without unleashing a host of unintended consequences that may make the world even less secure and stable is proving to be difficult. The acceptance of the trade-off between inequality now for the promise of disarmament later suggests that the logic of the NPT is powerful. India and Pakistan may be morally correct in the arguments about discrimination, but may also have important security-related motives for refusing to sign the NPT.

The discrimination argument was rendered even more questionable by arguments that India should sign the NPT as a nuclear weapons state. If the treaty is discriminatory, and if India therefore should not sign it as a matter of principle, how could it uphold that principle if India were prepared to sign the treaty in a position of "superiority" as a nuclear weapon state, but not when in a position of "inferiority" as a non-nuclear weapon state? The hypocritical aspects of such reasoning would be quickly pointed out by Indian analysts, if offered by others for India to accept.

The argument that nuclear possession somehow granted a country prestige has for years been undercut by the wide acceptance of the NPT, and now by its indefinite extension. If over 160 countries thought that the acquisition of nuclear weapons bestowed prestige, why would they sign it? The notion that nuclear weapons somehow bestowed prestige has also been undercut by the actions of states such as Japan and Germany, whose status, far from being diminished, has been enhanced in the eyes of many by adhering to the NPT. Strong, rationalized economies have dome more for Germany and Japan than nuclear weapons ever could, and India may garner the same status as it follows suit. In contrast, it would make little sense to suggest that South Africa rose in any state's estimation by its admission that it had fabricated six nuclear weapons. That achievement did not obscure the negative aspects of apartheid, nor did it bestow any international approval on the white regime. Quite to the contrary, when South Africa eliminated its arsenal, it gained substantial international approval.

Discrimination and prestige are weak reeds to support India's opposition to the NPT, but perhaps a better case could be made that signing the NPT would somehow undermine India's national security. Given that Pakistan has already committed itself to signing the NPT if India does so, the burden is on India to determine whether such a step would hurt or enhance its security. Coupled with a unilateral no-first-use pledge by China, Indian accession to the treaty would not jeopardize Indian security vis-à-vis Beijing. Many would consider it foolish to accept Chinese reassurances at face value, but diplomatic improvements between New Delhi and Beijing since Rajiv Gandhi's initiatives, as well as the border agreement and follow-on negotiations, may set the stage for a diplomatic resolution to Sino-Indian disagreements.

Furthermore, by playing a more active role in international arms control efforts, India could put pressure on China to conform to internationally agreed-upon standards, rather than be continually nagged about its own recalcitrance. The nuclear-related security threat posed by China has not prevented India from achieving its desired ends in foreign policy, such as integration into the international economy, improved standing at the United Nations, a leading role in the nonaligned movement, or a dominant position in South Asia. Maintaining a defense option against a quiescent enemy may distract or divert India from these important objectives.

With respect to the threat from Pakistan's nuclear capability, the behavior of Iraq and North Korea certainly would remind New Delhi that a signature on the NPT does not prevent nuclear mischief. In isolation then, neither India nor Pakistan could feel confident that the joint signing of the NPT would allay its legitimate concerns about the other's nuclear capabilities. Attached to any agreement could be a set of inspections, though, which would provide the verification necessary to guarantee against cheating on either side.

Reciprocal Inspections

Given that India and Pakistan have declared their nuclear facilities under the terms of the No-Attack Agreement, an inspection regime would disclose nothing new, but would reassure both sides about the other's activities. It might be useful and more acceptable to arrange this on a piecemeal basis, at least at first. Additional information about already-disclosed sites would become available as a result of the inspections, depending on the extent of access each side allowed. Rather than beginning with inspections of sensitive facilities such as Pakistan's uranium enrichment installations or India's reprocessing plants, an agreement could begin with something as simple as mining operations or fuel fabrication or uranium conversion facilities. Given Pakistan's reactions to U.S. proposals for inspections in the spring of 1994, only a tiered approach would have any hope of gaining acceptance.

Although these inspections could usefully complement a commitment to the NPT, they need not be so linked and could be negotiated without either side joining the NPT. (India's refusal to modify its opposition to the NPT makes such linkage unlikely anyway.) The security benefits of a reciprocal inspection regime may be substantial. If narrowly considered from the Indian point of view, access to and consequent restraint on Pakistani developments would be a net security benefit. India's need for nuclear weapons against Pakistan remains in doubt; thus New Delhi would be giving up little security in allowing Pakistan access to Indian facilities. The symbolism of such a step might grate on Indian sensibilities, but the advantages in terms of Pakistani restraint and Indian confidence of that restraint ought to be decisive.

If India were prepared to arrange some kind of fuel-cycle facilities inspections, this would be an important and valuable step toward a secure and stable arms control regime in South Asia. Pran Chopra has argued that if the nuclear weapons states agree universally to a no-first-use pledge, which is then added as protocol to the NPT, all states that claim their nuclear programs are only meant for peaceful purposes (i.e., India and Pakistan) should affirm their willingness to open their nuclear establishments for inspection by IAEA.[18] The problems that a no-first-use pledge would create for Pakistan have been detailed already, but a global no-first-use pledge would not necessarily create the same problems. If tied to negative security assurances (i.e., assurances to non-nuclear weapons states that they would be protected against nuclear threats from third parties), Pakistan's concerns might be met, and inspections could become a reality.

A Regional Nuclear Test Ban

A regional test ban would have little impact on Indian thinking about the national security benefits of nonproliferation measures in South Asia. Pakistan has never claimed to have tested a nuclear device, yet for a number of years has asserted or implied that it has a nuclear weapons capability. There is by now a certain amount of unclassified information available about nuclear weapon design; many scholars feel that a first generation atomic weapon could in fact be fabricated without benefit of a nuclear test.[19] Banning tests, therefore, might not prevent Pakistan or India from deploying at least some nuclear weapons if either chose to do so. From other than the security perspective, however, a test ban might provide some psychological and symbolic reassurance to both sides—precisely the intent of confidence-building measures.

The Clinton administration has endorsed a Comprehensive Test Ban Treaty (CTBT), and negotiations are underway toward that end. India and Pakistan have tended to lump proposals for a regional nuclear test ban with the NPT as inherently discriminatory. There is no disputing the inequity, but India may find itself in a position to gain some security benefits vis-à-vis China by taking the lead on the testing issue. As noted above, a regional South Asian test ban would not particularly benefit India's security with regard to Pakistan. With a global CTBT a significantly more likely prospect, however, India could steal a march on the process by engaging Pakistan in a regional ban. Indeed, such an agreement could play a powerful role in pushing the Western states into agreement on a CTBT. If New Delhi is prepared to join a global CTBT anyway, negotiating a regional ban would cost little, assuming that India is making no plans to conduct nuclear tests.[20] China has not shown any enthusiasm for a CTBT, and Beijing's ongoing test program suggests improvements are being made in its weapons program. India, of course, may choose to sit back and watch as China improves its nuclear capabilities. The opportunity to shift the focus of attention to China, however, and perhaps to put Beijing in a defensive position regarding nuclear testing should not be overlooked. Again, the issue of arresting technical development, avoiding a costly and inevitably wasteful arms race, and freezing Pakistan and China in place (all of which benefit Indian security) argue in favor of Indian arms control initiatives.

Although the prospects may not be good, either India or Pakistan could unilaterally announce that it would not conduct any nuclear tests, either at all or for a specified duration, as Pervez Hoodbhoy and K. Subrahmanyam have proposed.[21] Such a declaration from Islamabad would offer India relatively little comfort, as Pakistan has by its own admission made significant headway in its nuclear developments without benefit of a nuclear test. Such a declaration by India would similarly provide little comfort to Pakistan, as India conducted its only test over two decades ago.

The point of CSBMs, however, is more modest than constraining the adversary absolutely codifying agreements. As a statement of peaceful intent, or as a means to send the message that one or the other side is ready to go no further in its nuclear program, foreswearing nuclear testing would be valuable. The question for India returns to the strategic merits of such a declaration, and the larger issue of enhancing its own security by walking down this road. The issue is China, not Pakistan. A unilateral Indian declaration not to test and the exploitation of that declaration to hurry a CTBT into existence could either isolate China or draw Beijing into the agreement.

A Fissile Material Cutoff

The issue of cutting off further development of fissile material is at the forefront of arms control discussions in the West. For countries already in possession of significant quantities of fissile material, banning further production has a greater symbolic than strategic value. Stockpiled materials are likely to be grandfathered in a cutoff treaty, so the security ramifications of a fissile material cutoff would be minimal.

For the United States, a fissile material cutoff makes a virtue of necessity. In South Asia, a cutoff need not require formalization in an arms control agreement, as either Pakistan or India could unilaterally declare that they would no longer produce fissile material. Pakistan's last two prime ministers have asserted that this has been done. What Pakistan's unilateral freeze includes remains unclear, and as with any unilateral declaration, there are no means of verification. It has not been reciprocated in any case.[22]

Because India probably has significant quantities of separated plutonium already, a unilateral declaration that it was ceasing production of fissile material could again turn the arms control spotlight on China. India is in a position to approach China as Pakistan has India: launch a peace offensive in the nuclear arena that shifts the burden to Beijing. Many

Indians rightfully argue that China has long ignored India and that the world has given China a free ride in arms control terms. As China shows renewed interest in mending relations with India, India should consolidate that interest with some pressure on the nuclear front. To the extent that India can neutralize the nuclear issue between itself and China, it opens up greater possibilities of returning the South Asian equation to one of conventional weapons, in which New Delhi holds the advantage over Islamabad. A unilateral declaration by India that it would cease reprocessing spent fuel for a limited time would be relatively cost free, would feed into the developing consensus in favor of a global cutoff, and would pressure China to do the same. Current reserves of separated plutonium should be more than enough for whatever mixed oxide fuel India is ready to produce, and with the Fast Breeder Test Reactor not yet finished, no sacrifice would be made by temporary self-restraint. India may choose to wait for a universal agreement before taking this step, but it would seem that such a delay would continue to give China a free ride in security and arms control terms.

Pervez Hoodbhoy has called for a unilateral freeze by Pakistan. In the concluding part of a series on nuclear issues in a Pakistani newspaper, Hoodbhoy argued that Pakistan should declare "that it will freeze the production of enriched uranium for a period of 18 months and will not conduct a nuclear test in this period." As noted, Pakistan's prime ministers have stated that the program has been frozen; more explicit declarations could well satisfy these recommendations. Hoodbhoy sees this as an important next step in Pakistan's continuing peace offensive, which he notes has had an effect on India. Quoting Praful Bidwai in the *Times* of India, he sees India in a defensive position as a consequence: "New Delhi has been unable to dispel the impression that it is merely stone-walling and resisting every reasonable [Pakistani] move."[23] The point is well taken on two counts: Pakistan benefits from such aggressive diplomacy, while India suffers in comparison. India could benefit equally, however, both by accepting Pakistani offers and by conducting the same kind of diplomacy toward Beijing. If inaction clearly served India's strategic regional interest, the lack of initiative would be understandable. It would seem, though, that an initiative such as this would enhance India's standing while compromising little in terms of security.

Skeptics on both sides would contend that a unilateral declaration with no verification provisions would be an empty gesture. Indeed it may be empty, if the promise is not kept. Confidence-building in an environment of mistrust and enmity must begin somewhere, however, and may well lead to the next step—a formal arms-control agreement codifying the unilateral measure and providing the necessary verification provisions. It may be possible, though, to reinforce unilateral steps and even bilateral agreements with third-party assistance. The United States may be able to support

CSBMs or arms-control agreements by providing verification expertise and technology as needed or desired by India and Pakistan. The U.S. experience in verifying arms agreements with the Soviet Union could be brought into play in a South Asian regional agreement.

A Missile Deployment Ban

Pakistan and India are both working on missile delivery systems. Pakistan is developing the *Hatf I*, and has contracted with China for the M-11. The short-range *Hatf I* is little more than an oversized artillery rocket and is an unlikely candidate for nuclear delivery. In a private interview, former Army Chief of Staff Mirza Aslam Beg affirmed this point, while denying that the M-11s would have a nuclear delivery role. He claimed that they were nothing more than a conventional deterrent to the Indian *Prithvi*, as F-16 aircraft were available for nuclear delivery.[24]

Indians also deny that the short-range *Prithvi* and long-range *Agni* have any nuclear role; the *Agni* is still under development and the *Prithvi* has not been formally deployed. Therefore, neither India nor Pakistan currently see their available or planned missiles as central to the Indo-Pakistani nuclear relationship. That is to say, regardless of either side's development or deployment of nuclear weapons, and even if both sides should choose to reject nuclear weapons, some missile capability would still be considered important as part of the conventional deterrent against the other, and for India against China.

Despite this argument, missile deployment could be an especially explosive change in the South Asian security environment. The U.S. proposals for regional missile control—in effect, no deployments—emerged from a concern that Indian and Pakistani confidence that the threshold for war is very high may quickly disappear if missiles are deployed. If either side's missiles were equipped with nuclear weapons, a dangerously unstable escalation might ensue, making the concern even sharper. Future crises, which may be unavoidable, would be increasingly difficult to manage the closer the missiles are deployed to each other's borders. The old NATO fear of tactical nuclear weapons being seized by an invading force would be as difficult to resolve in South Asia as it would have been in Europe. Discussions between India and Pakistan on a regional INF treaty, even before deployment, might significantly enhance both sides' confidence in their ability to manage crises.

Conclusion

The U.S. approach to nonproliferation in South Asia seems to still be to first cap, then reduce, and finally eliminate weapons of mass destruction and their delivery vehicles. But as long as initiatives come from Washington rather than from New Delhi and Islamabad, their chances of success will depend too much on extraneous factors. In ironic but different ways, both India and Pakistan continue to depend on those extraregional factors: Pakistan continues to want to draw outside powers, in particular the U.S., into the peace process in South Asia, and India refuses to get involved in regional arms control arrangements unless they are part of a global regime or include China. The result is a brittle standoff while each side takes unilateral military-oriented steps to achieve security.

The prospects for a nonproliferation regime depend on the will on the subcontinent. If nonproliferation continues to be an American preoccupation yet never becomes a front-burner issue for India and Pakistan, proposed solutions may never take root in South Asian soil. For nonproliferation to become a central issue for India and Pakistan, proposals and solutions must be based upon the security of each state. The concern expressed by the former director of central intelligence James Woolsey that "the arms race between India and Pakistan poses perhaps the most probable prospect for future use of weapons of mass destruction, including nuclear weapons"[25] may turn out to be mistaken. If it turns out to be correct, however, it would be the Indians and the Pakistanis who would suffer through a nuclear catastrophe. Ultimately, therefore, it is an issue that Indians and Pakistanis must manage on their own. Pakistan's fixation on the Kashmir issue and India's on global equity are quite understandable, but they should not block arms control and nonproliferation measures, which may provide as much if not more security than independent, potentially technically unstable or unreliable nuclear weapons arsenals.

A Guarded Prognosis

Although there is room for optimism that a nonproliferation regime can be worked out in South Asia, at best it can be described as guarded optimism. India and Pakistan continue to feel vulnerable to powerful neighbors, and in a global environment where the threats to international order are increasing daily and where nuclear weapons continue to be the coin of the security realm, it becomes all the more difficult for states to abandon independent means for providing self-defense and security. For those states with the means, nuclear weapons continue to fulfill those needs.

Yet a number of states (South Africa, Argentina, Brazil, Kazakhstan, Belarus, and Ukraine, for example) have chosen alternative tools for security than nuclear weapons. Furthermore, the "disutility" of nuclear weapons in solving domestic problems was made evident as the Soviet Union dissolved. Although neither is faced with imminent dissolution, India and Pakistan face serious internal security threats that cannot be resolved with nuclear weapons. Forgoing nuclear weapons will not eliminate those internal threats, of course, but to the extent that the acquisition of nuclear weapons causes other states to keep a distance—in terms of aid, trade, technology, military assistance, etc.—these internal problems will become increasingly burdensome. It is a trade-off that sovereign states make all the time, and one that India and Pakistan to some degree have already made.

In the context of global regime change, however, with the likely negotiation of a CTBT and some kind of fissile material cutoff, optimism for nuclear nonproliferation—or perhaps to put it more accurately, a return to nonproliferation—in South Asia gains more substance. Whether negotiations are conducted bilaterally between each state and the United States or with each other, agreements to limit nuclear growth may provide a first step toward the elimination of nuclear weapons.

Thus optimism produced by regional conditions and regional confidence is countered by pessimism at the global level. At the same time, inactivity at the regional level is countered by a number of initiatives at the global level. As global conditions change, and as movement toward arms control becomes increasingly visible around the globe, the sense of confidence within South Asia that Indians and Pakistanis are able to resolve their differences on their own may yet result in security pledges and formal agreements that will enhance security and maintain regional and international stability without recourse to nuclear weapons.

Notes

1. Seymour M. Hersh, "On the Nuclear Edge," *New Yorker*, March 29, 1993, pp. 56–73; William E. Burrows and Robert Windrem, *Critical Mass* (New York: Simon and Schuster, 1994).

2. Douglas C. Makeig, "War, No-War, and the India-Pakistan Negotiating Process," *Pacific Affairs*, 60, no. 2 (summer 1987), contains an excellent review and analysis of a number of Indo-Pakistani agreements, including the Simla Accord.

3. The text of the Simla Accord can be found in appendix 1 of this volume.

4. For a more complete analysis of this agreement, see Imtiaz Bokhari and Thomas Thornton, *The 1972 Simla Agreement: An Asymmetrical Negotiation*, FPI Case Study no. 11 (Washington, D.C.: Johns Hopkins School of Advanced International Studies, 1988).

5. "Gandhi Ends 3-Day Visit to Pakistan," *New York Times*, January 1, 1989, p. 3.

6. Joint Publications Research Service, *Near East & South Asia*, JPRS-TND-92-002, January 31, 1992, p. 20.

7. The text of the No-Attack Agreement can be found in appendix 2.

8. See Bennett Ramberg, *Destruction of Nuclear Energy Facilities in War: The Problem and Implications* (Boulder, Co.: Westview, 1980).

9. U.S. Department of State, "Report to Congress on Progress Toward Regional Nonproliferation in South Asia," 1993.

10. "Report to Congress," p. 6.

11. Selig Harrison has argued that Pakistan would be unlikely to make a no-first-use pledge unless it were linked to conventional arms control. Other links to formalized arms control agreements may be necessary for mutual security pledges to take on greater weight.

12. Public lecture, Indo-US Conference at the University of Pennsylvania, Philadelphia, October 4, 1993.

13. Raja Ramanna, *Years of Pilgrimage: An Autobiography* (New Delhi: Penguin, 1991), pp. 88–96.

14. Pakistani Foreign Secretary Sheharyar Khan stated on February 6, 1992, that Pakistan had "elements which, if put together, would become a [nuclear] device," including highly enriched uranium cores. See R. Jeffrey Smith, "Pakistan Official Affirms Capacity for Nuclear Device," *Washington Post*, February 7, 1992, p. A18.

15. Some aspects of a bilateral initiative to Pakistan were discussed in "South Asian Lands Pressed on Arms," *New York Times*, March 23, 1994; and "The United States Proposes Sale of F-16s to Pakistan," *Washington Post*, March 23, 1994. A more complete picture is found in the three Department of State reports to Congress on progress on nonproliferation in South Asia.

16. Peter J. S. Duncan, *The Soviet Union and India* (London: Royal Institute of International Affairs, 1991), p. 123.

17. George Perkovich, "A Nuclear Third Way in South Asia," *Foreign Policy*, 91 (summer 1993), pp. 85–104.

18. Pran Chopra, "For Effective and True Non-Proliferation," unpublished paper prepared for the American Association for the Advancement of Science conference on Advanced Weapons in the Developing World, Cairo, Egypt, February 23–26, 1993.

20. See for example Howard Morland, *The Secret That Exploded* (New York: Random House, 1981); and Robert Serber, *The Los Alamos Primer* (Berkeley: University of California Press, 1992).

20. [Editor's note: In late December 1995, allegations were made that India was in fact making preparations for a second nuclear test. Indian spokesmen initially characterized these allegations as "purely speculative." Subsequently the Indian minister for external affairs, Pranab Mukherjee, categorically denied any such preparations. See Prem Shankar Jha, "India Can't Be Cowed Down on Nuclear Issue," *India Tribune*, January 20, 1996, p. 2.]

21. Pervez Hoodbhoy, *The News* International (Islamabad), March 22, 1993; K. Subrahmanyam, "Nuclear Policy, Arms Control and Military Cooperation," unpublished paper presented at the Conference on India and the United States after the Cold War, March 7–9, 1993, p. 20.

22. Zahid Qureshi, "Who Capped the Nuclear Programme?" *The News* International, December 8, 1993; this article also appeared in *Nawa-i-Waqt*, November 26, 1993.

23. Hoodbhoy in *The News* (International).

24. Personal interview, May 31, 1993.

25. "Testimony by Director of Central Intelligence James Woolsey," Senate Governmental Affairs Committee, Washington, D.C., February 24, 1993.

8

Transparency Measures

Pervaiz Iqbal Cheema

Three major wars and innumerable border clashes are an unenviable record for any two neighboring countries, especially two developing countries with very low income levels.[1] Deep-rooted suspicions, mutual distrust, and antagonism continue to bedevil Indo-Pakistani relations even after the passage of nearly fifty years. Despite the fact that economic and political developments in South Asia have reached a stage where one might begin to contemplate with hope and optimism the prospects of a normal neighborly relationship, the conflicting interpretations of normalcy and priorities seem to be taking a continually heavy toll on the security and mutual confidence of the two countries. Although both countries acutely realize the need for normalcy, economic cooperation, and regional stability, they most often make only minor concessions in peripheral areas. At the declaratory level, most leaders of the region have repeatedly asserted desires to work for peace, but at the practical level any such efforts have been viewed with suspicion and cynicism. With the departure of the cold war and the augured emergence of the "new world order,"[2] however, countries are looking more seriously for ways to implement the process that effectively reduced the East-West tension.

The signing of the Helsinki Accord introduced confidence-and security-building measures (CSBMs) to Europe. These measures very quickly began to pay dividends. The adoption of CSBMs at the Madrid meeting (1983) and their subsequent inclusion in the Stockholm (1986) and Vienna (1990) documents further highlighted the usefulness of CSBMs in reducing tensions.[3] Yet despite the success of the European example, the CSBM process has not yet been fully used in South Asia. This chapter will look at the factors that impede the adoption of CSBMs in South Asia. It will then analyze transparency measures as part of the overall process of implementing CSBMs. Finally, it will explore the practicality and usefulness of transparency measures within the specific context of South Asia.

Confidence- and Security-Building Measures

The goal of confidence- and security-building measures is to reduce or eliminate the causes of mistrust, fear, tension and hostilities. But the most important aspect of CSBMs is to create a climate in which even the most complicated issues are subjected to analysis and discussion aimed at resolving them. Military CSBMs, such as the Indo-Pakistani agreements not to strike each other's nuclear installations, to prevent airspace violations, to permit over-flights and landings of military crafts in each other's country, and to give advance notice of military exercises and troop movements along mutual borders, have substantially enhanced each country's confidence in security affairs. Similar CSBMs in the political arena could lead to greater rationality and stability in relations between the two countries.

During the dialogues that have been initiated to promote CSBMs and achieve some sense of normalcy in the bilateral relationship, questions have been raised regarding the major obstacles impeding the process of normalization. Broadly speaking, four sets of obstacles tend to hinder progress in this area and discourage constructive efforts at both individual and collective levels. These impediments are 1) historical problems, 2) mutual misperceptions, 3) domestic developments, and 4) concurrent disputes.[4]

Historical Problems

The cold war between India and Pakistan predates the British departure from the Indian subcontinent and can easily be traced back to colonial rule and to the rivalry between the Indian National Congress and the Muslim League. After partition, this rivalry evolved into conflict following the hasty partition of the subcontinent. Issues such as mass migration and refugee problems, evacuee properties, water disputes, the division of financial and military assets, and the problems of integration of princely states took their toll on Indo-Pakistani goodwill. The Kashmir dispute arose out of partition and continues to impede almost all normalization efforts. Both sides have repeatedly stressed that without a resolution of the Kashmir issue, peace is unlikely to make honorable entrance to the South Asian scene.

Mutual Misperceptions

Conflict and tension have also arisen in South Asia because of differing perceptions and different images the protagonists have of each other.

Misperceptions tend to paint a totally different picture than that which actually exists. Sometimes these distorted perceptions are acquired because of a lack of information. At other times, misperceptions by leaders and decision makers are deliberate.

Perceptions or misperceptions need to be considered at two levels, public and governmental. Perceptions tend to give sustenance to varying interpretations and misinterpretations. For example, Pakistan's sense of insecurity during the initial days of independence prompted it to enter into the Western defense alliance system. India saw this as an attempt to upset the power balance and to challenge Indian authority in South Asia. Because India envisaged for itself a central role not only in South Asia but also in Asia more broadly, the arrival of an outside equalizer upset its entire design.

Domestic Developments

Domestic pressures and upheavals also tend to disrupt many constructive international processes and are known to have contributed substantially to major foreign policy shifts in most countries of the world. Governments commonly use external events to divert attention from pressing internal political, economic, social and even security crises. Hostile external responses make it relatively easy to enhance internal cohesion by employing emotional and sentimental jargon. One does not have to look too deeply into the prevailing situations in India and Pakistan to see the existence of strong pressures generated by various internal crises. Indian and Pakistani leaders have almost always exploited the other's internal turmoil and tensions for their own advantage. Three types of situations have tended to develop most frequently: the periodic emergence of minority governments (Bhutto in Pakistan, Singh and Rao in India); an incumbent government, unable to resolve an internal crisis, that begins to rely too heavily on diversionary tactics (the concept of the "foreign hand"); and the development of excessive influence by certain vested interests (the business community, religious groups, etc.).

Current Regional Disputes

Among the ongoing disputes that are taking a continually heavy toll on bilateral relations are Kashmir, the Siachen Glacier, the Wullar Lake Barrage, and the nuclear weapons programs on both sides of the border. India's nuclear program is far more advanced and more comprehensive than Pakistan's. India has already tested a nuclear device, established a large fleet of bombers, and secured the requisite missile technology, and is now rushing to perfect long-range missiles and satellite capabilities. Although the government of India has always stressed the peaceful orientation of its nuclear program, informed press reports have periodically suggested that India never abandoned its nuclear weapons program. Pakistan, on the other hand, while it has also proclaimed its peaceful nuclear program, recently acknowledged that it has acquired the technical capabilities to make a nuclear device.

Transparency Measures

Etymologically, transparency means capable of being seen through. In the context of international relations, transparency means that the chances of misinterpretation, whether deliberate or inadvertent, are reduced to a minimum. The concept of transparency is probably the most attractive form of the notion of open diplomacy. And just as open diplomacy managed to remove many apprehensions on the part of adversaries, the concept of transparency can help lessen the temptations of exaggerated estimates and misinterpretations in military matters. Transparency implies the systematic release of information covering almost all aspects of military activities. By making such information public and promoting accessibility to requisite information, transparency measures (TMs) reduce uncertainties that could breed apprehensions that could, in turn, produce tensions.

Transparency measures are perhaps the most effective restraint on arms transfer. Under full transparency, both the supplier and the recipient would have to negotiate in full view of all sides. TMs also limit arms sales by enabling states to evaluate accurately their security situations and, consequently, to keep their arms procurement list in line with realities on the ground. Thus the realistic assessment of security needs that follows from transparency would not only save resources but also facilitate justifying any threatening procurement before the world community.

The choice of which transparency measures to adopt depends on the objective. If the objective is to educate and increase public awareness, all one needs to do is to establish regular channels of information. These channels could be set up at both national and regional levels. If the objective is to strengthen already adopted and operative CSBMs, the approach has to be tailored to the visible dividends paid by these prior CSBMs. Such an approach might be more step-by-step than comprehensive.

A certain level of political will is crucial to a successful disarmament negotiation process. Even though political and disarmament negotiations are sometimes viewed as independent processes, the underlying linkage between threat perceptions and the overall political situation cannot just be brushed aside. To assess threat, one has to dwell rather heavily upon perceptions, which can deviate from reality as a result of preconceived ideas or the professional bias of the perceiver. Threat assessment involves contextual imperatives as well as an adversary's capabilities and intentions.

Capabilities are essentially relative and easier to assess than intentions. Although exaggerated claims have made assessment of capabilities rather difficult in the past, the advent of modern monitoring and satellite technology has greatly facilitated accurate assessments of an enemy's capabilities. The enemy's ability to inflict harm is related to the target's ability to defend itself. Any enemy will find it difficult to impose his will upon an adversary that possesses capabilities that can counter or nullify those the aggressor has. An accurate assessment of intentions involves close scrutiny of past behavior, a cold-blooded evaluation of the existing political situation, and evaluation of the enemy's capabilities.[5] A potential aggressor thus depends heavily upon the perceived capabilities relationship between himself and his adversary.

Several types of useful TMs can be envisaged given this situation. Among them, perhaps the most important is the publication of annual defense budgets that clearly spell out the allocations for various arms. If a particular allocation has been increased, it should be adequately highlighted, giving the reasons for the increase. This would remove all grounds for misinterpretation by the adversaries. Attempts to disguise legitimate defense expenditures under other subheadings within the overall budgetary exercises should be avoided. For example, sometimes the expenditure for strategic roads is listed in the communication rather than defense sector. Admittedly, roads have a dual purpose and they could be listed legitimately under communications, but roads whose use is exclusively military should be listed under the appropriate subheadings of the defense budget. Efforts should be made to clarify, as far as possible, any dual-purpose items in order to lessen chances for misinterpretation. A detailed discussion of the defense budget in the Parliament could contribute enormously the desired level of openness. Detailed coverage of parliamentary debate on defense in the national press could further enhance openness. Increased awareness could also stimulate renewed thinking within and outside the government. The publication of annual defense budgets and consequent detailed press coverage of parliamentary debates is a form of direct communication not only with the nation in question but also in other interested nations. Information regarding the size, structure, weapons, cantonments, future inductions, purchases, and movements of forces would be shared with all interested parties, both inside and outside the country.

A second extremely useful TM is the publication and circulation among interested parties of an annual calendar of exercises. This calendar could mention the areas in which the exercises are to be held. Exercises could be prohibited in areas that are either too close to the border or viewed as extremely sensitive. Constraints could also be established on the frequency, size, or types of military exercises. In addition, spelling out the objectives of particular exercises in detail would be helpful. For example, a particular exercise might be described as testing of new terrain and new tactics, or as introducing new weapons, or a combination thereof.

Third, an agreement to invite observers from an adversary state to witness military exercises could be extremely useful to further enhance openness. This tool would work best if exercises were viewed as part of defensive rather than offensive preparations. In 1989, when Pakistan undertook its military exercise, it invited many military attachés from various embassies, including from India. This tended to confirm the nonhostile intention of Pakistan's exercises.

Fourth, all unscheduled movement of troops, whether caused by internal crisis or an emergency on a border, need to be notified as quickly as possible. A regularized pattern of notification tends to generate confidence in the openness of a country's policies. Sudden movement during emergencies may entail delayed notification, but then the nature of emergency could itself provide sufficient justification for delayed notification. The basic requirement is for the establishment of a regular and open system of quick notification of all forms of troop movements, including peacetime movements such as the transfer of units from one place to another.

Fifth, tests covering all aspects of sophisticated weaponry need to be announced publicly. Development of weapon systems requires periodic testing, but if these tests are not secretive, unnecessary apprehension is unlikely to surface. Particular attention should be paid to tests of nuclear and missile technology. The nuclear weapons applications of missile technology and the fact that there are currently no effective defenses against missiles make the development and testing of missiles a cause for significant concern in adversary countries.

Sixth, higher military training institutions should invite attendance and participation from perceived and known adversaries. Inviting an Indian participant to Pakistan's National Defense course or a Pakistani to a similar course in India would be a CSBM that would clearly indicate the course structure and objectives. A fixed quota of seats for foreign participants, including at least one or two from the perceived adversary, would certainly prove to be a useful transparency measure. Collaborative training schemes could even be devised, especially in technical areas. Joint courses could be organized at a regional level that would enable all the regional countries to explore the avenues of collective defense of the region.

Seventh, a method of annual information exchange among interested states could be devised.[6] This could be done in two ways: Either a comprehensive defense book could be published, indicating the existing strength of active and reserve forces, various weapons, defense production, and other aspects of defense preparedness, or a regional or bilateral agreement could be signed in which countries agree to supply the desired information on demand. A comprehensive defense book could be published either by the individual countries or by a regional organization employing a commission of military experts from member states.

Eighth, all arms procurement agreements, including those containing transfer of technology, could be made public. For example, all arms sale transactions could be published in a UN register,[7] which would enable each side to verify transactions when it is deemed necessary. Alternatively or in addition, a regional register of arms imports and exports could be maintained. Both the UN and regional organizations could launch projects to collect and publish information regarding defense procurement, allocation of resources, existing strength of men and material, etc. The existing UN system of standardized reporting of military expenditure should be encouraged to be adopted by almost all members of the UN.

Ninth, exchange visits of high military officials and regular meetings of officers at lower levels could be encouraged. Ordinarily, military officers meet only following an ugly incident or just before or after a major catastrophe occurs. The establishment of regular contact between high officials and other officers in peacetime is likely to reduce tension. Military attachés could be invited to security-related discussions at public forums; continuous hounding of these personnel by intelligence agencies could be discouraged. Regular meetings of military attachés with their counterparts in the host country would provide a useful channel of communication, establishing a dialogue regarding security issues. Defense ministers, or at least high officials of defense ministries, could also meet regularly to highlight new developments that endanger the security of their respective countries, describe measures that are likely to be undertaken to meet the perceived security threats, and inform each other of the rationale of certain defense-related actions.

Tenth, to satisfy each other's inquisitive instinct and allay apprehensions, a system of inspections on demand could be introduced. The underlying assumption here is that the inspection would only be required if the requesting party is not satisfied by the explanation of the target state. The involved state need not be extremely sensitive about the inspection. Sometimes an inspection is required merely to satisfy a government's highly developed sensitivities and is not meant to cast doubt on the other country's explanation.

Eleventh, an open skies treaty (a system of aerial observation in which the collected data could be shared by both the observer and the observed) can be extremely useful in promoting openness of military forces and activities.[8] The concept of open skies is not meant for gathering detailed technical intelligence. However, it can be a useful tool in collecting basic information on an adversary's military activities and capabilities. The number of overflights and the nature of sensors could be mutually agreed upon.

Twelfth, all conventional defense production units could be opened for visits of officials from other countries, including those of adversaries. Apart from legitimate precautions for industrial espionage, major products and technological breakthroughs improving weaponry could be quickly made public.

Thirteenth, advanced research regarding the prevention of nuclear accidents and the thorny problem of nuclear waste disposal could be made public. Alternatively, collaborative joint programs could be initiated, aimed at preventing nuclear accidents and devising means for the safe disposal of nuclear waste.

Transparency Measures and South Asia

Undoubtedly, transparency measures covering military activities could be extremely useful for all the regional states in strengthening their policies of restraint. However, it must also be pointed out that CSBMs, including TMs, are not a panacea providing quick healing to all ailments. Not only are CSBMs not supposed to solve all problems, but they are also prone to be exploited for deception and disinformation. Furthermore, it is difficult to predict smooth sailing for CSBMs (including TMs) in all regions of the world, primarily because of differences in prevailing geopolitical environments, peculiar regional characteristics, and domestic compulsions. What was successful in Europe may not register a similar level of success in South Asia. Each region has its own distinct characteristics and its own strategic needs. A comparative analysis of Europe and South Asia clearly highlights the contrasting elements. First, in Europe the contending groups were more or less equal, whereas in South Asia, India occupies a predominant position in both economic and military strength.[9] Second, whereas an ideological controversy was the focus of contention in Europe, the historical experience of more than a thousand years of communal and religious differences has been the root of tension in South Asia.[10] Third, in Europe the experience of world wars and the fear that the next war might be nuclear considerably influenced thinking, whereas in South Asia the dangerous implications of nuclear war have yet to make a convincing impact. Despite having experienced four major wars, South Asia still seems far from a firm commitment to avoid the next war.[11] Fourth, the chances of premeditated war in Europe were and still are extremely remote and thus the apprehensions of the European states revolved primarily around the possibility of accidental war. In South Asia, on the other hand, the chance of intentional war is much greater than the chance of one due to misunderstanding, although the possibility of accidental war cannot be ruled out altogether.[12] Finally, the promotion of CSBMs in Europe occurred within the context of the Conference on Security and Cooperation in Europe (CSCE), whereas in South Asia no such process exists.[13]

In the wake of recent communal riots and the gradual deterioration of Indo-Pakistani relations,[14] the prospects for CSBMs, including TMs, appear bleak. But the major goal of CSBMs is to break such deadlocks and put the adversaries on the road to normalcy. One redeeming feature of the situation in South Asia is that both India and Pakistan are not averse to positive initiatives. Already a system of continued dialogue exists at the secretarial level. This, of course, is not enough. Because it is the largest country in the region, the onus seems to be on India to undertake a major initiative. But the weak position of India's current leadership makes it unlikely that New Delhi will undertake any major initiative that might endanger the government's position in terms of voter appeal. Unless and until an initiative emanating from internal, regional, or extra-regional sources gains the support and blessing of India, the desired dividends are unlikely to surface.

The unofficial dialogues that have been started are indeed useful. An informal exchange of views always leaves a positive effect and even helps erode any existing rigidity. While there is no denial of the fact that unofficial dialogues are extremely beneficial, the introduction of TMs is heavily dependent upon official pursuits. The agreements to prevent airspace violations and permit overflights and landing by military aircraft, to ensure advance notice of military exercises and troop movements along mutual borders, and to refrain from striking each other's nuclear installations are all the product of official negotiations. The success of such agreements tends to generate an aura of optimism and hope. Highlighting new measures with clearly analyzed practicabilities could induce the governments to consider seriously more such measures. In considering each of the previously mentioned transparency measures in the Indo-Pakistani context, the following considerations need to be taken into account:

1. Not only could the annual defense budget be thoroughly discussed in the Indian and Pakistani parliaments, but the budget estimates could be published in detail along with a rationalization of any intended increases. It is a well-known fact that both India and Pakistan are spending a disproportionate part of their resources in maintaining huge armed forces, while education, health, social welfare, and other social and economic sectors receive a very small share of available resources. A proper cost-benefit analysis could only be undertaken if budgetary details were made available, details including not only the exact allocation of resources to various arms of the defense forces (i.e., army, navy, air force, etc.) but also the allocation to various sections of a particular arm. It would not be very difficult for the Indian and Pakistani governments to make all the details gradually available to the public and to their respective representatives.

The availability of relevant information and the openness regarding defense budgets are much better in India than in Pakistan. The Indian Ministry of Defense publishes an annual defense report containing information regarding all aspects of its defense policies, current force structure, and future plans. In addition, the members of parliament are provided with requisite information during the defense debates in Lok Sabha. They also discuss the defense budget more openly than their counterparts in the Pakistani National Assembly.[15] The situation in Pakistan is much more bleak; there is no tradition of publication of ministerial reports, nor is any detailed information regarding the defense sector given to the parliament, not even during the actual debates on defense budgeting. Were information made available to public representatives in Pakistan, not only would the level of parliamentary debate attain impressive heights, but part of the information would also find its way to national news outlets. With the steady strengthening of democratic practices, it should not be all that difficult for the Pakistani authorities to open up and begin releasing desired information to both the public and elected representatives. Once a detailed presentation of the defense budget becomes a regular feature of parliamentary debates, the defense ministry might begin to contemplate publishing an annual report for public consumption.

2. The publication of an annual calendar of exercises is another quite feasible proposition. An agreement on prior notice of military exercises has already been completed.[16] As a result, both national exercises and joint exercises, such as cooperative exercises with the United States, have been announced well in advance. Even before this agreement, national exercises like India's Brasstacks in 1987 and Pakistan's Zarb-e-Momin in 1989, were also well publicized. Publishing an annual calendar of such exercises would not be too difficult a step to take. It would merely institute a regular practice of communication and sharing information.

3. The next step after notification of such exercises would be the inviting of observers, including military observers from potential or existing adversaries, to witness the exercises. Pakistan's invitation in 1989 to the Indian military attaché to attend briefings was a step in the right direction. Since a start has already been made, it is only a question of systematizing and regularizing of this useful practice, which could be extremely helpful in securing the desired level of openness and transparency.

4. An agreement to invite participants from the other country to attend a higher level of defense courses in their respective defense-training institutions is also a step that can easily be classified as within reach. Both countries have already allowed many outsiders to attend high-level courses at their respective national colleges. Allowing a perceived adversary's high officials to do the same would be the next desired step. In addition, the regular exchange of high-ranking military officials could further promote

the desired atmosphere of openness. Visiting military officials could also be invited to deliver regular talks at the respective national defense colleges.

5. To generate further confidence and institutionalize the arms procurement process in the region, a process for registering all weapon sales agreements with a regional organization such as the South Asian Association for Regional Cooperation (SAARC) could be established. Alternatively, all weapons-related sales agreements could be registered with both the UN and SAARC, providing the regional states with sufficient openness to share information regarding weapons acquisition and the transfer of technology. Such a step would considerably curtail unnecessary apprehension.

6. An open skies treaty could be signed within the region after detailed discussions are held to determine its perimeters. Such a treaty would improve mutual understanding and confidence by giving all participating countries, regardless of size, a direct role in gathering basic information on the military capabilities and activities of other participating countries.[17] South Asia is a geographically compact area in which an open skies agreement is not only feasible but desirable, certainly from the viewpoint of civil aviation authorities. Such an agreement would also open options for new interstate routes for all the region's air companies. A regional organization could be entrusted with the task of monitoring the operation of the treaty and resolving the problems that would arise from time to time. The treaty would imply territorial openness within the agreed limits and would include agreements on sensors to be installed on aircraft and on the sharing of information gathered by the participating countries.

7. An agreement to open ordnance and other defense-related factories to regional visitors is not beyond the realm of possibility. To begin with, the agreement should cover a limited number of identified factories. It could later be enlarged to bring in more and more such factories. Obviously such a proposal would face considerable difficulties, because India's arms-production base is much larger than Pakistan's. But setting a limited number of factories to be included should help lead the parties to some level of agreement.

8. An agreement to undertake joint security studies covering issues such as the prevention of nuclear accidents or the development of safe methods to dispose of nuclear waste, along with other pressing security problems, is not an elusive goal. Some joint studies have been undertaken already to cover aspects of security scenarios in South Asia.

The above-mentioned are just some of the measures which are not only feasible but are also desirable to enhance the security of South Asia. Some of the suggested measures can be pursued quite easily; others may take some time to secure a desired level of consensus.

Notes

1. For details, see Pervaiz Iqbal Cheema, "India and Pakistan: Problems of Normalization," *Pakistan Journal of Social Science* 6, no. 2 (July–Dec. 1980), pp. 75–88.

2. Much has been written about the death of the cold war and the emergence of the new world order. To me it appears that things are still in a state of flux and the new order has not yet taken a concrete form. Indeed the disappearance of the East-West confrontation has not only improved the overall international environment and atmosphere but has also substantively enhanced prospects for solutions to some of the acute regional conflicts.

3. See Syed Zakir Ali Zaidi, "CSBMs in the South Asia Region," Disarmament Topical Paper no. 7 (New York: United Nations, 1991), pp. 110–20.

4. See Pervaiz Iqbal Cheema, "Confidence Building in India-Pakistan Relations," *The News*, March 19, 1992. Also see Cheema, "India and Pakistan: Problems of Normalization."

5. For a detailed analysis of threat perceptions, see Pervaiz Iqbal Cheema, "Pakistan's Threat Perceptions," in Rais Ahmad Khan, ed., *Pakistan-United States Relations* (Islamabad: Area Study Centre, Quaid-i-Azam University, 1983), pp. 107–24.

6. See Pierce S. Corden, "Building and Strengthening Confidence and Security in Asia," Disarmament Topical Paper no. 10 (New York: United Nations, 1992), pp. 166–73.

7. See Friedrich Ruth, "Transparency and Confidence-Building," Disarmament Topical Paper no. 3 (New York: United Nations, 1990), pp. 63–65.

8. For details see Peter Jones, "Open Skies: A New Era of Transparency," *Arms Control Today*, May 1992, pp. 10–15. Also see "Open Skies Treaty," in *U.S. Department of State Dispatch*, March 30, 1992.

9. See Corden, "Building and Strengthening Confidence and Security in South Asia," p. 168; and Zaidi, "CSBMs in the South Asia Region," pp. 110–11.

10. Zaidi, "CSBMs in the South Asia Region," pp. 110–11.

11. Three wars were fought between India and Pakistan and one between China and India. In addition, the South Asians have experienced innumerable border clashes, including major ones (e.g., the Rann of Kutch clash in April 1965) that could be classified as war.

12. Zaidi, "CSBMs in the South Asia Region," p. 111.

13. Zaidi, "CSBMs in the South Asia Region," p. 111.

14. The demolition of the Babri Mosque on December 6, 1992, by Hindu militants and the consequent communal riots in which more than two thousand died and thousands were rendered homeless elicited strong reaction in Pakistan. As a consequence, relations between India and Pakistan took a downward dip. Minor disputes over the return of the bodies of two Pakistanis who were tortured to death and over the control of Jinnah House in Bombay also contributed to the existing tension.

15. See Indian Ambassador H.E.S.K. Lambah's statement regarding the defense allocations for 1993–94 in *The News*, March 17, 1993. Also see *The News*, March 1, 1993.

16. For details of agreement see *A Handbook of Confidence Building Measures for Regional Security*, Handbook no. 1 (Washington, D.C.: Henry L. Stimson Center, 1993), pp. 46–47.

17. See "Open Skies Treaty."

9

Military Postures, Risks, and Security Building

Jasjit Singh

The search for confidence- and security-building measures (CSBMs) among states is closely linked to the reduction of mutual threat perceptions, mistrust, and risks that arise out of confrontation, tension, and disputes. A state's military and security policies, postures, and activities can all too easily translate tense situations into conflict, violence, and outright war. CSBMs are aimed at preventing such escalations.

Dangerous military activities are a product of military postures and strategic doctrines; these, in turn, stem from politics and political direction. The historical experience heavily influences the perceptions that underlie political and military decisions. It is therefore necessary that the focus on military-related risk factors be situated in the context of politics and historical experience.

Military-related CSBMs evolved in Europe out of the cold war confrontation that produced two of the world's most heavily militarized regions (central Europe and northeast Asia). Although the example of European confidence- and security-building is useful in that it establishes certain principles and approaches, viable CSBMs will also need to take specific regional factors into account. This is certainly so in the South Asian context. Furthermore, although most of the steps taken for confidence- and security-building will need to be bilateral, the CSBM framework must address concerns beyond the bilateral equation.

In South Asia, the historical approach to building confidence and security among neighbors has relied almost entirely on political rather than military measures. The Sino-Indian *Panchsheel* (Five Principles of Peaceful Coexistence) and the Indo-Pakistani Simla Agreement are two classic examples. Only in recent years have some attempts at classical military CSBMs started to take shape.

Nature of Military Risks

The pattern of past wars and conflicts provides an indication of the nature of risks associated with military-related activities. There have been a number of wars and battles between Pakistan and India since 1947.[1] A number of features common to these historical experiences are relevant to security and confidence building.

First, all the wars started off as irregular warfare/armed conflict under ideological imperatives, and later escalated into regular inter-military wars. The critical point of risk and crisis management, therefore, is more at the preliminary and intermediate stages—during the irregular war period and at the escalation points. At these points, it is also clear, the measures that would need to be adopted are more in the political arena rather than purely military. However, the military implications and concurrent military risks of escalation deserve attention as potential CSBM areas.

Second, it also stands out that India was not the initiator in all the wars and conflicts.[2] A closer examination of the driving force for this reveals three basic factors at the root: ideology, state goals and objectives driven by ideology (with regime goals at times taking precedence), and politico-military doctrines for the application of force in international relations.

Third, external political and military support, as well as perceptions thereof, has been a crucial factor in escalation to war. For example, U.S. military aid to Pakistan after 1954 generated perceptions of military (especially technological) superiority, and after India's defeat in the 1962 war with China, created the incentive for Pakistan to initiate the 1965 war.[3] More important, perhaps, were the miscalculations arising out of the events of April 1965. Pakistan presumed that India, even if pressed hard in Jammu and Kashmir, would not retaliate across the international border in Punjab, as it had done in 1947–48. Similarly, expectations of external support and of a favorable international response were important in India's decision to escalate Pakistan's civil war, leading to the 1971 war and the independence of Bangladesh.

Fourth, overall mutual political mistrust has intensified over the years. Each country perceives a threat from the other, although the nature of the threat perception is different on either side. It can be argued that the legitimacy and the basis of these perceptions is questionable. Thus the two could benefit from starting a dialogue on the subject of threat perceptions itself.

Parallels can also be drawn from the Sino-Indian war of 1962. That war was an escalation from clashes between patrols along a difficult and disputed terrain; it was propelled by China's politico-military doctrine of "teaching lessons" for ideological and state reasons; and it had an external dimension (in reverse, to demonstrate the international isolation of India). In fact, all the wars in the region since 1947 have revolved around disputed sovereignty. In addition, all these wars have had one singular characteristic: They have been the most restrained and limited wars of the twentieth century. This fact alone indicates a strong potential for CSBMs.

The answer, therefore, lies in serious dialogue to discuss historical experiences and mutual threat perceptions. Unless these are aired—at least nationally, and preferably in a bilateral framework—and in some cases exorcized, there is little hope of improving the security environment. Dialogue becomes even more important in the context of crises arising out of perceived mobilizations, as the U.S.-Russian dialogue on the Cuban missile crisis of 1962 has shown. In the South Asian context, three crises have arisen out of just such military maneuvers: the 1986–87 incident on the Sino-Indian border, the "Brasstacks" incident in January 1987, and the spring 1990 crisis.

In 1987, while the Pakistan-supported separatist militancy in Indian Punjab intensified, India perceived military moves by Pakistan as seriously threatening.[4] Theoretically, Pakistan could have been contemplating a swift, broad pincer by its two strike corps. But from a practical standpoint, such a move was not so easy, especially as long as India was able to deploy defensive ground troops. It is also highly unlikely that General Zia would have risked a war with India at a time when the Soviets were still in Afghanistan, or that the United States would have let Zia proceed down that line. Most important, Pakistan would have stood out as the aggressor—and General Zia ul Haq was hardly the type of person to take such risks. The brinkmanship was, no doubt, highly risky. Its aims were perceived in India to be political and more related to encouraging separatist violence in Punjab, disrupting a planned and advertised military exercise, and, above all, to use a 'crisis' to achieve credibility for the nuclear weapons program while incurring minimum costs.

The events of spring 1990 have attracted even greater attention than the 1987 "Brasstacks" incident, especially since the impression has been created that India and Pakistan were on the brink of nuclear war in 1990.[5] The Pakistan-based Jammu and Kashmir Liberation Front (JKLF) separatist movement, which had escalated to armed militancy in July 1988,[6] was further intensified in early December 1989. By January 1990, the militancy had assumed the dimensions of a full-fledged proxy war. When Pakistan raised the ante further during February and March, the situation appeared similar to that at the end of August 1965. The Pakistani army chief, General Aslam Beg, had also asserted the previous year that the lack of strategic vision that had been blamed for Pakistan's earlier failures to take Kashmir by force had now been rectified. The India response to Beg's provocations was to maintain a completely defensive posture and to keep the United States in the picture.[7] India's strategy of war prevention denied Pakistan the opportunity to trigger another war like that of 1965.

Political Goals and Objectives

Most assessments of military activities, and hence also of military CSBMs, revolve around assessments of capabilities and the demonstration of those capabilities. Such assessments, given their intangible bases, are usually inadequate to provide any real guidance to the intentions of the potential adversary. Yet capabilities and intentions are intrinsically linked; intentions drive capabilities, and capabilities provide the means by which intentions are pursued. Furthermore, intentions, and the adversary's perceptions of those intentions, have a powerful influence on the risks and dangers arising out of military postures and activities. The conceptual framework for addressing risks and dangers, therefore, has to be built around political aims, objectives, perceptions, ideologies, and actions.

At a fundamental level, ideologies continue to be a source of conflicts. The high profile of the cold war led the world to believe that the East-West ideological conflict was the only such conflict of any significance. The reality, however, is that ideology has been playing an increasing role in international relations and conflicts. Empirical evidence indicates that ideology has been the primary factor in over two-thirds of the armed conflicts since World War II, and by some assessments, has played an important role in over 90 percent of these conflicts.[8] Nationalism as an ideology has been a powerful factor in anti-colonial and border wars. A large number of conflicts have arisen out of dissatisfaction with the arrangements for decolonization or with the outcomes of independence.

The revival of ethnicity and religion in the political domain has given an impetus to political ideologies. Ethnicity has traditionally influenced political power and reinforced nationalism. It has also led to irrational nationalism, as in the case of Nazi, Khmer Rouge, Afghan, and Serbian ethnoreligious nationalism. The political use and exploitation of religion has often led to a particularly vicious method of pursuing ideological fundamentalism. These developments are of special significance to multi-ethnic and multi-religious cultures, pluralistic states, and evolving nation-states.

South Asia has been afflicted by competing and conflictual ideologies, which themselves were responsible for the partition of the subcontinent in the 1940s: "The ideologies of the two nations are diametrically opposed—India is based on secularism and nationalism, while Pakistan is founded on the two-nation theory which insists that religion cannot be separated from politics."[9] A fundamental dissonance and conflict, therefore, has been built into the Indo-Pakistani situation. Ethnicity has further complicated the ideological issues, and has been an important factor in increasing internal tensions and insecurities, especially in Pakistan, where the thrust toward "Islamic ideology" has been used to counter movements based on ethnic identities.[10] This in itself was a major factor for the Pakistani leadership's avoidance of adult franchise-based parliamentary democracy, which would have left a greater share of power resting with Bengali East Pakistan (a dilemma that was resolved only by the separation of East Pakistan).[11] Political instability has also led to military control of the power structure for most of Pakistan's history. As long as the "Pakistani Army has a casting vote, it is hard to see how relations between Pakistan and India can ever be peaceful. . . ."[12] Progressive Islamicization has invariably increased the discord and mistrust between the two neighbors. Under Zia ul Haq, Pakistan moved significantly closer to an ideology in which Islam is seen as the basis of the state itself.[13] In fact, this renewed deployment of Islamic ideology led U.S. scholars in the early 1980s to forecast that ideology would inevitably raise the Kashmir issue to the conflictual level once again.[14]

Ideological differences also existed between the People's Republic of China and India. But here, an early attempt was made to attenuate ideological contradictions through the principle of peaceful co-existence (as articulated in the *Panchsheel*). This effort was not sufficient to avert the war of 1962, however, and the communist ideology of export of revolution was perceived by India as supporting the separatist militancy and insurgency in India's northeast until the mid-1970s. (Termination of this support was an important factor in starting the thaw in Sino-Indian relations.)

At the same time, the resurgence of religion is playing an important role in politics, even in states that have pursued liberal democratic or socialist ideologies.[15] The combination of religion, nationalism, and politics is potentially highly destructive. Empirical evidence and trends in the growth of ethnoreligious nationalism point out some implications of the resurgence of religion for states (especially those with liberal democratic political systems), state-building, and security. First, the growth of ethnoreligious nationalism as a factor increasing the potential for intra- and inter-state conflict must be addressed. Most of the states in which ethnoreligious nationalism is growing, including India and Pakistan, are heterogenous. And in places where nationhood starts to be defined solely on ethnicity and/or religion, at times even ignoring civilizational and cultural identities, it creates powerful sources of instability. The breakup of Pakistan in 1971 (and, for that matter, of India in 1947), the fragmentation of and subsequent war in Yugoslavia, and the collapse of the Soviet Union, for example, owe in no small measure to this trend. More recently, China has had to face new concerns about its nationalities. Second, external support to internal discord and separatist impulses remains an important element in increasing instability and conflict. As Evan Luard points out, "Often the seriousness of such [modern, localized, civil] wars is hugely intensified by intervention of that [external] kind. In a few cases external interference is mainly responsible for there being any war at all; as when a rebel force that would have had no significance but for outside assistance is built up to contest an existing government's rule [the Pakistani-created revolt in Kashmir in 1965, the U.S.-orchestrated and financed rebellion in Nicaragua from 1981 onward]. . . ."[16] The Pakistan-supported separatist militancies in Punjab and in Jammu and Kashmir have been seen by some as serious threats to Indian stability.

Third, ethnoreligious ideology not only goes against the fundamental tenets of democratic norms and values, but its transnational dimension has a destabilizing effect on democratic processes, especially when that ideology is pursued through support of violence, militancy, or terrorism.

The question that these facts give rise to is this: Can anything be done to reduce the impact of ideological conflict without questioning or altering cherished beliefs in either case? The fundamental problem between Pakistan and India (and between China and India) is a deep-rooted political mistrust, which in itself makes confidence building an important exercise. Yet one of the difficulties this mistrust creates is a tendency not to adhere to international agreements. (Pakistan's record in this respect does not generate confidence.)[17] This raises questions about the credibility and reliability of any confidence- or security-building agreement that might get negotiated.

In this context, then, security and confidence building between Pakistan and India needs to be based on the following precepts:

1. Bilateral declaration of political commitment to the independence, sovereignty, integrity, stability, and prosperity of both states. India should have no difficulty in initiating this process through unilateral commitment to the stability and integrity of Pakistan.
2. Bilateral declaration of political commitment to the identification of and cooperation on issues for which a convergent approach can be adopted. This could be implemented at international, multilateral, regional, and bilateral levels. Fruitful areas might include nonmilitary dimensions of security, trade and techno-economic issues, or global disarmament issues.
3. Bilateral commitment to peaceful co-existence. This would permit the countries' competing ideologies to exist without a conflict of military power or other instruments of violence.

4. An unambiguous and unqualified re-affirmation of political commitment to the 1972 Simla Agreement as the basis of the bilateral relationship. In particular, the following principles need to be re-emphasized:

a. A commitment to the principles of equal sovereignty, noninterference, and peaceful resolution of disputes;

b. The establishment of normal and liberal relations in the areas of cultural, trade, and personal contacts. India should move away from the principle of 'reciprocity' and should, if necessary, liberalize its rules unilaterally. This would, over time, help move the two sides from the existing "negative" reciprocity toward positive reciprocity; and

c. The establishment of a healthy trade and commercial relationship, so that both countries can develop faster.

Politico-Military Doctrines and Threat Perceptions

It is clear that any attempts to improve the security environment between India and Pakistan and to reduce the risks associated with their military activities will succeed only if they are placed in the appropriate political context. One of the important issues to be addressed is that of politico-military doctrines. The examples of the 1987 and 1990 "crises" reveal a remarkable degree of restraint and discretion on the part of India. In the process, Indian doctrine shifted, unannounced, from the traditional territorial defense to the prevention of war. The political philosophy behind this doctrine has retained its earlier "defensive defense" orientation, but it no longer seems to hinge on the defense of every inch of territory. This shift has been reinforced by the changing nature of war.

Pakistan's military doctrine, on the other hand, has been constructed on the philosophy of "offensive defense."[18] In its actual application, "Pakistan has not hesitated to be the first to employ the heavy use of force in order to gain an initial advantage."[19] At the same time, Pakistan has advocated a military strategy of war based on "instilling terror into the hearts of the enemy," during prewar, war, and war-termination stages.[20] This entails a strategic doctrine that rests heavily on the use of terrorism and unconventional modes of conflict. It also entails a reliance on nuclear weapons as an instrument of policy. It is interesting to note that in 1989 when General Aslam Beg formally announced the doctrine of offensive defense, he also linked it to the use of nuclear deterrence for military purposes, and exhorted his senior officers to use terror as a weapon in accordance with the interpretation of the Quran. Pakistan's doctrines have also placed a great deal of emphasis on guerrilla warfare. Unlike the United States, whose doctrine was concerned with *suppressing* a guerrilla war, Pakistan's doctrine was framed "in terms of *launching* a people's war against India."[21]

China's strategic doctrine has undergone a shift from the traditional "people's war" to the "people's war under modern conditions." The new doctrine is apparently weighted more heavily toward the offensive.[22] At the same time, there are no signs of China having given up its traditional concept of using military force for "teaching lessons"—a patently offense-dominated philosophy. Thus there is a clear need for a serious dialogue on the issue of politico-military doctrines and their implications, at least among the strategic communities of the countries of South Asia. Some degree of harmonization of strategic doctrines will greatly enhance mutual confidence and security.

The levels of risk in dangerous military activities depend in large part on the perceptions of threat by the other country involved. These perceptions, of course, tend to be heavily biased by subjective factors. But in general, dangerous military activities include the following:

1. An increase in levels of tension that upset stability and pose risks of escalation;
2. Threatening miliary postures, deployments, or force levels; and
3. A lack of transparency that may lead to errors of assessment and judgment.

Reducing tensions is essentially a political process and was addressed earlier. But what is lacking in South Asia is an appropriate forum, at the bilateral as well as multilateral regional level, to facilitate reducing tensions. A suitable model may be an instrumentality similar to the Conference on Security and Cooperation in Europe (CSCE), suitably modified to the regional and local environment. The case for a "Conference on Security and Confidence Building in South Asia" should be closely examined. It would need to include the regions of South Asia and Central Asia and countries such as China, Iran, Afghanistan, etc. At the same time, dialogue among the strategic communities of each country involved needs to be established and pursued with a degree of continuity.

Peacetime Deployments The greatest payoff in reducing the risks and perceptions of threatening postures may come from addressing the issue of peacetime deployments of military power. In many cases normal peacetime deployments reinforce threat perceptions because they convey a powerful signal of a country's military posture. At the same time deployments are an indication of mobilization capabilities, and therefore can be an important element in creating an almost permanent strategic surprise capability, if the deployments are close enough to expected operational areas. One of the serious problems in shaping an Indian response to the

1986–87 incident on the Sino-Indian border was the perception by India of a significantly increased Chinese force level in Tibet.

The situation on the Indo-Pakistani borders is symbolic of the problem. Pakistan's two armored strike corps are located at Kharian (a base 40 km from the border with India) and Multan (140 km from the border). A third armored division is believed to have been raised and located around Bahawalpur—a mere 90 km from the international border. Thus the mobilization period for an armored strike formation is very short indeed. Even the movement of these divisions for routine exercises is bound to be watched with great suspicion by India. The two Indian armored divisions, on the other hand, are deployed 250 km and nearly 800 km by road or rail from the international border, respectively. This asymmetry has always been a source of concern to India, and is an important element in threat perceptions.

Pakistan has routinely claimed its lack of geographical depth as a serious handicap to rearranging such deployments. However, the critical element is the time taken to deploy forward; and although it may not be possible to arrive at an equal figure for both countries' deployments, there is a need for some compatibility between the two. This criteria could form the basis for reviewing peacetime deployments. Deployments set back behind major rivers would further help. Similar principles could apply to other components of military power.

It has also been suggested that all the cantonments in Pakistan are close to the Indian border, and hence the peacetime locations of major formations are close to the border. But even a cursory examination shows that substantive relocation of the major offensive (and hence the most threatening) armored strike formations is a feasible proposition, even in the existing cantonments. For example, one strike corps could be relocated to Mardan, Peshawar, or Kohat instead of Kharian. Similarly, the Multan strike corps could be relocated west of the Indus River, possibly in the area of Dera Ghazi Khan. The Bahawalpur strike formation could be shifted closer to Karachi.

Dislocation from the present situation and the consequent costs of such redeployments in peacetime locations will naturally be a factor. One way of meeting the financial burden of relocation could be through international finance and aid; such measures would serve a greater purpose than simply building up military capability.

Redeployments of forces across the Sino-Indian frontier are more problematic because of the terrain differences and the fact that the deployments on both sides are essentially infantry-centered forces. Thus the approach here has to rely more on political commitments based on the principle of mutual and equal security and the already agreed principle of maintaining peace and tranquility on the borders. Within the framework of these principles, it is possible to arrive at agreements for force reductions in the areas close to the line of control. Since technical verification will not be viable, reliance will have to be placed on politically binding commitments, joint mechanisms to deal with the problems of inadvertent or willful violations. Allowing trans-border movement of people, aerial reconnaissance, and regular sharing of data and information are some of the steps that would increase confidence in such CSBMs. The existing direction and pace of dialogue between India and China indicates the great promise and utility of such an approach.

Setting peacetime deployments adequately back from the borders would itself become an important indicator of reduced threat and risks. This is where exercises and maneuvers would have different implications than at present, when any exercise, especially by India, has been perceived/projected as a threat. At the same time, definitive measures are required to reduce the risk of surprise; and many of them are feasible. For example, aerial surveillance of areas extending up to 100 km inside each other's territory could be instituted. This would bring all forward deployments under surveillance, and adequate warning of any attempts to launch a major offensive would then be available. With such an agreement in force, there would be little chance of crises like those of 1987 and 1990 taking place.

The most important measure to support CSBMs would be reduction in offensive forces. Broad consensus on what constitutes "offensive" weapons is now available through the CFE Treaty. There seems little reason why the two sides cannot mutually agree to cutbacks on the order of one thousand tanks, four hundred heavy artillery, four hundred ICVs, and agreed numbers of strike aircraft each, and abolition of armed helicopters. This magnitude of cutbacks would take the two countries to their pre-1971 levels,[23] and would help to reduce the threat perceptions and force levels without compromising the security of either side. If a fixed-quantity agreement is not acceptable, other bases, like equal proportions or reductions to fixed numbers to maintain what Stephen Cohen has called a "balanced imbalance," could be considered.

The wars between India and Pakistan have been some of the most restrained ones in the twentieth century. The philosophy of restraint is one of the most powerful safeguards against dangerous military activities, and hence needs to be encouraged. Institutionalization of restraints on war would be a major CSBM. Thus the agreement for non-attack on nuclear installations should be extended, at an early date, to include population centers and economic targets.

Miliary-Related Risks Past wars between Pakistan and India were preceded by guerrilla war or militant activities. Even the 1962 Sino-Indian war was preceded by clashes that, at least on the Indian side, involved non-military, para-police organizations. It is therefore important to pay attention to military-related activities that tend to enhance the dangers and risks of military confrontation.

The role and impact of guerrilla warfare (or low-intensity conflict, as it has come to be called) was discussed earlier. Such conflict has been perceived by many countries to be a "low-cost option" short of open warfare, and received both legitimacy and a boost in the Afghan war. State-of-the-art techniques and technology of unconventional war were fine-tuned over a decade in the conflict between the two superpowers; the combatants—and more important, managers of the war—simply belonged to other states.[24] As it is, we may already be seeing an increased incidence of irregular warfare (as opposed to regular, military-to-military wars); all the twenty-six armed conflicts going on in the world during 1993 were of the irregular, low-intensity, unconventional type.

The critical factor for the efficacy of future CSBMs will be the management of such military-related activities and forestalling their escalation to regular military conflicts. The foundation of this level of conflict lies in factors such as ideology, politico-miliary strategic doctrines, and the type of weapons and forces needed for prosecuting such conflicts. The first two factors have already been discussed.

The proliferation of small arms and minor weapons has made it easier to prosecute irregular, low-intensity wars. The wars in Vietnam and Afghanistan have given a strong boost to the qualitative and quantitative growth of such weaponry. These weapons—including arms of up to 50 caliber, sophisticated shoulder-fired surface-to-air missiles, land mines, high-rate-of-fire machine guns, very high energy explosives, and modern communication sets—now provide the means to sustain armed conflict at levels of low intensity but high lethality. Allowing, abetting, and encouraging the proliferation of small arms and minor weapons and their transfer across borders has emerged as one of the most dangerous military activities in the contemporary world.

The problem, of course, is that such proliferation has been consciously pursued by states in search of strategic policy objectives, in addition to trade through normal, grey, and black markets. Drug money provides another means to buy and transfer such weapons. Retrenchment in military power, especially in Eastern Europe, the former Soviet Union, and China, has made large stocks of surplus weapons available to those with the means to purchase them. During the cold war, the United States, Saudi Arabia, the Soviet Union, China, and other countries pumped huge quantities of small and minor weapons into the region. Pakistan was a conduit for U.S.-supported arms supplies of which a mere 40 percent reached the Mujahideen. The Soviets left behind massive supplies of sophisticated weaponry in Afghanistan. Massive quantities of such weapons now exist in the Pakistan-Afghanistan region, creating a dangerous situation in which these weapons are used to wage transnational wars. There is extensive evidence of the use of Afghan war-surplus weapons in the proxy wars against India in Punjab and Kashmir. Pakistan's active involvement in terrorist acts abroad finally led the United States to place it on the watch list of states sponsoring terrorism abroad. Since 1989, trained militants and sophisticated weapons have been pumped into the Indian state of Jammu and Kashmir; recoveries include upward of ten thousand AK-series Kalashnikov assault rifles, machine guns, rocket-launchers with over a million rounds of ammunition, and hundreds of sophisticated communication sets and detonators.

The problem that arises from the availability of such weapons is that governments have rapidly lost their traditional monopoly over the instruments of violence. The spread of these weapons not only threatens to destabilize states, but seriously undermines peace and security in society itself. Such highly lethal weaponry provides the means to pursue ideologies and political aims through violence. These weapons are the primary tool of terrorists and militants—from Mr. Kansi outside the gates of CIA headquarters, to Somali warlords, Serbian fighters, Afghan Mujahideen, and the insurgents in Kashmir and Punjab. Nevertheless, states must continue to bear the responsibility for the actions of non-state actors.

Another military-related activity that has aggravated tensions in the past is the hijacking of Indian civilian aircraft. Two more notable instances were the February 1971 and August 1984 hijackings of Indian Airlines planes to Pakistan. In the former case, the aircraft was torched at Lahore; in the second case, the unarmed hijackers received weapons in Lahore before the plane was allowed out of the country. Compared to nearly two dozen hijackings over the past two decades from India to Pakistan, there has been none in the reverse direction. But it is still necessary to establish joint procedures for action in such cases, especially to ensure that the hijacking is not allowed to contribute to bilateral tension.

The proliferation of small arms and minor weapons poses a greater threat to peace and security than perhaps even nuclear proliferation. Nuclear weapons may or may not get used, but small arms are being used every day, threatening the peace and security of society itself in addition to undermining the state, especially when linked to ideological motivations. CSBMs in this context will not be easy to institute. As in other areas, a degree of cooperation with the adversary is necessary. Some of the measures that could be instituted between India and Pakistan (where the problem is the most acute, but which can be the model for other agreements also) are briefly noted below:

1. A bilateral agreement to curb the spread and proliferation of small arms and minor weapons to non-state actors. This would be a logical corollary to the SAARC agreement to curb terrorism.

2. Review and revision of national gun-control laws in the two countries so as to completely deny individuals access to such weapons. Where important persons require protection with such weapons it should be provided by the state. Possession of such weapons by individuals should attract severe exemplary punishment.
3. A concerted drive to recover such weapons within each country and place them under strict state control.
4. The sharing of information on current holdings of such weapons by states.
5. Dialogue on improved border management to restrict flow of arms.
6. Establishment of a register for small arms and minor weapons (on the lines of the UN Register for Arms Transfer), which should also include national production.

Risk-Prone Activities Border incidents and violations have the potential to escalate tension and conflict. These assume a particularly dangerous dimension when they occur across cease-fire lines and lines of control, particularly when there is no agreement to maintain peace and tranquility across them (like the Sino-Indian agreement), or when one side is seen to disassociate itself from an earlier commitment to do so(as is the case with the Indo-Pakistani agreement of 1972). Thus it is necessary to establish binding political commitments to the inviolability of borders and lines of actual control, regardless of any variances in perception, differences in interpretation, or claims across these lines. It should be noted that the inviolability of borders was a fundamental element of the Helsinki process, on which most of the successful CSBMs in Europe were constructed; the deviation in the former Yugoslavia triggered unmanageable conflict in the region.

Military exercises are traditionally considered one of the dangerous activities that increase the risk of conflict; at times they are aggravated by an overreaction due to assumptions of worse-case scenarios. In recent years military exercises and maneuvers by China, India, and Pakistan have been perceived by the other side as intriguing at the minimum and threatening at times. It has often been difficult for these countries to assess accurately the intentions of the others. Such situations contain a high risk of miscalculation. Bilateral agreements to give notice of exercises and maneuvers could greatly reduce the potential for overreaction. Some agreements on advance notification have already been reached between India and Pakistan following the CSBM package proposed by India in 1990. Limitations on the scale of military exercises in the regions close to the borders, as well as prenotification of exercises are the obvious solution. Such agreements will continue to suffer from significant limitations, however, as long as major formations, especially mobile armored ones, are located close to the borders during peacetime.

Nuclear and Missile Risks The ambiguous nuclear postures of Pakistan and India make it difficult to devise measures to reduce the risks normally associated with nuclear weapons and accidents. It would be useful for both sides to shed their ambiguity, but given the international situation and the perceived need for a nuclear option on both sides, it is highly unlikely that either side will move in that direction. However, there is significant potential for enhancing stability by limiting nuclear weapons capability. At the same time it should be possible (at least conceptually) to marginalize the role of nuclear weapons.

An important element in both strategies is the attitude toward the use and utility of nuclear weapons. China has always maintained that it would not be the first to use nuclear weapons. India and Pakistan should make similar commitments. Since neither country admits possessing nuclear weapons, the logical agreement to reach would be one of no first use of their nuclear capabilities against each other. Such an agreement would reduce the risks normally associated with nuclear weapons without requiring any confirmation of the possession of such weapons.

The countries could further circumscribe the potential role of nuclear weapons through bilateral and multilateral agreements not to attack each other's population centers, economic targets, and chemical industries (which could produce disastrous fallout like that in the accident at Bhopal in 1984). Such agreements would be a logical extension of the Indo-Pakistani agreement not to attack each other's nuclear installations, which came into force in 1993. A regional convention calling for the outlawing of nuclear weapons as a crime against humanity would also help to delegitimize nuclear weapons.

More than fifteen thousand ballistic missiles have been fired since 1943 in various wars, and every one of them carried a conventional warhead. Ballistic missiles, by their very nature, are highly destabilizing. The uncertainties about the type of warhead they might carry increase this instability. The continued existence of such missiles in the absence of any credible defense against them is a powerful incentive for proliferation. China, for example, has deployed thousands of ballistic missiles, and they have been deployed increasingly in other countries in the region. Both Pakistan and India have the capability to deploy such missiles. In this context, it is difficult to agree with the view that missile tests constitute a dangerous military activity, at least in South Asia. India gives notice of its missile tests internationally. Furthermore, all India's missile tests have been conducted in the Bay of Bengal, away from Chinese or Pakistani territory. It would nevertheless be useful to formalize a regional agreement whereby all missile tests are announced in advance and are not carried out in the direction of the other countries.

Implementation Problems and Prospects

One of the key prerequisites for the implementation of CSBMs is greater transparency. The lack of transparency lies at the root of misperception. Legitimate concerns about the security of defense information arise in all countries. But a great deal of transparency is possible without compromising national security. Substantive changes will be required to increase the transparency of military postures; a start could be made by publishing on a regular basis comprehensive details of defense expenditures and military activities, exchanging information on major weapons system acquisitions, and providing schedules of military exercises, maneuvers, etc.

Given the high level of mutual mistrust, especially between India and Pakistan, any CSBM agreement would still raise the problem of verification. CSBMs could rapidly become counterproductive if violations start taking place and cannot be arrested in time. But both India and Pakistan have very limited technical means of verification, and it is highly unlikely that third party assistance in this field would be acceptable to either side. This is why there is a need for countries such as the United States to support the strengthening of national technical means of verification in India and Pakistan. Increased verification capabilities would make it easier for both countries to consider the Open Skies proposals favorably, at least up to 100 km from the borders.

Finally, we must address what perhaps is the most crucial question: Should improvement in political relations and "political CSBMs" precede military CSBMs? The optimum answer, as in most cases, lies somewhere in the middle. CSBMs that are more technical and military in nature will have limited potential unless there is a corresponding improvement in mutual confidence and trust in the political domain. Until such confidence is built up, states tend to agree only to such measures that are less substantive and more cosmetic, and to those that do not require giving up any perceived advantage. Only in the case of activities or areas that have an obvious element of risk that the dangers involved may not be manageable can we expect military CSBMs to readily precede political ones. And it will remain debatable whether such measures really improve mutual confidence or whether they only help to stabilize some particular aspect of the confrontation. The case of the Indo-Pakistani agreement on non-attack of nuclear installations readily comes to mind in this regard. Proposed by India in 1985 because of Pakistan's perception of a threat of attacks on Kahuta, it took over eight years to be hammered out and implemented. In the meantime, we have seen relations between the two countries plunge to their lowest levels.

What is required most is a comprehensive approach whereby the improvement of political relations and mutual trust and confidence in the overall policies of potentially hostile countries remains the central objective, even of the military-technical CSBMs. In specific areas the latter should receive greater emphasis, so that strategic stability is enhanced. The example and experience of the Helsinki process and approach would be highly valuable in this regard.

Notes

1. The military conflicts between Pakistan and India since independence include the following:

1947–48: Jammu and Kashmir; irregular warfare through tribal invasion escalated into full-scale war.

April 1965: Rann of Kutch; border skirmishes.

Aug.–Sep. 1965: Jammu and Kashmir; Pakistani guerrilla operations launched on August 1, escalated into full-scale war when Pakistan launched operation Grand Slam on September 1, 1965.

1971: Civil war in East Pakistan, escalated into regular war; resulted in creation of Bangladesh.

1984–87: Saltoro Ridge conflict (west of Siachen Glacier).

1984–92: Proxy war in Indian Punjab. Significant cutback in Pakistani support to militancy in 1989 helped control the conflict.

1988– : Proxy war in Kashmir, beginning in July 1988; escalated in December 1989.

For a more complete discussion, see chapter 1 in this volume, and also Šumit Ganguly, *The Origins of War in South Asia*, 2nd ed. (Boulder, Co.: Westview, 1994).

2. For a Pakistani account of the 1947–48 war, see Maj. Gen. Akbar Khan, "The Kashmir War 1947–48," *Defence Journal* (Karachi), September 1983; for the 1965 war, see the then army commander-in-chief Gen. M. Musa, *My Version* (Lahore: Waji-d Alis, 1983), and Field Marshal Michael Carver, *War since 1945* (London: Weidenfeld and Nicolson, 1980), pp. 223–24; for the 1971 war, see Sidiq Salik, *Witness to Surrender* (Karachi: Oxford University Press, 1977), and Maj. Gen. Fazal Muqueem Khan, *Pakistan's Crisis in Leadership* (Islamabad: National Book Foundation, 1973).

3. Stephen P. Cohen, *The Pakistan Army* (New Delhi: Himalayan Books, 1984), p. 139.

4. The Pakistan army's main strike corps, normally stationed at Kharian (40 km from the border), had moved out to operational positions on the border by December 1986. In mid-January 1987, the second and only other strike corps was observed moving out of its peacetime location of Multan to the international border, where Pakistan has a salient across the river Sutlej. India's one strike corps was in its peacetime deployment in Haryana-Punjab, over 200 km from the border; elements of India's second (and only other) corps were beginning to move out of their peacetime location near Jhansi (800 km from the border) for exercise Brasstacks, which was scheduled for late February/early March. It is in this context that infantry units from across India were quickly moved to defensive positions on the border. By January 24 the Multan strike corps was returning to its barracks and the crisis was over.

5. The most colorful Western article on the subject is Seymour Hersh, "On the Nuclear Edge," *New Yorker*, March 29, 1993.

6. Interview with Ammanulla Khan, president of the JKLF, in *Newsline* (Pakistan), February 1990.

7. See interview with the chief of staff of the Indian army, General V. N. Sharma, "It's all bluff and bluster," *Economic Times*, May 18, 1993, p. 7.

8. Kalevi J. Holsti, *Peace and War: Armed Conflicts and International Order, 1648–1989* (Cambridge, U.K.: Cambridge University Press, 1991).

9. Christina Lamb, *Waiting for Allah* (London: Hamish Hamilton, 1991), p. 262.

10. Hamza Alavi, "The State in a Crisis: Class and State," in Hassan Gardezi and Jamil Rashid, eds., *Pakistan: The Roots of Dictatorship* (London: Zed Press, 1983), pp. 57–58.

11. Omar Noman, *The Political Economy of Pakistan 1947–85* (London: PKI, dist. by Routledge & Kegan Paul, 1988), p. 9.

12. Lamb, *Waiting for Allah*, p. 270.

13. For a Pakistani exposition on the subject, see Hamood-ur-Rahman, *Reflections on Islam* (Lahore: Islamic Book Foundation, 1983), especially the chapter "Ideology of Pakistan." In another chapter the author argues that the Islamic system provides for the separation of powers by "allocation of Legislation to Almighty; Executive to the Community and Judicature to the Qazis" (p. 174).

14. Shirin Tahir-Kheli, "In Search of Identity: Islam and Pakistan's Foreign Policy," in Adeed Dawisha, ed., *Islam in Foreign Policy* (Cambridge, U.K.: Cambridge University Press, 1983), p. 81.

15. Emile Sahliyeh, ed., *Religious Resurgence and Politics in the Contemporary World* (Albany: State University of New York Press, 1990).

16. Evan Luard, *The Blunted Sword: The Erosion of Military Power in Modern World Politics* (London: I. B. Tauris, 1988).

17. Jasjit Singh, "Politics of Mistrust," in Jasjit Singh, ed., *India-Pakistan: The Crisis of Relationship* (New Delhi: Lancer International, 1990).

18. K. C. Pant, "Philosophy of Indian Defence," in Jasjit Singh and V. Vekaric, eds., *Non-Offensive Defense: The Search for Equal Security* (New Delhi: Lancer International, 1989). For Pakistan's doctrine, see Cohen, *The Pakistan Army*, and Mushahid Hussain, "The Strike of a True Believer: Pakistan Tests New Doctrine," *Jane's Defence Weekly* 12, no. 22 (December 2, 1989), pp. 1230–31.

19. Cohen, *The Pakistan Army*, p. 145.

20. Brigadier S. K. Malik, *The Quaranic Concept of War* (Lahore: WajidAlis, 1978), pp. 58–59.

21. Cohen, *The Pakistan Army*, p. 65.

22. Maj. Gen. D. Banerjee, "Modernisation of China's Military Doctrine," *Strategic Analysis* 12, no. 9 (December 1989).

23. There is support for the idea among strategic experts of Pakistan and India. See for example Nazir Kamal, "Defensive Security in Regions other than Europe," *Disarmament* (UN) 15, no. 4 (1992), pp. 136–52.

24. Brig. Mohhamad Yousaf and Maj. Mark Adkin, *The Bear Trap: Afghanistan's Untold Story* (Lahore: Jang, 1992).

10

Crisis Management and Confidence Building

C. Raja Mohan

Two major politico-military crises in the last seven years are widely believed to have brought India and Pakistan to the brink of a full-scale war. The first crisis resulted from Pakistan's military response to India's Brasstacks military exercise during the winter of 1986–87. The second crisis between India and Pakistan, the so-called spring 1990 crisis, was also seen by some analysts as having the potential to escalate into a nuclear exchange. Some members of the U.S. intelligence community have argued that these crises brought the world closer to a nuclear war than it had been at any time since the Cuban missile crisis in 1962. Although other American actors involved in the management of the 1990 crisis have discounted this assessment, there clearly was potentially dangerous nuclear activity during the 1990 crisis that needs to be fully understood.

Irrespective of final judgments on the nature and gravity of these two crises, it is essential that New Delhi and Islamabad pay greater attention to creating more systematic and institutionalized mechanisms for managing future political and military crises. Six factors make this imperative. First, the emergence of real but undeclared nuclear capabilities in both countries has made the danger of crises escalating to nuclear conflict a real probability. The U.S. intelligence community has publicly announced its belief that both countries could assemble nuclear weapons in short order. Coupled with the shortage of official and public discussion in both countries regarding how this nuclear factor could interact with military and political crises between the two countries, there is a strong tendency to reach gloomy forecasts regarding the future of Indo-Pakistani relations.

Second, recent years have witnessed a tragic deterioration in Indo-Pakistani relations, probably to the lowest level in their independent histories.

Even basic civility in the conduct of bilateral relations has become impossible to maintain. Attacks on and harassment of each other's diplomats have become routine. The treatment of each other's citizens has become unpredictable. Moreover, the events that followed the demolition of the mosque in Ayodhya in December 1992 have brought unbearable strain to the relationship.

Third, it does not appear that the question of Kashmir, the basic source of political tension between India and Pakistan, is amenable to a mutually acceptable solution in the near future. Both countries have far too much at stake and far too little maneuvering room to negotiate an amicable compromise. Islamabad cannot hope to wrest Kashmir out of India through military means. And New Delhi is finding it difficult to return the Kashmir valley to normalcy and revive the stalled political process in the state.

Fourth, despite recent pressure for reducing military expenditures and cutting down the size of armed forces, it does not seem realistic to expect a significant scaling down of the military competition between India and Pakistan. On the contrary, both countries are on the verge of deploying advanced weapons systems, such as short-range missiles, that could even reduce military stability.

Fifth, the domestic politics of both countries have reached a stage of extreme fluidity and instability. The era of strong political leadership appears to have past; a succession of weak political leaderships has taken root. Both countries are experiencing a rise of extreme religious ideas and movements that have helped harden domestic public opinion against the other country. These religious movements have also acquired the power to block even the minimal adjustments required for a stable military situation on the border.

And finally, the end of the cold war has disoriented the traditional foreign policies of both countries, resulting in greater insecurity in the region. New Delhi and Islamabad are currently in the process of redefining their relations with the great powers, and this process is proving to be more complex than most have assumed. In fact, although the disappearance of the Soviet Union has in some ways strengthened the arm of American diplomacy in the region, both India and Pakistan have been more defiant than malleable in responding to American attempts to coax or coerce a regional arms control and nonproliferation regime. Defiance of the United States on key national security issues has become a political necessity for the very survival of the weak governments in both India and Pakistan, thus preventing a more sustained and fruitful dialogue on tension reduction and confidence building.

With no reasonable prospects for improving relations, the persistence of ideological and political disputes, and the continuing military instability, decision makers in both countries may find it necessary to devote significant energies toward the management of crises and the avoidance of war. For the international community, too, achieving regional military stability and arms control have become important objectives given the new emphasis on preventing the proliferation of weapons of mass destruction.

This chapter first briefly delineates some of the basic notions of the doctrine of crisis management and the problems associated with it. It looks at some lessons learned from the Soviet-American experience with crisis management and confidence building. Next, it examines the problem of strategic stability in the context of the small but undeclared nuclear arsenals of India and Pakistan. The final section looks at some of the confidence- and security-building measures (CSBMs) and institutions relating to crisis management that the two sides could consider as part of a larger confidence-building regime.

Crisis Management

Crisis management is an activity that political leaders, diplomats, and soldiers have been engaged in since the emergence of organized state conflict. In the twentieth century, however, two factors have made crisis management both necessary and vital. The first is the advent of the nuclear age and the devastating social annihilation that could result from the use of nuclear weapons. The onset of the nuclear era has dramatically enhanced the need to manage international crises below the threshold of war. The second factor is the increasing recognition that normal organizational and operational processes come under severe stress during international crises.

Crises are extraordinary situations between peace and war where conflict between the national interests of two or more countries calls for action in a compressed time frame and involves the use or threat of force. Such crises require coordination between military and political leaders in each country and often involve other nations as well.

Effective crisis management involves complex decision making to resolve the basic tension between the goals of defending the national interests thought to be at stake and avoiding military conflict or unnecessary escalation. The objective of each side is not necessarily the avoidance of war at any cost; to attain that objective, one state need only yield to its adversary's desires. Crises happen, persist, and recur because states participate in them, choosing to defend their interests rather than acquiesce. A state could also attempt to go beyond protecting its interests; it could try to advance those interests in a crisis, by seeking to gain a relative advantage without risking escalation to an unacceptable level.

In pursuit of their goals in a crisis, states must have sufficient military capabilities as well as the political will to use them. These capabilities and the will to resort to them must also be communicated to the adversary.

Signaling resolve may raise the risks of war, but nations often take such risks to protect their fundamental interests in the hope that they can control the risks and avoid unwanted costs.

Decision makers face a number of tasks and challenges during crisis management. The tasks are, in essence, information collection, assessment, definition of options, deliberation and decision making, and execution of the decisions made. The great number of ambiguous signals generated during a crisis makes faulty perceptions based on incomplete or inaccurate information the biggest problem in crisis management. The enormous expansion of the ability to generate intelligence information has not solved the problem of information management during a crisis. Too much information tends to crowd the judgment, prudence, and wisdom of decision makers during a crisis.

Even with good information, decision making remains a major challenge. In the United States, for instance, the frequent turnover of top-level decision makers and the inexperience of political leaders in crisis diplomacy are seen as two significant drawbacks. Decision making in a crisis also involves conflicts over knowledge, expertise, and authority that must be resolved quickly and decisively. This need is counteracted by the tendency for "group think," a reluctance to look at alternate viewpoints, and an unwillingness to confront evidence in favor of other views. Thus, an efficient balance between consensus and divergence of views is an important requirement for decision making in a crisis.

Civil-military relations also come under enormous stress during a crisis. There is a basic tension between the importance of civilian control over military operations at the tactical level and avoidance of the dangers of civilian micromanagement of military forces during a crisis. The intense physical stress of a crisis is also known to degrade the skills of key decision makers, making crisis management unpredictable.[1]

Communication between adversaries during a crisis is another important element of crisis management. This communication includes regular diplomatic interaction, the public pronouncements of both states, and the use of the military idiom to signal one other (i.e., the movement of troops, the shifting of forces to higher alert levels, etc.). The escalation or de-escalation of crises is a product of the communication between adversaries, whether intentional or not and whether understood correctly or not. Communication can be difficult for technical, cultural, structural, and psychological reasons and because signals can be ambiguous, confusing, or even provocative. During the Cuban missile crisis, for example, Moscow and Washington found that they had no reliable technical means of direct communication, and certain key messages were delayed by hours.

Communication through the military idiom creates the classic security dilemma during crises. Military actions that one side takes to enhance its security are often perceived by the other side as a threat that requires some countermeasure; such a response, in turn, is seen as a threat by the other side. Incorrect anticipation of the reaction can compound the problems of misperception and can lead to an escalating action-reaction dynamic—a "deadly spiral."

The use of military force to signal political resolve, commitments, and intentions is a dangerous but unavoidable element of crisis management. Military alerts, movements of troops, and other actions are integral to coercive diplomacy and crisis management. But such military actions often result in escalation and competitive risk taking. This kind of crisis diplomacy entails two risks in particular: the first is a growing perception that war is inevitable, thus encouraging the consideration of preemption; the second is that the adversaries lose control of the situation, thus stumbling into an inadvertent war.

A number of political and operational requirements for crisis management have been identified. Politically, the limitation of objectives pursued in a crisis and the limitation of the means employed on behalf of those objectives are crucial in managing and defusing crises. Operationally, each side must maintain top-level civilian control over military options; the tempo of military movements must be slowed down in order to provide for diplomatic exchanges; military movements must be coordinated into the diplomatic strategy; military signals of resolve must have consistently limited diplomatic objectives; moves that give the impression of a resort to large-scale warfare, given an incentive for preemption, need to be avoided; options that signal a way out of the crisis other than through military action should be chosen; and proposals should be compatible with the opponent's fundamental interests. Other scholars have provided similar rules of thumb for crisis management. Hillard Roderic offers four general lessons: slow down the leadership's reactions; ensure correct perceptions; ensure full control of the military; and be alert for unpredictable events.[2]

Clearly, there is no "how to" guide for policy makers engaged in international crisis management. No theory of international relations can provide such a guide to the practitioners. But experience and a substantial body of literature on crises and their management can provide some useful first steps in exploring the dangers of escalation into wars that no one wants.

Nuclear Crisis Management and CSBMs

The widespread interest in crisis management following the Cuban missile crisis may not have produced a general theory with guidelines for the future management of nuclear crises between the superpowers, but it did help generate intensive thinking about maintaining strategic stability between the nuclear arsenals of Moscow and Washington. The key question was how to stabilize nuclear deterrence during crises while reducing the risks of accidental or inadvertent war. This involved reducing the prospects for preemption, loss of control, and unwanted escalation, each of which could have lead to a nuclear war that neither side wanted. The management of the deterrent relationship between the former Soviet Union and the United States, in particular nuclear crisis management, became not only an important part of strategic thought in Washington, but a policy preoccupation as well. In the wake of the Cuban missile crisis, the two sides embarked on a course of instituting a whole range of confidence- and security-building measures (CSBMs) to stabilize nuclear deterrence and prevent the drift toward an unwanted nuclear exchange during a crisis. These measures were described earlier in this volume.

The various arms control treaties implemented between the United States and the Soviet Union can be usefully separated into two categories: structural and operational.[3] Whereas the objective of the former is force reduction, the latter is preoccupied with regulating certain military activities. The agreements on reducing the Conventional Forces in Europe (CFE) can be seen as structural arms control and the agreements flowing out of the Conference on Security and Cooperation in Europe (CSCE) are essentially operational arms control. Extrapolating from these and other leading definitions, CSBMs can be defined as "those operational arms control measures that are intended to reduce or eliminate misperceptions while fostering greater military transparency, all in pursuit of the ultimate goal of reducing the chance for military conflict or escalation."[4]

Over the last three decades a large number of East-West CSBMs, bilateral as well as multilateral, have been concluded.[5] But despite the apparent success of the U.S.-Soviet CSBMs, one must not forget the primary limitation of CSBMs. As James Goodby, who lead the U.S. delegation to the Stockholm CSBM negotiations, noted, "generally speaking, confidence-building measures are useful when neither side wants a war. Will they prevent a war someone does want? The answer is obviously no."[6] However, even with this in mind, the effectiveness of CSBMs in preventing and managing potential crises during the cold war cannot be discounted.

The efforts to improve crisis management during the cold war were not limited to negotiating reliable communication channels and other CSBMs between the superpowers. In fact, the bilateral effort was marginal in comparison with the energies that the United States devoted to unilaterally improving its ability for managing crises. These efforts involved debating the means for reducing the vulnerability of its armed forces, strengthening the command and control of nuclear forces, preventing the accidental or unauthorized use of nuclear weapons, and improving the technological and organizational elements of the decision making structure.

Did the institution of the CSBMs discussed above improve the overall ability of the superpowers to avoid war? This question cannot be answered definitively. If the first two decades of the nuclear relationship between Washington and Moscow were marked by recurring crises, the next two were remarkably free of crisis, despite the oscillation of the relationship between detente and confrontation. Since the Middle East crisis of 1973, when Soviet and American forces were placed on alert, there has been no major nuclear crisis. Clearly, both sides learned to respect certain broad rules of prudence in their relationship. But the very process of thinking about crisis management and the institutionalization of CSBMs contributed to this learning of nuclear coexistence.

Nuclear Deterrence and Strategic Stability in South Asia

The central strategic concerns of superpower nuclear crisis management, such as preemption, loss of control, and miscalculated escalation, also happen to be the chief justifications in American strategic thinking for preventing the spread of weapons of mass destruction to the developing world. In a recent survey of the American nonproliferation literature, Peter Lavoy listed ten specific concerns about nuclear weapons proliferation:

1. The vulnerability of new nuclear forces invites military preemption
2. The command and control arrangements in the emerging nuclear states are inadequate, thus increasing the prospects for accidental or inadvertent launch and detonation of nuclear weapons
3. The tenuous arrangements for command and control threaten the loss of nuclear weapons to either terrorists or disgruntled elements in the armed forces
4. Military competition among new nuclear powers creates "arms race instability," increasing the likelihood of war
5. Given the underlay of ideological, political, and territorial disputes, a conventional war could quickly escalate into a nuclear exchange
6. An ambitious Third World leader might resort to nuclear coercion or war
7. New nuclear states will assist other states toward proliferation
8. As a consequence of (7) there could be a chain reaction leading to the spread of weapons of mass destruction
9. Nuclear proliferation among conflict-prone states would draw the superpowers into a cataclysmic nuclear war
10. The spread of nuclear weapons to new states would inhibit military intervention by the United States against the new nuclear states, thus complicating American regional security planning.[7]

As we can see, the first six points relate to the sense that the balance of terror among the new nuclear states would be "delicate," making the dangers of preemption, escalation, and loss of control almost unmanageable among the new nuclear states. Underlying this thinking is the sense that the nascent nuclear powers may not adhere to rules of the "nuclear game." This basic conviction has guided policy formulation on issues of nonproliferation in general and South Asia in particular. In recent testimony before the Senate Committee on Governmental Affairs, the director of the Central Intelligence Agency said that "the arms race between India and Pakistan poses perhaps the most probable prospect for future use of weapons of mass destruction, including nuclear weapons.[8]

There has been a small but articulate school of thought in the United States that has challenged the basic assumptions of nonproliferation thinking.[9] These "nuclear realists," who make the case for "managing" proliferation as opposed to preventing it, have argued that nuclear weapons will induce caution among political and military decision makers, irrespective of the geographic and technological conditions of the security environment in question. It may be useful here to review the arguments and counterarguments between the "proliferation pessimists and deterrence optimists"[10] on the key issues relating to crisis management in a nuclear South Asia.

Prevention and Preemption

It is widely assumed that the proliferation of nuclear weapons increases the temptation for preventive actions by threatened states in order to nip in the bud the nuclear activities of their rivals. The Israeli destruction in 1980 of the Osirak reactor in Iraq is the classic example of this preventive action. In the mid-1980s, there was significant concern in Pakistan that India could launch a similar preventive attack against Kahuta to destroy the emerging nuclear weapons capability of Pakistan.[11]

The mainstream argument in the West is that these temptations for preventive actions are real and that they increase tensions and conflict among emerging nuclear nations. But this need not always be true. There is no evidence that China considered a preventive action against the emerging nuclear capabilities of India. After the 1974 Indian nuclear explosion, India and China did not drive themselves into fears of preemption, despite their hostile relationship. In the Indo-Pakistani context, rather than contemplating a preventive war against Pakistani nuclear capabilities, India proposed an agreement in 1985 prohibiting attacks on each other's nuclear facilities in an effort to assuage Pakistani concerns about Indian moves toward nuclear prevention.

American worries regarding preemption are rooted in a strong analytical argument. It is believed that, given the small size and inherent vulnerability the emerging nuclear forces, they invite preemption, increase the fears of a surprise attack, and foster crisis instability. It has been argued that New Delhi and Islamabad may have "strong incentives to strike first in a severe crisis or conventional war in anticipation of preemption by the other," given the significant asymmetries between Indian and Pakistani capabilities.[12] The country with inferior capabilities, in order to prevent preemption, may want to attack first, while the one with superior capabilities, knowing the vulnerabilities of the other and their tendency to preempt, may likewise want to attack first.

Other analysts disagree, arguing that small nuclear forces could be preempted "only if the would-be attacker knows that the intended victim's warheads are few in number, knows their exact number and locations, and knows that they will not be moved or fired before they are struck."[13] The costs of incomplete prevention or preemption are so high, it is argued, that states will be inhibited by "the impossibility of knowing for sure that a disarming strike will totally destroy the opposing force and in the immense destruction even a few warheads can wreak."[14] The Indian and Pakistani leaders are not unaware of the costs and consequences of a nuclear strike and can make as rational an assessment as any one else in the world. Dispersal of nuclear weapons is the simplest means of reducing the incentives for surprise attack, by ensuring that a sufficient retaliatory force survives a first strike.

Loss of Control

The ability to disperse nuclear capabilities, which is so central to assuring a retaliatory capability and the stability of deterrence, presents questions of reliable and responsible command and control of nuclear weapons. Clearly the tasks of dispersal and control raise conflicting demands. Can the new nuclear states, with their primitive technological capability, manage their nuclear forces? Many analysts assume that new nuclear nations would not be able to develop adequate command and control systems to control their forces, thus allowing escalation and increasing the prospects for an accidental or inadvertent war. The arguments along this line envision a range of issues and scenarios.

One is that the new nations may not be competent enough to handle complex technological systems thus increasing the risk of a catastrophic accident. Two, terrorist groups in these countries could seize control of nuclear weapons. Three, ethnic tensions in these countries could weaken the central government's control of nuclear weapons. Four, it is far more difficult to guard against unauthorized use of nuclear weapons. Five, a severe tension between civilian and military authorities may result in the loss of civilian control over nuclear weapons. Six, a loss of control within the military to lower level commanders may occur. Seven, there may be the inability to manage the tensions between "positive control" (i.e., the ability to deliver the nuclear weapons when required) and "negative control" (i.e., preventing the unauthorized use of nuclear weapons).

In approaching the problem of loss of control in South Asia, it may be wise not to presume that reliable command and control would be automatic. Nor is it necessary to accept the alarmist assessments of traditional nonproliferation thinking. There are dangers in uncritically extrapolating to South Asia the ideas and concepts related to command and control that arose in the context of the Soviet-American nuclear arms race.

Strategic thinking in the subcontinent does not imitate American strategic thinking in relation to the size and operational requirements of stable deterrence. The superpowers believed gargantuan arsenals were necessary to satisfy the operational requirements of stable deterrence. New Delhi and Islamabad do not have the necessity or the capability to create such large arsenals; instead they depend upon the doctrine of minimum deterrence. Thus their requirements of command and control are not of the same magnitude. Unlike the superpowers, India and Pakistan need not integrate their nuclear weapons into their armed forces during peacetime; nor do they need to deploy these weapons worldwide on land and at sea.

Furthermore, there are no nightmares about 'bolt-from-the-blue' attacks in South Asia. As crises and confrontations evolve over long enough periods of time, both countries should have ample time to prepare for a nuclear exchange. India and Pakistan could keep their nuclear weapons in unassembled form, separate from their delivery systems, thus greatly reducing the dangers of loss of control.

This need not preclude greater discussion of the issues relating to loss of control within and among the strategic communities of India and Pakistan, however. Clearly, the confidence surrounding control and stability of deterrence is not going to be automatic, and it needs to be generated over time. The physical safety of nuclear material and nuclear weapons, the prevention of accidental detonations, the creation of reliable operating procedures, and the education of political leaders and the military leadership regarding the control of nuclear forces are some of the issues that the strategic elites in the subcontinent need to consider.

One major issue in relation to loss of control remains to be discussed in the political context of South Asia: civil-military relations. A recent study suggests that "the more stable the civil-military relations, the more delegative the command and control system; the more volatile the civil-military relations, the more assertive the command and control system."[15] This typology presents a number of problems in assessing the situation in South Asia. In India, where there are conditions of stable civil-military relations and the civil control of the military is unchallenged, we should expect a control system with a bias toward positive control or delegation to the military. In reality, however, the Indian military has remained almost entirely outside the nuclear decision making realm. Even when headed by General Sundarji, the well-known proponent of the Indian nuclear option, there is no evidence to suggest that the Indian armed forces have gained any influence in government debates concerning nuclear weapons. This in fact may be a major problem in India, where the armed forces are not encouraged to think about nuclear weapons, the doctrine of employment, or the relevance of arms control. India may have carried its doctrine of nuclear ambiguity to an extreme, as there is no substantive thinking within its key institutions on a range of issues relating to nuclear weapons. General Sundarji, after retiring as chief of staff of the Indian army, said, "We do not have an integrated planning or command and control mechanism at the top. That's one of our conspicuous failures."[16]

In the case of Pakistan, the argument cited would suggest a tendency toward an assertive or negative control of nuclear weapons. The argument that volatile civil-military relations should lead to tighter controls over nuclear forces appears to be rational. It may have been the reality under the strong leadership of General Zia ul Haq, who as supreme leader of Pakistan most likely exercised strong control over nuclear policy and doctrine. But since Zia's death in 1988, there has been a fragmentation of political authority into an unstable troika of the president, the prime minister, and the army chief. In other words, there has been no clear sense of the nature of control over Pakistan's nuclear weapons program since the death of General Zia.

Indeed, in a 1992 interview, Benazir Bhutto implied that as prime minister she had little control over the nuclear program.[17] It has also been reported that during her visit to the United States in 1989, the Bush administration had arranged a briefing from the CIA director, who allegedly gave Bhutto more information on the Pakistani nuclear program than her own military was willing to report to her.[18] There is no need here to go into a detailed argument about the nature of civil-military relations in Pakistan and their implication for nuclear command and control in that country. However, greater transparency about the nature of control in Pakistan could be a useful step toward more confident crisis management on the subcontinent.

Escalation and De-escalation

Controlling escalation is one of the most important aspects of crisis management, as miscalculated escalation is one of the routes to a war that neither side wants. Many American analysts of South Asian affairs seem convinced that there was a significant military escalation during both winter 1986–87 and the spring 1990 Indo-Pakistani military crises. Many also believe that during the 1990 crisis, India and Pakistan came very close to a nuclear exchange. Moreover, it has been suggested that the American intervention through the Gates mission during the spring of 1990 helped defuse the nuclear crisis and prevent a war. Given continuing tensions between India and Pakistan, and the dismal state of their bilateral relations, there is widespread conviction in the West that the danger of a conventional conflict escalating to the nuclear level is real in the India subcontinent. However, many in the Indian subcontinent and a few in the United States have questioned the basis of this judgment. Clearly there is not enough authentic information regarding these crises to make a final assessment of the nature and evolution of these crises.

The 1986–87 crisis did involve a large Indian military exercise, Brasstacks, a corps-level triennial exercise conducted with some flair by the then Indian army chief, General Sundarji. In response to these Indian exercises, Pakistan deployed its army, including its armored forces, in forward positions. The Indian army in response occupied its traditional defensive positions, thus completing the escalation. It appears that elements of brinkmanship, crisis manipulation, and escalation were all present. However, the leadership in both countries was successful in de-escalating the crisis.

It was also during this crisis that we may have seen, for the first time, the unveiling of the nuclear factor. Pakistan chose the occasion of the crisis to hint at its nuclear weapons capabilities. At the peak of the crisis, an Indian journalist, Kuldip Nayar, was given access to A. Q. Khan, the head of the Pakistani nuclear weapons program. Dr. Khan allegedly suggested that Pakistan had succeeded in building the bomb and had gained a deterrent capability: "Nobody can undo Pakistan or take us for granted. We are here to stay and let it be clear that we shall use the bomb if our existence is threatened."[19] Indian strategic analysts saw this as an attempt to convey a nuclear signal at the peak of the crisis. But the story did not appear until March 1, 1987, by which time the crisis had largely subsided. Seymour Hersh has claimed that India had made its own nuclear moves during Brasstacks. He suggests that General Sundarji probably integrated tactical nuclear weapons into the exercises.[20] This appears to be a total misconception, however. There is little reason to believe that India had built tactical nuclear weapons, or for that matter that it had any nuclear weapons ready for use in 1987.

Seymour Hersh has attempted to make the most compelling case for the view that New Delhi and Islamabad were on the brink of a nuclear exchange during the 1990 crisis.[21] Prior to the appearance of the Hersh article, a number of similar assessments from a number of sources, including the CIA, surfaced.[22] While assessments of a nuclear exchange have come largely from CIA sources, some regional experts within and outside the U.S. government believe that there was a "hyping-up" of the crisis and that de-escalation had started well before the Gates mission was undertaken. In the subcontinent, too, there has been a general discounting of the alarmism surrounding the impending nuclear exchange between the two nations.[23]

In particular, the 1990 crisis saw the unfolding of a sequence of events. The Pakistan Army had begun the conduct of a large exercise, Zarb-e-Momin, in December 1989. Towards the end of 1989, a major uprising in Kashmir took place, just as the new government of V. P. Singh was beginning to settle in. There was tough talk regarding Kashmir from both sides, with an expectation in Pakistan of the impending independence of Kashmir and a fierce determination in New Delhi to prevent it. The Indian army is said to have deployed three additional divisions in Kashmir and one extra division in Punjab to forestall any Pakistani military adventures. It is not known whether these defensive moves by India were seen as indicating an aggressive intent in Islamabad, thus resulting in an escalation of the crisis. It is now believed that to indicate its defensive intent, India allowed the U.S. ambassador, William Clark, and his military attachés to look at the disposition of the Indian forces. This moves appears to have helped clarify and defuse the situation.

However, there are a number of unanswered questions in relation to the nuclear factor. Seymour Hersh reports that the U.S. had observed Pakistani F-16s on a full nuclear alert.[24] The NBC account suggests that the Pakistani army had "flipped" the nuclear switch during the 1990 crisis.[25] It is not clear what motives led Pakistan to alert its nuclear forces. Did Pakistan fear an Indian attack across the line of control aimed at the campus used for training Kashmiri militants? Were such fears reasonable? There have also been some intriguing assertions in Pakistan that the nuclear threat allegedly conveyed by Islamabad forced India to back down. After a discussion with the key Indian players involved in the 1990 crisis, however, Subrahmanyam wrote, "Whatever Mr. Gates may have discussed with the Pakistanis, no policy maker in India recalls his raising the issue of nuclear confrontation."[26] General Aslam Beg, who was the army chief in Pakistan during the 1990 crisis, also has denied suggestions of a Pakistani nuclear threat.[27]

It would appear that the prospects for miscalculated escalation leading to a nuclear war could be limited. Some Indian analysts have made a compelling case suggesting that there already is evidence hinting at considerable caution against the dangers of escalation. Subrahmanyam has argued that "there is consciousness in India that in [the] future Pakistan cannot be driven to a position where it would seriously consider the exercise of a nuclear option. That consciousness is already evident in India not repeating the strategy of hot pursuit adopted in 1965 against Pakistan-despatched armed gangs across the line of control in the state of Jammu and Kashmir."[28] He has also suggested that Pakistan is also aware of the risks of allowing escalation. The Pakistani army was called out to stop the proposed marches by the Kashmiri militants across the line of control in the early 1990s. Subrahmanyam argues that the intense military confrontation on the line of control in Kashmir has broken down only once, in 1965.

CSBMs for Crisis Management between India and Pakistan

Most analysts outside South Asia show little optimism about proliferation on the subcontinent. Within India and Pakistan, however, many analysts are confident about the prospects of maintaining a stable structure of deterrence. They tend to dismiss Western alarmism regarding the dangers of nuclear war on the subcontinent. One of the few areas on which Indians and Pakistanis agree is in their total rejection of Western efforts to impose a nonproliferation regime on the subcontinent. Elites in both countries strongly resent the condescending and paternalistic attitudes of the West regarding the nuclear issue. Defense of national sovereignty on the nuclear issue has wide popular support in both countries, and few politicians are willing to risk the consequences of running counter to this popular sentiment.

Western analysts are perplexed by the peculiar nature of the nuclear debate in South Asia, where both New Delhi and Islamabad constantly complain about the nuclear weapons capabilities of the other without being willing to do very much about addressing the dangers associated with nuclear weapons. To put the paradox in the words of George Quester, South Asians tend to "assume the worst about the adversary's capabilities on the nuclear front, and the best about his intentions."[29] Quester offers three possible explanations: first, that South Asians are utterly ignorant of nuclear weapons and the dangers they present; second, that South Asians are aware of the threat but feign a lack of concern; and third, that the relationship between India and Pakistan is more sophisticated, and that their historical ties give them some intangible reassurance that nuclear proliferation will not lead to nuclear war.[30]

Although there are grounds for being optimistic about the emergence of a stable structure of deterrence in the subcontinent, as shown in the previous sections, there is no room for complacency in efforts to avoid nuclear war in the region. Unlike those analysts whose specialty is in nonproliferation, many regional experts are less alarmist and more hopeful about the nuclear problem in the subcontinent.[31] Nevertheless, there is a strong case for negotiated arms control and confidence-building to ensure that nuclear deterrence remains stable. Both sides should devise mechanisms that reduce the temptations for preemption, prevent loss of control, avoid the dangers of escalation, and maintain adequate capabilities for communication during a crisis. Several means of enhancing stability in the region are possible.

Covert or Overt Nuclear Posture?

The reluctance of India and Pakistan to formally announce their nuclear weapons status and their continued claims of using nuclear technology only for peaceful purposes raise important questions of strategic stability between covert nuclear forces. Covert nuclear weapons programs entail grave dangers, including a lack of broad scrutiny over decision making, the dominance of the military in the formulation of doctrine, a tendency for bias toward offense and preemption, strained crisis management and nuclear signaling, and a lack of knowledge of the other's nuclear status and doctrine.[32] Hence the calls for transparency or openness in the nuclear postures of India and Pakistan are received warily in U.S. policy circles.

There are some, however, who see the utility of the current nuclear ambiguity in the subcontinent. Clearly any call for overt nuclear deployment in India and Pakistan runs counter to the current international efforts to limit the spread of mass-destructive weapons and to the formal American policy of rolling back nuclear weapons on the subcontinent. Some even argue that nuclear ambiguity has given diplomatic flexibility to both India and Pakistan in dealing with nuclear issues at home and abroad,[33] or that a form of "non-weaponized nuclear deterrence" has developed between India and Pakistan.[34]

These arguments assume that the current nonproliferation regime will remain in perpetuity and that South Asia's nuclear posture would be carefully managed. However, a major shock to the nonproliferation system, involving the nuclearization of Iran or North Korea or unpredictable events in China could set in motion a dynamic that could transform the nuclear environment of the subcontinent. Such an occurrence would undermine both the international nonproliferation regime as well as the current inhibitions in India and Pakistan against overt nuclear weapons deployment.

Even assuming that there would be no major external factor transforming the nonproliferation environment, it should not be impossible to separate the questions of the de jure nuclear weapons status for India and Pakistan and the practical recognition of their de facto nuclear capabilities. But in both India and Pakistan there is a continuing reluctance to come to terms with the need for peaceful nuclear coexistence. For effective crisis management, it may be essential for India and Pakistan to acknowledge each other's nuclear capabilities and initiate a dialogue aimed at learning to live in a nuclear neighborhood. Regardless of the final decisions regarding the deployment or non-deployment of nuclear weapons, negotiating

CSBMs for the prevention of war in general, and crisis management in particular, has an independent merit of its own.

From Tacit to Explicit Bargaining

The current state of relations between India and Pakistan should not lead us to ignore the long record of bilateral negotiation and problem solving between the two countries.[35] Although this has been seriously impaired in recent years, the past record of negotiating CSBMs provides a good foundation to build on. But clearly recent events, including the destruction of the Babri mosque, the communal rioting in Bombay, and the Charar e Sharief fiasco, have disrupted the dialogue. The transformation of the domestic situations in both countries, marked by the rise of the religious right and the hardening of popular animosities between the two nations, makes it necessary to open up and institutionalize the negotiation of CSBMs.

In fact, external pressures, primarily from the United States, on the nonproliferation issue may have prevented a more open discussion of the nuclear issue on the subcontinent. Many Pakistanis harbor strong resentment over the imposition of the Pressler amendment, which they see as discriminatory. And in India, there has been a sense of unremitting American pressure to force India into the NPT or the Five Power Conference on nonproliferation in South Asia. Much of South Asia's diplomatic energies have been directed toward stalling American pressure while avoiding the key issues relating to the prevention of nuclear war. The United States, as noted earlier, has now begun to emphasize war-avoidance. It is also urging India and Pakistan to initiate a direct, high-level dialogue on the nuclear issue.

Washington has formally outlined a detailed agenda on nuclear and non-nuclear CSBMs for India and Pakistan to consider.[36] The proposals include measures that would cap nuclear capabilities in the region, introduce a nuclear restraint regime, prevent war, and generate transparency. Over the last two years there have been a number of unofficial proposals detailing possible CSBMs for the subcontinent.[37] Our concern here is with only those measures that relate to crisis management. These measures can be unilateral, bilateral, or multilateral.

Preventing Preemptive Strikes

The 1988 agreement not to attack each other's nuclear facilities has been an important CSBM that has effectively reduced the fears of nuclear preemption on the subcontinent. It grew out of Pakistani fears during the mid-1980s regarding Indian plans to take out the uranium-enrichment plant at Kahuta. The proposal for the non-attack agreement had come from outside the Indian government, from K. Subrahmanyam, then the director of the Institute for Defence Studies and Analyses, as part of a proposal for nuclear confidence-building between India and Pakistan.[38] In their meeting in December 1985, Rajiv Gandhi and General Zia ul Haq agreed in principle on the idea. The agreement was signed during Rajiv Gandhi's visit to Pakistan in December 1988. Under the agreement,

> each party shall refrain from undertaking, encouraging or participating in, directly or indirectly, any action aimed at causing the destruction of, or damage to, any nuclear installation or facility in the other country (Article I.1).

The agreement also mandates that each country provide the other with a list of the latitudes and longitudes of its covered nuclear installations and facilities at the beginning of every year and whenever any changes are made (Article II).

Other measures to reduce prospects for preemption might include dispersal of forces, mobility, hardening, and improving readiness levels, all of which were used by Washington and Moscow during the cold war. It would be prudent for both countries to decide not to keep all their special nuclear material in one place. Neither country is in such a position as to be overly apprehensive about all its delivery systems being wiped out in a single preemptive strike by the other. Nevertheless, both might consider hardening the shelters of their nuclear strike aircraft, and both already have deployed mobile missiles.[39] Improving readiness levels would tend to loosen control over nuclear forces and may be unnecessary for India and Pakistan.

No Early Use

Declarations and pledges on preventing the first or early use of nuclear weapons could be useful instruments in stabilizing nuclear deterrence in the region. Indian analysts have been calling for such agreements between India and Pakistan, as well as on a wider basis involving China, Russia, and the United States.[40] But in Pakistan there seem to be apprehensions that, given India's conventional superiority, promulgating a no-first-use pledge could undermine Pakistan's ability to deter Indian conventional aggression. This is similar to the arguments used by the NATO alliance to argue against no-first-use agreements during the cold war. However, neither NATO's past fears nor the current Pakistani fears can be considered justified. First, if the very national survival of Pakistan were to be threatened by an Indian aggression, none of the CSBM agreements would have much relevance or would in any way hamper Pakistan from defending itself by all available means. Second, many of Pakistan's worries regarding India's supposed freedom to launch conventional attacks under a no-first-use pledge could be addressed under a broader regime of military CSBMs aimed at reducing the possibilities of a conventional war. Third, as noted earlier, there is an emerging sense in India that, given the nuclear capability of Pakistan, India can no longer afford to push Pakistan beyond a point; the deterrent effect of Pakistani nuclear capabilities is real and is unlikely to be undermined by pledges for no early use or no first use.

Crisis Communication

Effective signaling and communication during a crisis could be improved by strengthening the existing communication channels and instituting new ones. The two sides have a hotline between the army directors general of military operations (DGMOs). There are now suggestions for a similar mechanism between the chiefs of air operations in the two air forces.[41] But these channels appear to be inadequate for crisis management, for a variety of reasons.

First, some forms of strategic signaling during a crisis may not be possible on the current hotlines. The attempt by Pakistan to signal its nuclear capability during the 1986–87 crisis took the form of providing an Indian journalist a meeting with Dr. Khan. But that interview was not published for weeks. Second, the military officials on both sides have complained that the hotline does not "work" when either side chooses not to let it work. This problem has hampered the speedy resolution of problems arising out of military incidents on the border.[42] According to U.S. sources involved in the 1990 crisis, there appears to have been a problem of "face" in deciding who would call first on the hotline between the DGMOs. The problem is said to have been sorted out by the two foreign secretaries agreeing to call each other in quick succession, thus circumventing the problem.[43] Since then, an informal agreement was reached that the two DGMOs would call each other every Tuesday on a regular basis.

Clearly, though, there is a need for upgrading and modernizing the existing DGMO hotline and for establishing additional ones. More important, however, may be the establishment of crisis management groups at the appropriate levels to ensure not only that incidents and accidents that have potential to escalate are at once brought to the notice of the other side, but also that decisions get made quickly enough to defuse the situation. Decision making, in India at least, involves a number of institutions and bureaucracies and the political leadership at the highest level, thus making it a slow process. Crisis management groups with the right authority may be able to quicken the pace of decision making. Effective crisis management groups would have to involve the military services, civilian defense officials, and diplomats. Establishing risk reduction centers on both sides could be one way of putting together responsible crisis management teams.

Preventing Loss of Control

A number of American analysts have suggested "nuclear stability assistance" for emerging nuclear nations as a way of reducing the dangers of accidents, terrorism, unauthorized use, and other forms of loss of control. These analysts argue that if the spread of nuclear weapons cannot be stopped, it may be a good policy to mitigate the dangers associated with nuclear weapons.[44]

Technical assistance that could be provided to new nuclear states includes the improvement of security over nuclear forces by providing PAL technology; improving the safety of nuclear weapons through better designs that avoid unintended nuclear explosions; enhancing the survivability of nuclear forces; and increasing the reliability of operational procedures. The proponents of stability assistance recognize that current international agreements and American domestic law prohibit giving such assistance to emerging nuclear states. Furthermore, new nuclear nations might not react favorably to the idea of receiving such technical assistance.[45] But India and Pakistan need not wait until the American government decides to help them through stability assistance. On their own, New Delhi and Islamabad could begin to strengthen the physical security and safety of their nuclear materials and facilities. They could also unilaterally work toward improving other elements of managing their incipient nuclear forces, such as command and control or safe storage issues.

Joint Military Commission

Expanding the exchanges between the two militaries could be a useful measure for managing crises. In a thoughtful assessment of Indo-Pakistani negotiations, Douglas Makeig has noted the collapse of the professional and social linkages that existed between the two armed forces in the early years of independence and their current inability to exercise "moderating influence" on the government as they once did in both countries.[46] He notes the fact that during the Rann of Kutch crisis of 1965, Air Marshal Asghar Khan's telephone call to his counterpart Arjun Singh resulted in a "gentlemen's agreement" not to employ their air forces in the military clashes taking place in the Rann of Kutch. The Indian and Pakistani army chiefs met twice in the aftermath of the 1965 war to work out disengagement procedures.

Today, however, it has become impossible for one army chief to accept an invitation to visit the other country. The negative reaction in the Pakistani media to the Indian government's 1992 invitation for General Asif Nawaz to visit India and Nawaz's consequent inability to accept that invitation indicate the near impossibility of renewing high-level regular military interaction between the two countries.

Any expectation of initiating military diplomacy akin to the Soviet-American "military diplomacy" that was established in 1987[47] would have to be tempered by the current political realities in the region. The interaction between the superpowers involved not only the discussion of military doctrine and regular high-level visits, but also the establishment of a joint military commission charged with periodically reviewing dangerous military activities and incidents, as well as procedures for defusing them. The establishment of a similar mechanism between India and Pakistan could be a useful way of maintaining a low-key, sustained technical dialogue between the two militaries—a dialogue that is at least partly insulated from the larger political dynamic. But it should be noted that the military exchanges between Russia and the United States began with the winding down of the cold war and flourished with each step down the ladder of confrontation. Such military exchanges could not have been visualized at a time of intense tension between the two nations. Given the current state of political tension between India and Pakistan, the agenda for South Asian CSBMs must clearly be modest. That brings us back to the basic paradox of arms control: It is least feasible politically when it most needed to avoid war, and it is relatively easy to accomplish when political relations are not hostile.

Notes

1. For an analysis of the impact of stress on policy makers, see Jerrold M. Post, "The Impact of Crisis-Induced Stress on Policy-Makers," in Alexander L. George, ed., *Avoiding War: Problems of Crisis Management* (Boulder, Co.: Westview, 1990), pp. 471–96.

2. See George, ed., *Avoiding War*, pp. 24–26, and Joseph Nye, Jr., "Nuclear Crisis Management," in Andrew Goldberg et. al., eds., *Avoiding the Brink: Theory and Practice of Crisis Management* (London: Brassey's, 1990), p. 13.

3. This categorization is drawn from Richard Darilek, "The Future of Conventional Arms Control in Europe: A Tale of Two Cities: Stockholm, Vienna," *Survival* 29, no. 1 (January/February 1987), p. 5.

4. This definition is developed in C. Raja Mohan and Louis J. Klarevas, "Building Confidence in Regions of Conflict: Replicating East-West CBMs in South Asia and the East Mediterranean," unpublished work in progress.

5.For more on East-West CSBMs, see John Borawski, ed., *Avoiding War in the Nuclear Age: Confidence-Building Measures for Crisis Stability* (Boulder, Co.: Westview,

1986); R. B. Byers, F. Stephen Larrabee, and Allen Lynch, eds., *Confidence-Building Measures and International Security* (New York: Institute for East-West Security Studies, 1987); Jonathan Alford, "Confidence-Building Measures in Europe: The Military Aspects," in Jonathan Alford, ed., *The Future of Arms Control, Part III: Confidence-Building Measures,* Adelphi Paper no. 149 (London: International Institute for Strategic Studies, 1979), pp. 4–13; Karl E. Birnbaum, ed., *Confidence Building and East-West Relations,* Laxenburg Paper no. 5 (Laxenburg, Austria: Austrian Institute for International Affairs, 1983); Alexander L. George, Philip J. Farley, and Alexander Dallin, eds., *U.S.-Soviet Security Cooperation: Achievements, Failures, Lessons* (New York: Oxford University Press, 1988); John Borawski, *From the Atlantic to the Urals: Negotiating Arms Control at the Stockholm Conference* (Washington, D.C.: Pergamon-Brassey's 1988); Carl C. Krehbiel, *Confidence- and Security-Building Measures in Europe: The Stockholm Conference* (New York: Praeger, 1989); John Borawski, *Security for a New Europe: The Vienna Negotiations on Confidence-and Security-Building Measures, 1989–1990 and Beyond* (Washington D.C.: Brassey's, 1992).

6. Quoted in George D. Moffett III, "Confidence-Building for Peace," *Christian Science Monitor,* September 24, 1992.

7. Peter Lavoy, "Learning to Live with Nuclear Weapons: Regional Arms Control and Nonproliferation Policy," paper presented at the annual meeting of the American Political Science Association, Washington, D.C., September 1991.

8. Testimony of James Woolsey, February 24, 1993.

9. See, for example, Kenneth Waltz, *The Spread of Nuclear Weapons: More May Be Better,* Adelphi Paper no. 171 (London: International Institute for Strategic Studies, 1981). See also Dagobert L. Brito and Michael D. Intriligator, "Proliferation and the Probability of War: Global and Regional Issues," in Dagobert L. Brito, Michael D. Intriligator, and Adele E. Wick, eds., *Strategies for Managing Nuclear Proliferation: Economic and Political Issues* (Lexington, Mass: D.C. Heath, 1983), pp. 135–143.

10. This is the felicitous expression used by Peter Lavoy in Lavoy, "Learning to Live with Nuclear Weapons," p. 9, although it is being used in a slightly different context here.

11. *Arms Control Reporter, 1984,* Section 454, p. B36.

12. Susan Burns, "Preventing Nuclear War," in Stephen Philip Cohen, ed., *Nuclear Proliferation in South Asia: The Prospects for Arms Control* (New Delhi: Lancer, 1991), p. 93.

13. Waltz, *The Spread of Nuclear Weapons,* p. 16.

14. Waltz, *The Spread of Nuclear Weapons,* p. 17.

15. Feaver, "Command and Control in Emerging Nuclear Nations," *International Security* 17, no. 3 (winter 1992–93), pp. 160–187.

16. As quoted in Michael O'Rourke, "Nuclear Stand-off: Interview with General K. Sundarji," *Far Eastern Economic Review,* September 13, 1990, pp. 24–26.

17. See the transcripts of the *NBC Nightly News* broadcasts of December 1 and 2, 1992.

18. Seymour Hersh, "On the Nuclear Edge," *New Yorker,* March 29, 1993, p. 61.

19. Quoted in Kuldip Nayar, "'We Have the A-Bomb,' says Pakistan's Dr. Strangelove," *Observer* (London), March 1, 1987.

20. Hersh, "On the Nuclear Edge," p. 59.

21. Hersh, "On the Nuclear Edge," pp. 56–69.

22. Gordon Oehler, the director of the CIA's nonproliferation section before the Senate that if India and Pakistan had gone to war in the Spring of 1990, "there was a real possibility that it could have gone to nuclear war." Testimony before the Senate Committee on Governmental Affairs, February 23, 1993.

23. K. Subrahmanyam, "Down Memory Lane," *Economic Times,* March 24, 1993.

24. Hersh quotes an American intelligence analyst as saying, "They had F-16s prepositioned and armed for delivery—on full alert, with pilots in the aircraft. I believed that they were ready to launch on command and that message had been clearly conveyed to the Indians." Hersh, "On the Nuclear Edge," p. 65.

25. See the transcripts of the *NBC Nightly News* broadcast of December 1 and 2, 1992.

26. Subrahmanyam,"Down Memory Lane."

27. Ikram Ullah, "Former Military Chief of Staff on Nuclear Program," originally appearing in the *News* (Islamabad), December 6, 1992. Reprinted in Joint Publications Research Service, *Nuclear Developments,* December 18, 1992, p. 17.

28. K. Subrahmanyam, "Nuclear Policy, Arms Control, and Military Cooperation," paper presented at a seminar on "India and the United States after the Cold War" organized by the India International Center and the Carnegie Endowment for International Peace, New Delhi, March 1993, p. 15.

29. Quester, *Nuclear Pakistan and Nuclear India: Stable Deterrent or Proliferation Challenge* (Carlisle, Pa.: U.S. Army War College, 1992), p. 3.

30. Quester, *Nuclear Pakistan and Nuclear India,* p. 4.

31. See, for example, Stephen Philip Cohen, "Nuclear Neighbors," in Cohen, ed. *Nuclear Proliferation in South Asia,* p. 12.

32. See Shai Feldman, "Managing Nuclear Proliferation," in Jed C. Snyder and Samuel F. Wells, Jr., eds., *Limiting Nuclear Proliferation* (Cambridge, Mass.: Ballinger, 1985), pp. 304–8; K. Sundarji, "Former Military Chief Discusses Nuclear Options," originally appearing in the *Indian Express* (Delhi), December 20, 1992, reprinted in Joint Publications Research Service, *Proliferation Issues,* January 7, 1993, p. 11; and Burns, "Preventing Nuclear War."

33. Neil Joeck, "Tacit Bargaining and Stable Proliferation in South Asia," *Journal of Strategic Studies* 13, no. 3 (September 1990), p. 79.

34. George Perkovich, "A Nuclear Third Way in South Asia," *Foreign Policy* 91 (summer 1993).

35. A comprehensive survey of the Indo-Pakistani dialogue is given in chapter 1 of this volume. See also Douglas C. Makeig, "War, No-War, and the India-Pakistan Negotiating Process," *Pacific Affairs* 60, no. 2 (summer 1987), pp. 271–94.

36. "Report to Congress on Progress Toward Regional Nonproliferation in South Asia," May 1993.

37. For a wide-ranging discussion of these proposed CSBMs, see Susan Burns, "Preventing Nuclear War," pp. 105–19.

38. K. Subrahmanyam, "Building Trust on the Bomb: What India and Pakistan Can Do," *Times* (India), July 30, 1985.

39. India's short-range missile *Prithvi* is capable of being deployed on mobile launchers. Pakistan has acquired Chinese M-9 and M-11 missiles, both of which are mobile. See Shirley A. Kan, *Chinese Missile and Nuclear Proliferation: Issues for*

Congress, Congressional Research Service Issue Brief (Washington D.C.: Congressional Research Service, 1993), pp. 4–5.

40. Subrahmanyam, "Building Trust on the Bomb."

41. According to some sources, such a link existed earlier but has fallen into disuse over the last two decades.

42. General K. M. Arif of Pakistan referred to some of these problems in the third round of the Neemrana meeting, which took place in Surajkund in May 1992. These problems have been confirmed by the Indian side as well.

43. Interview with a former U.S. official.

44. Feaver, "Command and Control in Emerging Nuclear Nations," p. 182.

45. See Lewis A. Dunn, *Containing Nuclear Proliferation,* Adelphi Paper no. 263 (London: International Institute for Strategic Studies, 1991), p. 49.

46. Makeig, "War, No-War," p. 274.

47. See Kurt M. Campbell, "The Future of 'Military Diplomacy' in U.S.-Soviet Relations," in George, ed., *Avoiding War,* pp. 519–544.

11

Prerequisites for Success

John Sandrock

The end of the cold war and, along with it, the end of the confrontation between the largest and most heavily armed alliances the world has ever known have produced fundamental changes in major security relationships in much of the world. Massive numbers of nuclear weapons no longer threaten the almost instant annihilation of millions, if not the entire world, and the ultimate threat to the national survival of much of the industrialized world has receded to the point where no one considers a massive exchange of nuclear weapons a serious possibility. The end of the East-West confrontation has permitted the turning back of the proverbial doomsday clock from five minutes before midnight.

But in another part of the world, where "Freedom at Midnight" is celebrated between the fifteenth and the sixteenth of August every year, and where *ahimsa* (nonviolence) and *satyagraha* (peaceful resistance) once brought an empire to its knees,[1] perhaps the most serious and potentially dangerous confrontation in the world today continues without any hope for an early or lasting rapprochement. The end of the cold war has had virtually no effect on the bitter and hostile relationship between India and Pakistan.

The end of the cold war confrontation was the product of many positive factors, but a key ingredient to the relaxation of tensions was the step-by-step confidence- and security-building process that was first formalized by the 1975 Helsinki Final Act and has been augmented and modified by the 1986 Stockholm Document and the Vienna Documents of 1990 and 1992. The process had a beginning, a middle, and, while it has not yet ended, appears on an irrevocable course to a brighter future.

Between India and Pakistan, there have been many beginnings but few middles, and there is no end in sight, nor is there a process that could lead to a lasting peace—at least not at the moment. Bilateral relations are worse today than at any time since the end of the last shooting war in 1971. The future is at best murky and uncertain and at worst could see the storm clouds of a major conflict, perhaps involving the employment of nuclear weapons.

India and Pakistan have acknowledged the fact that both nations have a capability to deploy nuclear weapons within hours, or, at most, within one to two days of a decision to do so and that they are on the verge of deploying prompt delivery systems (missiles) that could carry nuclear weapons. As a result, their confrontation must be and is considered a threat that affects not only the survival of their ancient civilizations, of which they are justly proud, but also the security of the entire region and far beyond.

No one pretends that the process that led to the Helsinki Accords or the modifications and refinements that have occurred since are a panacea for all the world's problems or even that Europe has become a totally benign and peaceful environment. One must look no further than the tragedy of the former Yugoslavia to recognize that this is not the case. But South Asian governments and strategic thinkers who dismiss the Helsinki process and the positive results it achieved for Europe with a simple "...it hasn't solved all the problems, ... the conditions are different here, ... the time isn't right" must recognize that the essential element of the Helsinki Accords was not the details, but rather the political will, the dedicated and continuing commitment, and the hard-won support of the populations of the contracting nations. There were no utopian answers nor any clearly charted path in Europe when the process began. Thus it is unrealistic to seek or expect to find utopian answers to the problems that plague South Asian relations. In Europe, the danger of violence has not disappeared, but there is a commitment and a process that has reduced the threat of international conflict to a minimum. A similar political commitment and process are missing in South Asia.

The threat of a major bilateral conflict in South Asia is omnipresent. While most South Asians on both sides of the Indo-Pakistani border may reject this notion, when normal diplomatic discourse has all but terminated, when each protagonist constantly accuses the other of serious meddling in internal affairs, when charges and countercharges fill a vitriolic press, when there are almost daily exchanges of cross-border fire, when territorial disputes appear unresolvable, and when troops face each other not across an international border, but across an "line of actual control" that neither side recognizes as a permanent boundary, there is a severe potential for conflict.

In much of the world, the end of the cold war has produced a relaxation of tensions. In South Asia, where previous tensions were not a by-product of the cold war confrontation, the old rivalries and problems continue unabated. The cold war in the West began in 1949 and is now over. India and Pakistan began their cold and occasionally hot war two years earlier. Its end is nowhere in sight.

The reasons for this are many and have been discussed at length in this volume. What has perhaps not been stated as forcefully as I would state it is that there has been a lack of will by both sides to achieve a peaceful and lasting resolution. Perhaps this is a lingering result of the colonial experience. Until 1947, South Asians were not responsible for their own destiny and did not have the authority or the right to make meaningful decisions. With independence came responsibility and, at the risk of angering some very dear Indian and Pakistani friends and colleagues, in my opinion no government in India or in Pakistan since independence has proved capable of meeting the most fundamental responsibility of government: guaranteeing peace and security for its people. In this most basic requirement, every government in India and Pakistan has failed miserably.

When a Gujarati village woman will not get on a commercial aircraft unless she is assured that it will not overfly Pakistan because she fears for her life, her government has failed her. When a Pakistani farmer tilling his field near the border believes that he requires arms to protect himself against an Indian invasion, which, in his mind, might come at any moment, his government has failed him. When soldiers face each other in utterly inhumane conditions on the heights of the world's most inhospitable battlefield—the Siachen Glacier—their governments have failed them. A thousand and more explanations and excuses can be offered to account for this, but the fundamental indictment is, in my opinion, irrefutable.

India and Pakistan have already fought three wars, experienced numerous crises, and continue to demonstrate their more or less complete disdain for one another at virtually every opportunity. While much of the rest of the world has managed to increase the level of international civility, coming ever closer to international peace and understanding, India and Pakistan appear locked in an intractable confrontation with little or no prospect for an early easing of tensions, much less a permanent resolution of their problems.

What is required is an agreed plan of action, a step-by-step approach that will begin to address systematically the issues that bedevil the relationship. In fact, this is what happened in the Helsinki process. When negotiations began, the parties were far apart on every issue. Each had totally different objectives. The vast gulf between them came to be bridged over time through a reasonable process in which each success, no matter how minor, fueled progress, and where no failure, no matter how large, stalled the process for long.

The United States and the Soviet Union were pivotal to the progress that led to the Conference on Security and Cooperation in Europe that first convened in Helsinki in 1972. The discussions and negotiations that led to this initial formal meeting were lengthy and difficult. When the first proposals for such a conference were made in the 1950s, the existence of the cold war had recently been recognized and bilateral relations between the United States and the Soviet Union were marked by deep suspicion and distrust. In the mid-1950s, Soviet proposals to limit force sizes in Europe were seen in the West as a blatant attempt to prevent Germany from joining NATO and to get as many U.S. troops off the continent as possible. The United States saw no advantage in pursuing this type of agreement because it believed that the Soviet proposals were little more than a ploy to gain complete control of Europe.

In the 1960s, renewed proposals from the East received a similarly cool initial reception in the West and, although some talks were held, the Soviet Union's 1968 invasion of Czechoslovakia interrupted the discussions. By 1969, however, partially as a new U.S. presidential administration and its search for a way out of the war in Vietnam, the United States took a more positive attitude. During a preparatory meeting the East listed three conditions: recognition of the inviolability of existing frontiers, the recognition that two Germanies existed and that both were sovereign nations, and the renunciation by West Germany of any ambitions to obtain or possess nuclear weapons. Within a month, NATO's North Atlantic Council signaled its willingness to participate in negotiations but soon thereafter also communicated certain preconditions that it felt must be met. These included a requirement to discuss conventional force reductions in Europe on a "mutual and balanced basis," i.e., reductions in U.S. forces in Europe could not result in a relative force advantage to the other side. A second Western requirement dealt with the status of Berlin, which at that time continued to exist under the threat of imminent Soviet intervention. Several other exchanges of notes and so-called precipitating events preceded the 1972 conference start date, but the essential goal of beginning a productive dialogue was maintained.

The multi-volume book that could be written about how the Helsinki process proceeded and how its results were achieved clearly is beyond the scope of this chapter. As mentioned above, however, the importance of the Helsinki process to South Asia's security situation lies not in the details but in the political commitment and the dedication by all concerned to progress toward a satisfactory solution. In the 1950s, 1960s, and even the 1970s no one could have foreseen how the process that led to a lasting rapprochement in Europe would play out, and discussions certainly were difficult, but there is little doubt that the overall goal of improving the security of Europe and its population remained in the forefront of the effort. Now a similar commitment and dedication to improving security is called for in South Asia.

Current Agreements between India and Pakistan

India and Pakistan have a decided advantage over the Europeans who started the Helsinki process almost forty years ago. In addition to gleaning the worthwhile and applicable lessons from the Helsinki process, South Asians have a ready-made and already agreed-upon starting point. Although not everyone may agree at first, the logical and most readily available starting point is the Simla Agreement, which was negotiated and signed by the prime ministers of India and Pakistan after their 1972 conflict. It is an internationally recognized and valid document that has formed the technical basis for the bilateral relationship since the agreement entered into force on August 4, 1972. One of the key provisions of this rather short document stipulates that

> the two countries are resolved to settle their differences by peaceful means through bilateral negotiations or by any other peaceful means mutually agreed upon . . . . Pending the final settlement of any of the problems between the two countries, neither side shall unilaterally alter the situation and both shall prevent the organization, assistance and encouragement of any acts detrimental to the maintenance of peaceful and harmonious relations.

This and other provisions of the agreement form a solid foundation on which to build. Unfortunately, lack of political will, misplaced national pride, the failure of government, an almost unconscionable acceptance of the status quo, and tolerance for violence have prevented any significant progress. To be sure, the commitment to settle "their differences by peaceful means" has, over the past twenty years, resulted in agreement on several confidence- and security-building measures (CSBMs). Most of these are moribund. The five most recently agreed-upon CSBMs, although technically still viable, are approaching a similar status. Although they have been discussed in greater detail in other chapters of this volume, in order to place the major points of this chapter into the proper context, a brief review of the provisions of the current CSBMs is in order.

Agreement on Advance Notice of Military Exercises, Maneuvers, and Troop Movements

Although periodic discussions and an earlier agreement regarding the prior notification of military exercises near the international border existed, it is generally accepted that this agreement grew out of the Brasstacks crisis of 1987.[2] Beginning in late 1986, Indian military forces engaged in a series of military exercises that involved major portions of the Indian army and air force and, to a lesser extent, the Indian navy. Pakistani leaders, concerned that the massive troop buildup near their borders could have been a prelude to an Indian invasion, chose to increase the readiness of their own forces. Escalating tensions prompted local and international concern that war was imminent. Although the tensions were defused, the fact that both armies have major exercise areas in proximity of the border and the underlying concern that a future exercise again could bring the two nations to the brink of conflict prompted the agreement to notify each other in advance of military exercises.

The agreement covers only relatively large military exercises—i.e., corps level or above along the international boundary and division level along the line of control (the size of naval and air force exercises are also defined). The efficacy of this CSBM remains to be determined, although there have been allegations that its spirit, if not its letter, has been violated. Large military exercises are extremely costly affairs and tend to accelerate equipment wear and tear. There are some reports that India's Brasstacks exercises consumed roughly two years' worth of training funds. For whatever reasion, since 1987 both armies appear to have avoided large exercises that would require prior notification.

The Direct Communications Link between the Directors-General of Military Operations

The hotline between the directors-general of military operations (DGMOs) was originally established in 1971. It received very limited use and, when it was used, disinformation was often relayed in an ill-conceived and unfortunate effort to gain a tactical advantage. The link was largely ignored by both sides until the two most recent bilateral crises (Brasstacks in 1987 and the latest Kashmir crisis, which began in 1989). The need to avoid misunderstanding of each other's intentions became particularly acute after India and Pakistan came close to conflict in 1990. Although it was theoretically available, the DGMO hotline was ineffective during the 1990 crisis because neither DGMO wanted to be the first to use it, apparently feeling that first use might be interpreted as a sign of weakness. The current agreement stipulates at least a weekly test of the hotline and requires the DGMOs to converse, even if only briefly.

How the hotline may impact a future crisis is unclear. Certainly, if it is used to clarify a particular action and notify the other side of a rapidly developing situation (e.g., an internal crisis that requires the rapid deployment of significant security forces), it can be quite useful. If, on the other hand, the DGMOs are concerned about appearances or about revealing operational details, or if the hotline is used in a deliberate attempt to pass incorrect or incomplete information, it will be of no benefit at all. One would hope that the precedent set between 1971 and 1990 will not be repeated.

In addition to its potential utility during a crisis, the hotline does provide an additional channel of communications that is readily available and could be used for situations that may not have urgency. Concerns regarding the implementation of any of the existing CSBMs could be raised via the hotline. It could also be used to anticipate and defuse possible misunderstandings. A simple test for determining whether a particular measure or action could be of concern might be to consider what that action would mean if it were contemplated or executed on the other side of the border.

Measures to Prevent Air Space Violations
and to Permit Overflights and Landing by Military Aircraft

The most recent agreement, signed in early April 1991, deals not only with inadvertent airspace violations, but also establishes what amounts to a no-fly zone for combat aircraft within ten kilometers of the international border.[3] Unarmed transport and logistics aircraft, unarmed helicopters, and "Air Observation Post" aircraft may fly up to 1,000 meters from the other's airspace. The agreement also routinizes other airspace-related activities and stipulates actions to be taken when an inadvertent airspace violation occurs.

The agreement on preventing airspace violations will become particularly important as the air defense capabilities of both nations improve. Improved low-level radar and more capable, longer-range surface-to-air missiles will increase the capability of air defense forces, although the speed of modern jet aircraft will still limit their reaction and decision time. The agreement may serve to create a climate in which inadvertent airspace intruders are given the benefit of the doubt and air defense reaction is limited by higher headquarters restrictions. So long as the offending intrusion is fully investigated and a satisfactory explanation is given to the other nation, this agreement should serve to ease border tensions.

Agreement Not to Attack
Each Other's Nuclear Installations and Facilities

This agreement, originally signed in 1988, went into force after both governments had ratified it and a list of the applicable installations had been exchanged. The agreement is significant because it recognizes the special dangers involved with nuclear installations. Interestingly, heavy water production facilities in India do not appear to be included in the agreement. Like all confidence- and security-building measures and any other agreements, this one is valid only as long as it is observed by both parties and so long as both are confident that all appropriate facilities have been included in the exchange of lists. There have been some reports that neither side believes that the facilities lists are complete. The impact of this distrust in the event of a future conflict is difficult to assess, but as long as the suspicion remains that the list is incomplete there is a danger that some nuclear facilities may be targeted either inadvertently or on purpose. Some type of verification such as a challenge inspection regime may be the only way both sides can be sure that all appropriate facilities are covered.

Joint Declaration by Pakistan and India on the Prohibition of Chemical Weapons

In this 1992 agreement, Pakistan and India reaffirmed their adherence to the 1925 Geneva Protocol on the Prohibition of the Use in War of Asphyxiating, Poisonous or other Gases, and of Bacteriological Methods of Warfare. They also declared their intent to become original parties to the Chemical Weapons Convention, which they have since signed.

This agreement is significant since it eliminates an entire class of weapons from potential use and it may be even more significant if it serves as a first step in reorienting the bilateral relationship. By agreeing to significant measures, a pattern of cooperation may be established that leads to a resolution of larger, more complex issues.

Re-establishing a Crisis Management Process

In order for current and future confidence- and security-building measures to be effective, they have to be seen as more than cosmetic. Thus both governments might consider how to improve understanding of their intended purpose and how better to implement the spirit and letter of CSBMs. Useful discussions on other forms of cooperation have taken place as part of the foreign secretary discussions. For example, India and Pakistan have worked in good faith toward an anti-hijacking treaty, a drug enforcement cooperation proposal, and other forms of expanded trade and cultural ties.

Recently, however, additional strains in the relationship have emerged, primarily as a feature of the continuing controversy over Kashmir. The immediate reasons for the deterioration in the India-Pakistan relationship are many, and include the destruction of the Babri Masjid in Ayodhya, an escalation of border tensions, communal rioting in Bombay and in other places in India, Indian allegations after the March 1993 bombings in Bombay, the recent closure of consulates in Bombay and Karachi, and continued vitriolic comment in both the English language and vernacular press.[4] Another feature of the current relationship appears to be a tit-for-tat cycle of response to actual or perceived provocations or insults. Any number of examples could be cited, but the cause of improved bilateral relations is clearly not advanced when "the foreign hand" is blamed for virtually every act of violence or unrest and when that perception prompts official or unofficial retaliation. The desecration and destruction of religious sites in one country in retaliation for an alleged similar act in the other, the continuing harassment of diplomats, and a thousand other such acts may be symptoms of the much larger disease of reciprocal hatred, but they also fuel the continued deterioration of relations and severely complicate or even prevent any meaningful steps that might improve the situation.

A Next Step: Verification and Compliance

A first step that should be considered in reversing the fundamental difficulties that plague the Indo-Pakistani relationship is how best to enhance the sense of national security that both nations require. Increasing the effectiveness of and trust in existing CSBMs and other crisis management measures may be that first step. In part, the problems of noncompliance with existing measures have led both sides to question the need for and efficacy of additional CSBMs and have contributed to rather than defused regional tensions. For this purpose, regular consultations to discuss problems as they arise and to discuss broader verification and compliance issues in a routine fashion rather than in a crisis atmosphere could be initiated as soon as possible.

Without some type of verification measures for certain CSBMs, it is unlikely that either nation will have the necessary confidence that the other is in compliance with already existing agreements and CSBMs. Such mistrust makes the conclusion of new agreements much more difficult. Yet a variety of technical verification capabilities are now readily available, and India and Pakistan already possess a limited, indigenous means for verification: both have ground receiving stations for SPOT and LANDSAT data (Pakistan, in Islamabad; India, in Hyderabad). In addition, India has its own remote sensing satellite, and Pakistan has four and India has nineteen known seismic stations. One of Pakistan's stations and two of India's are part of the Worldwide Standardized Seismograph Network.[5] However, considerable human and economic costs may face both India and Pakistan if they attempt to modify or expand existing capabilities into a comprehensive verification system. Thus, it may be appropriate to consider some type of outside assistance as a means of enhancing local capability. Without "outside" help, both nations will face significant start-up costs for technical verification systems that may make early implementation of any verification regime virtually impossible.

Besides cost-related obstacles, India and Pakistan will need to discuss legitimate techniques of verification and information-gathering. If some type of inspection regime is agreed upon, will it allow only routine inspections or will there be provisions for challenge inspections? Are other forms of information-gathering acceptable? An Open Skies–type agreement for the verification and implementation of CSBMs has been discussed in non-governmental settings, but it is unclear if the governments have adequately considered this option or whether it can provide a basis for increased trust in South Asia. Both governments should investigate the potential costs and benefits of this type of system. In *Nuclear Proliferation in South Asia*, it is suggested that the lessons from cooperative monitoring in the Sinai may be applicable to South Asia.[6] These "lessons" include

1. The use of unmanned sensor fields located at entrances and passes (so as to be able to detect and identify intruding vehicles and people),
2. Manned surveillance posts at passes,
3. Demilitarized buffer zone monitored by a third party,
4. Weekly reconnaissance overflights, and
5. Regular on-site inspection teams.

Although not all of these measures may be applicable or acceptable in verifying Indian and Pakistan agreements and CSBMs, all available options should be considered in a joint, cooperative atmosphere. Only through in-depth discussions will it be possible to discern what may or may not be acceptable to both parties and to what extent the parties are willing to consider third-party involvement.

Pending a comprehensive agreement, cooperative monitoring for verification should utilize existing capabilities while recognizing the inherent strengths and vulnerabilities of the region.[7] Next, a measure such as an "open skies" agreement could build on the existing airspace violations agreement. Although an open skies agreement will not be a universal panacea, since airborne or spaceborne sensors cannot see inside buildings or underground and will be subject to other inherent limitations, it can nevertheless provide significant assurances especially relevant to the type of threat most likely in a South Asian security context.

Because of the limits of both sides' technical capabilities, other suggestions may need to be discussed. This could include the use of an international satellite monitoring agency, or the cooperative use of Russian or U.S. national technical means.

Obstacles to Implementation

In light of past experience and the broader confrontation, some of the obstacles that may prevent the adoption and successful execution of additional CSBMs include

1. the insistence by one side or the other that progress on any issue depends upon progress on another, single issue;
2. a discussion of "red flag" issues and a rehash of perceived past injustices to the exclusion of any new ideas;
3. unwelcome third-party involvement; and
4. a propensity to seek broad international approval for one position to the detriment of the other party.

One or both sides may want to discuss Kashmir, but Kashmir has become such an emotional lightning rod that substantive discussion on this issue may best be deferred. Without diminishing the importance of an eventual resolution to the Kashmir problem, other more manageable yet still important issues should be addressed before tackling Kashmir. A host of other issues such as getting the troops off Siachen Glacier and resolving issues such as the Wullar Barrage or Sir Creek disputes, may lend themselves to early resolution, particularly because the points of controversy are well understood by both sides and they are not as emotionally charged as Kashmir.

Conclusion

Almost fifty years of hostility are a formidable obstacle that cannot be overcome overnight. There is no magic wand nor are there any pat answers. But, all the tools are there. Increased international understanding and heightened national and regional security—peace—has broken out in many parts of the world. It is inappropriate, impractical, and probably impossible for India and Pakistan to attempt to copy exactly the successes in improving security enhancement processes that have succeeded elsewhere. Nevertheless, there are lessons that should be studied and benefits that can be derived. Process and dedication is what is missing in South Asia.

Without a doubt, some of those reviewing this volume will be able to identify a whole host of obstacles and conditions that could and, unfortunately, most likely will prevent early action. One can always find excuses or reasons for inaction. Accepting and maintaining the status quo involves little risk of failure. However, it does not lead to success. Any effort to resolve a problem, no matter how small it may be, introduces an unknown element and at least some risk of failure. Only a cursory examination of the past fifty years of South Asian history is required to recognize that in the bilateral relations between India and Pakistan, inaction and accepting the status quo have been a dismal failure. Accepting a bit of risk to initiate and nurture a peace process can pay huge dividends. Statesmen take initiative and accept risk, politicians sit back on their heels. More than anything, today's South Asia requires statesmen.

South Asian and foreign observers of the current Indian and Pakistani political situations have become fond of saying that neither nation's government currently is capable of exercising any initiative or assuming any risk if it values its political life. Others, including this author, would contend that the political difficulties facing the current Indian and Pakistani governments exist precisely *because* they are averse to taking the risk necessary to improve their relationship and thus enhance their security. The current governments and their predecessors have failed in their most fundamental obligations to their citizens in not providing for their collective security, instead apparently focusing more on preserving their own political security. Rather than a time for political conservatism, this is a time for activism that could and would lead South Asia out of an a fifty-year-old morass.

The lessons on how to do this are available. Perhaps the most important teacher of this lesson, a former leader who seldom receives full credit for his courage and wisdom, should be studied. No, I refer not to Gandhi, Nehru, or Jinnah. Anwar Sadat, Egypt's former president, showed the brand of courage that is required in South Asia today when he traveled to Israel for the first time and changed the history of the Middle East. Much maligned in the Arab world and eventually assassinated for his willingness to chart a risky, innovative course that would bring peace and security to his people, Sadat's personal courage, wisdom and foresight should serve as an example to South Asia's leaders. South Asia needs such a statesman.

In sum, the time has come for South Asian officials and strategists to examine the Helsinki process, the experience in the Middle East, and the positive aspects of how other nations and regions are dealing with their long-standing security problems. In looking at these examples, the focus should be not on what may be wrong with those efforts or on why those experiences may not apply to South Asia, but rather, on what parts *may* apply, and what lessons can be modified to have a positive effect in South Asia. The time has come for Indians and Pakistanis to look at the contents of the Helsinki glass not as half or even three-quarters empty, but perhaps as a glass that is at least a quarter of the way full.

Notes

The author wishes to acknowledge the fact that portions of this paper benefited from previous work sponsored by and completed for the United States Arms Control and Disarmament Agency.

1. Nonviolent civil disobedience, the combination of *ahimsa* and *satyagraha*, were the guiding philosophies of Mohandas Gandhi and became the force that he and his followers applied to rid South Asia of its British colonial masters. In Gandhi's words, *satyagraha* is "the force which is born of Truth and Love or nonviolence."

2. The earlier agreement on notification of military exercises near the border grew out of the Tashkent Agreement that ended the 1965 Indo-Pakistani conflict.

3. The agreement makes an exception for combat aircraft operating from airfields located in the immediate vicinity of the border. Aircraft operating from the Indian airfields at Jammu, Pathankot, Amritsar, and Suratgarh and the Pakistani airfields at Pasrur, Lahore, Vehari, and Rahim Yar Khan may not fly within 5 km of the border.

4. Anti-propaganda measures have been at the forefront of Indo-Pakistani cooperative proposals. The presses in both countries are notorious for inflaming passions among the populace. Indian and Pakistani officials have tried to curb hostile propaganda since as far back as 1948, with the 1948 Accord and the Liaqat-Nehru Agreement.

5. Stephen Philip Cohen, ed., *Nuclear Proliferation in South Asia: The Prospects for Arms Control* (Boulder, Co.: Westview, 1991), pp. 247–48.

6. Cohen, ed., p. 101.

7. For example, verification efforts could be complicated during monsoon season or in dense tropical forests along the western Indian coast (these are a considerable distance from potential targets). However, both India and Pakistan are near the equator and therefore are prime for geostationary satellite monitoring.

Appendix 1

Simla Agreement on Bilateral Relations and Statement on Its Implementations (The Simla Accord)

(Adopted at Simla, India, July 3, 1972; entered into force, August 4, 1972)

Agreement on Bilateral Relations Between the Government of India and the Government of Pakistan Signed in Simla by the Prime Minister of India, Mrs. Indira Gandhi, and the President of Pakistan, Mr. Z. A. Bhutto

I. The government of India and the Government of Pakistan are resolved that the two countries put an end to the conflict and confrontation that have hitherto marred the relations and work for the promotion of a friendly and harmonious relationship and the establishment of a durable peace in the sub-continent, so that both countries may henceforth devote their resources and energies to the pressing task of advancing the welfare of their peoples.

In order to achieve this objective, the Government of India and the Government of Pakistan have agreed as follows:

1. That the principles and the purposes of the Charter of the United Nations shall govern the relations between the two countries.

2. That the two countries are resolved to settle their differences by peaceful means through bilateral negotiations or by any other peaceful means mutually agreed upon between them. Pending the final settlement of any of the problems between the two countries, neither side shall unilaterally alter the situation and both shall prevent the organization, assistance or encouragement of any act detrimental to the maintenance of peaceful and harmonious relations.

3. That the pre-requisite for reconciliation, good neighbourliness and durable peace between them is a commitment by both countries to the peaceful coexistence, respect for each other's territorial integrity and sovereignty and non-interference in each other's internal affairs, on the basis of equality and mutual benefit.

4. That the basic issues and causes of conflict which have bedeviled the relations between the two countries for the last 25 years shall be resolved by peaceful means.

5. That they shall always respect each other's national unity, territorial integrity, political independence and sovereign equality.

6. That in accordance with the Charter of the United Nations, they will refrain from the threat or the use of force against the territorial integrity or political independence of each other.

II. Both governments will take all steps within their power to prevent hostile propaganda directed against each other. Both countries will encourage the dissemination of such information as would promote the development of friendly relations between them.

III. In order progressively to restore and normalise relations between the two countries step by step, it is agreed that:

1. Steps shall be taken to resume communications—postal, telegraphic, sea, land including border posts and air links including over-flights.

2. Appropriate steps shall be taken to promote travel facilities for the nationals of the other country.

3. Trade and cooperation in economic and agreed fields will be resumed as far as possible.

4. Exchange in the fields of science and culture will be promoted. In this connection, delegations from the two countries will meet from time to time to work out the necessary details.

IV. In order to initiate the process of establishment of a durable peace, both Governments agree that:

1. The Indian and Pakistani forces shall be withdrawn to their side of the international border.

2. In Jammu and Kashmir the line of control resulting from the cease-fire of December 17, 1971, shall be respected by both sides without prejudice to the recognised position of either side. Neither side shall seek to alter it unilaterally irrespective of the mutual difference and legal interpretations. Both sides further undertake to refrain from the threat or the use of force in violation of this line.

3. Withdrawals shall commence upon the entry into force of this Agreement and shall be completed within 30 days thereafter.

V. This agreement shall be subject to ratification by both countries in accordance with their respective constitutional procedures and will come into force with effect from the date on which the Instruments of Ratification are exchanged.

VI. Both Governments agree that their respective Heads will meet again at a mutually convenient time in the future and that, in the meanwhile, the representatives of the two sides will meet to discuss further the modalities and arrangements for the establishment of a durable peace and the normalization of relations, including the questions of repatriation of the prisoners-of-war and the civilian internees, a final settlement of Jammu and Kashmir and the resumption of diplomatic relations.

Appendix 2

The No-Attack Agreement between India and Pakistan

(Text of agreement on the prohibition of attack against nuclear installations)

The government of the Islamic Republic of Pakistan and the Government of the Republic of India, hereinafter referred to as the Contracting Parties:

Reaffirming their commitment to durable peace and the development of friendly and harmonious bilateral relations;

Conscious of the role of confidence building measures in promoting such bilateral relations based on mutual trust and goodwill; have agreed as follows:

ARTICLE I: Each party shall refrain from undertaking, encouraging or participating in, directly or indirectly, any action aimed at causing the destruction of, or damage to, any nuclear installation or facility in the other country.

The term "nuclear installation or facility" includes nuclear power and research reactors, fuel fabrication, uranium enrichment, isotopes separation and reprocessing facilities as well as any other installations with fresh or irradiated nuclear fuel and materials in any form and establishments storing significant quantities of radioactive materials.

ARTICLE II: Each Contracting Party shall inform the other on January 1 of each calendar year of the latitude and longitude of its nuclear installations and facilities.

ARTICLE III: This agreement is subject to ratification. It shall come into force with effect from the date on which the Instruments of Ratification are exchanged.

Appendix 3

Statement of Government of India on Confidence-Building Measures between India and Her Neighbors

The importance and content of confidence-building-measures (CBMs) in the conduct of inter-state relations has grown in recent years. The international environment has become more responsive to the contribution of CBMs in safeguarding peace and international security. While the subject has been on the agenda of UN for almost two decades, progress has often been slow because of the fact that regional specificities demand their own unique prescriptions.

Conceptually, building confidence amongst states implies that the conduct of states shall become more predictable thus reducing the risk of mis-perception while preserving each state's right to maintain its legitimate security capabilities. CBMs are not a substitute for disarmament but can help create a positive political atmosphere and reduce tensions. With her long-standing commitment to peaceful co-existence, India has set into motion a process of instituting CBMs with her neighboring states. India's relations with her neighbors vary in accordance with the political dynamics of each bilateral relationship and consequently the nature of CBMs introduced in each instance are different thereby highlighting the fact that regional specificity is an essential prescriptive and CBMs are not an assembly line production item.

India's Approach

India has approached the exercise of confidence building with her neighbors with the following objectives:

1. To provide an assurance of non-aggressive intent;
2. To prevent any attempts at misrepresentation of regular activities for political ends;
3. To reduce the likelihood of escalation of tensions; and
4. To create an environment for reduction of weapons through negotiations.

The history of CBMs in different parts of the world shows that progress in concluding and implementing CBMs is often slow even though the objectives may be ambitious. To overcome this hurdle, it is essential that CBMs be taken to be complementary to national security. Negotiations on CBMs must be focussed, with precise mandates, and decisions have to be made by consensus with both or all parties on the basis of realization that implementation of such measures would enhance the collective security of all participants.

In India's experience with her neighboring states, the range of CBMs appears to cover three broad categories:

1. *Political:* These include 'declarations of intent', discussions on security related concepts and doctrines, measures aimed at improving people-to-people contacts, and developing a broad base for bilateral relations;
2. *Communications:* These include the provision of communication links such as hot lines, dedicated channel links, risk reduction or conflict prevention mechanisms, periodic meetings at official level to discuss issues and defuse tensions; and
3. *Technical:* These would include activities relating to arms limitation and transparency, i.e. prior notifications, constraints on military activities in certain zones, ceilings on military equipments etc.

The following indicate the cross-section of CBMs which are in place between India and her neighboring states.

Pakistan

Relations with Pakistan have not been smooth. With three wars having taken place between India and Pakistan in 1948, 1965 and 1971, and the Kashmir issue outstanding, relations between the two countries are characterized by a high degree of mistrust, apprehension, hostility in public statements and even violent incidents on the border. With this background, India is attempting to put into place a number of CBMs in order to

1. improve the content of bilateral relationship and
2. means to prevent escalation of tensions through institutionalized links including communications.

In 1983, India and Pakistan reached an agreement on the establishment of a Joint Commission between the two countries to meet annually, with a view of promoting cooperation in "the economic, trade, industrial, education, health, cultural, consular, tourism, travel, information, scientific and technological fields." Subsequently, four Sub-Commissions were set up under the Joint Commission. The third meeting of the Indo-Pak Joint Commission was held in 1989. India maintains that regular meetings of the Sub-Commissions and Joint Commission and implementation of the cooperative activities identified by these bodies would serve to reduce mutual mistrust and provide greater people-to-people contacts among the two countries.

At the first round of the Foreign Secretary level talks in July 1990, India put forward an integrated package of CBMs. The package included CBMs in all the three categories -political, communication and technical. It provided for information-sharing on military exercises as a means of promoting transparency and reducing misapprehensions, improving communications among military commanders, joint border patrolling, exchanges of delegations of armed forces and at the political level, reiteration and reaffirmation to settling disputes through peaceful means and bilateral negotiations, ceasing hostile propaganda, respecting the Line of Control and refraining from acts detrimental to maintenance of peaceful harmonious relations and non-interference in each other's internal affairs.

The six rounds of Foreign Secretary level talks have focussed on carrying forward elements of the CBM package and also helped formalize the Agreement on Prohibition of Attack on Nuclear Installations and Facilities signed in December 1988. The instruments of ratification of this Agreement were exchanged in January 1991 and later, on January 1, 1992, India and Pakistan exchanged the lists of nuclear installations covered under the Agreement.

At the fourth round of Foreign Secretary level talks, an Agreement was signed on Advance Notice on Military Exercises, Manoeuvres and Troop Movements. Also at the fourth round of Foreign Secretary level talks, an Agreement between India and Pakistan was signed on "Prevention of Air Space Violations and Permitting Overflights and Landings by Military Aircraft". The instruments of ratification of these two Agreements were exchanged at the sixth round of Foreign Secretary level talks. Both these Agreements will go a long way in reducing misapprehensions. Implementation experience with these Agreements will indicate the areas where additional measures will be needed.

At the fifth round of Foreign Secretary level talks, it was agreed that India and Pakistan would consider issuing a Joint Declaration on Prohibition of Chemical Weapons. Such a Declaration was issued at the conclusion of the sixth round of Foreign Secretary level talks. Under this Declaration, both countries have undertaken not to develop, produce, acquire or use Chemical Weapons and also to refrain from assisting or encouraging others from doing so. Both countries have also reiterated their resolve to become original States Parties to the Chemical Weapons Convention being currently negotiated at the Conference on Disarmament.

Communications between the two countries have also been improved. Following the third round of Foreign Secretary level talks in December 1990, it was agreed that Director General of Military Operations of both countries shall remain in telephonic contact over the telephone hot line on a weekly basis. As a step towards transparency, a formal invitation was extended to the Chief of Army Staff of Pakistan to visit India. This invitation was conveyed during the sixth round of Foreign Secretary level talks.

With a view of taking concrete measures to contain terrorism, drug trafficking and smuggling and illicit border crossing along Indo-Pak border, it was agreed in 1989 that the DG of Pakistan Rangers and IG of BSF shall meet bi-annually to review implementation of agreements in this field in addition to maintaining the boundary pillars.

While India would have preferred a speedier implementation of these CBMs with a view to building upon them, it is clear that by their very nature, the pace of CBMs cannot be forced and must reflect genuine political will on the part of the states concerned.

Nepal

At the political level, relations between India and Nepal have been extremely close. Even though differences in the economic, trade, water sharing etc. field, have arisen, the existence of effective and responsive institutional level exchanges and extensive contacts among the leaders, have helped in resolving these issues through peaceful means.

The Indo-Nepal Treaty of Peace and Friendship continues to provide the underpinning of the special relationship between the two countries with its provision for national treatment of Nepalese citizens in India (except for political rights) and an affirmation of shared security perceptions. This special relationship is characterized in the open border that India shares with Nepal which gives the Nepalese citizens the right to enter India without a visa, seek employment and also enjoy rights of residence.

The Indo-Nepal relationship is characterized by frequent high level political exchanges. The gamut of bilateral relations between India and Nepal are covered under the Indo-Nepal Joint Commission set up 1988 with three Sub-Commissions dealing with Trade and Transit, Economic and Industrial Cooperation and Water Resources.

Bhutan

India's relationship with Bhutan falls into a special category and is governed by the 1949 Friendship Treaty. With Bhutan too, India has an open border and Bhutanese nationals have the right to the same treatment in India (except for political rights) as Indian nationals, i.e., right to work, right to residence and right to travel freely. The relationship between India and Bhutan is characterized by frequent high level political exchanges which act as CBMs and help in resolving any outstanding issues.

China

Normalization of relations between India and China, after the 1962 conflict, has been a slow process. A new beginning was made in 1988 when Prime Minister Rajiv Gandhi paid a goodwill visit to China at the invitation of Prime Minister Li Peng. The Joint Communique issued at the conclusion of the visit emphasized that principles of Panchsheel as guiding the conduct of "bilateral relations between the two countries - mutual respect for sovereignty and territorial integrity, mutual non-aggression, non-interference in each other's internal affairs, equality and mutual benefit and peaceful coexistence."

A significant achievement of the 1988 visit was the setting up of a Joint Working Group on the boundary question and another Joint Group to deal with issues regarding cooperation in the fields of economic relations, trade, science and technology. The process of consolidation of political relationship has continued. During the visit of Premier Li Peng to India in December 1991, an Agreement was signed on the re-establishment of Consulates General in Shanghai and Bombay, a Consular Convention between the two countries was concluded and MOUs signed for the resumption of border trade. In May 1992, President Venkataraman paid a State Visit to China. The joint statement at the end of the visit reflected the firm resolve of the two countries to settle the boundary question through peaceful negotiations and continue progress for enhancement of confidence building between the two countries in the border areas.

The India-China Joint Working Group on boundary issues has met four times and is also looking at technical and communication linked CBMs. At the fourth meeting in February 1992, it was agreed that military personnel of both countries would hold regular meetings in June and October at Bumla Pass (eastern sector) and Spanggur Gap (western sector). Supporting communication links are being established in both sectors. In addition to the regular scheduled meetings, additional meetings of border personnel would be held as and when required. Discussions in the Joint Working Group have focussed on technical aspects of CBMs in the areas along the Line of Actual Control, such as prior notification regarding military exercises. In the statement released during the visit of President Venkataraman, it was noted that CBMs would contribute significantly to the creation of a favorable and positive atmosphere for an early, fair, reasonable and mutually acceptable settlement of the boundary question between the two countries.

Exchanges between the National Defense College in India and the National Defense University of China; between the Institute of Defense Studies and Analyses and Beijing Institute of Strategic Studies have provided for greater contacts and exchange of views. High level defense visits have been exchanged between the two countries and the Indian Defense Minister visited China for the first time in July 1992.

Bangladesh

Indo-Bangladesh relations, despite occasional irritants, reflect shared values and common interests. Characterized at the political level by frequent high level exchanges, the institutional mechanisms between the two countries effectively function to prevent any differences from escalation. The land boundary between India and Bangladesh was demarcated in May 1974 and joint guidelines were issued the following year for the border authorities, namely, the BSF and the Bangladesh Rifles. These guidelines are intended to help the two para-military organizations to tackle problems of unauthorized movements of persons, inadvertent crossing of land and riverain boundaries, smuggling, communications while in hot pursuit of criminals, curbing traffic in illicit weapons and dealing with border crimes. Significantly, the two countries have agreed that no defensive works, e.g., trenches etc. shall be permitted within 150 yards on either side of the international boundary. Annual border coordination meetings are held between the two para-military organizations with more frequent meetings at the sector and sub-sector commander levels.

Specifications for flag communications and telephone communications have been laid down to ensure reliable contact between the border security agencies.

A number of training slots are provided on a regular basis to Bangladesh defense personnel in Indian training establishments, at all levels. A program of exchange of goodwill visits has begun with the first visit of the Indian Chief of Army Staff to Bangladesh in July 1991.

A Joint Economic Commission was set up in 1982. Cultural and academic exchange programs provide greater people-to-people contact between the two countries.

Myanmar

Despite fluctuations in Indo-Myanmar relations during the last three decades, there remain strong links of shared historical, cultural and ethnic ties between the peoples of the two countries. As with other neighboring countries, a Treaty of Friendship was signed between India and Myanmar in 1951. Myanmar, as founder member of the Nonaligned Movement, and India also shared common perceptions on international issues. Agreements on delimitations of land boundary and the maritime boundary signed in 1967 and 1986 have yet to be followed through to completion.

A major political effort to improve relations was undertaken during former Prime Minister Rajiv Gandhi's visit to Myanmar in 1987. However, some of the momentum was lost due to internal developments in Myanmar leading to the emergence of new political leadership. It is hoped that demarcation, as provided for in the boundary delimitation agreement, can be completed following inspections of the boundary pillars on the border.

Faced with common problem of trans-border terrorism, bilateral meetings between Area Commanders of the border security forces have been instituted. These meetings take place twice a year, with the objective of exchanging information and coordinating to the extent possible, anti-insurgency operations in the border areas.

Maldives

Indo-Maldives relations have seen a steady improvement since 1976 when a Maritime Boundary Agreement between the two countries was signed settling the issue of competing territorial claims over a part of Minicoy Islands. Bilateral political relations showed an upswing following the visit of former Prime Minister Rajiv Gandhi in 1986. Since then, exchange of high level visits between the two countries has continued on a regular basis.

An Indo-Maldives Joint Commission, set up in 1990, provides the framework for expanding bilateral economic and technical cooperation and improving people-to-people contacts. Health, welfare, communications, human resource development, infrastructural projects are some of the areas of activity under the Indo-Maldives Joint Commission.

The strong ties between the two countries was reflected in India's timely assistance to the Maldives Government during the 1988 crisis. Defense cooperation has also been expanded since 1988. It now includes provision of training slots in Indian establishments for Maldives defense personnel. In 1991, the practice of holding joint coastguard exercises between the services of the two countries was instituted.

Sri Lanka

Despite contentious and difficult issues relating to the Tamil refugee problem, Indo-Sri Lankan relations reflect a high degree of inter-action across a broad range of issues testifying to the functioning of institutional mechanisms. A major landmark in the bilateral relationship is the Indo-Sri Lanka

Agreement of July 1987 in which India is committed to the establishment of peace and normalcy in Sri Lanka with a view to preserving its character as a multi-ethnic, multi-lingual and multi-religious plural society. India has also assured Sri Lanka that its territory shall not be used for activities prejudicial to the unity, integrity and security of Sri Lanka.

The close relations between the armed forces of the two countries, are promoted through the provision of a number of training slots in Indian defense training establishments for Sri Lankan officers at all levels. Close cooperation between the Navies and Coastguard forces of the two countries has been instituted to curb paching, fishing in each other's territorial waters, smuggling etc. The Navies of the two countries have also cooperated with regard to the repatriation of Sri Lankan refugees.

To provide broader content, an Indo-Sri Landan Joint Commission was established in 1991. Initially, two Sub-Commissions on Trade, Investment and Finance and Social, Cultural and Educational Affairs were set up. An addition was soon made by instituting a third Sub-Commission to deal with Science and Technology. In recent years, there are growing interests in looking for joint ventures in industries and services.

Conclusion

The short review of CBMs instituted between India and her neighbors in recent years, reveals a wide spectrum. In a sense, it is a reflection of the dynamics of the bilateral relationship in each instance. The geography also conditions the issues in each relationship. In certain cases, India shares a long land boundary with its neighbors; in others there are religious, ethnic or linguistic links among populations on both sides of the international border which creates the problem of tracking refugee movements and infiltration. A number of neighboring states are much smaller than India and special efforts are needed to provide necessary reassurances to these states guaranteeing their territorial integrity and sovereignty. With such a broad spectrum of issues, clearly CBMs need to be explored and tailor-made to suit specific requirements. Imposing an uniform pattern may be counter-productive because it is only in one-to-one discussions and negotiations that India is in a position to be able to respond to concerns animating each bilateral relationship.

Confidence must be enhanced on all fronts and in tandem, if security has to be enhanced. Political declarations are significant but these must be supported by actions that reflect a desire for just and secure peace; actions that discard the option of military solutions, overt or covert, to resolve political problems; actions that reject military postures that are perceived as hostile. Continuance of hostile acts and inflammatory statements diminish the value of political CBMs. In a region where wars have taken place, a desire for peace must demonstrate a change in priorities, reflected through increasing intercourse among institutions, among public interest groups and among people through cultural, communication and economic linkages.

India will continue its efforts at building upon the existing CBMs in a step-by-step and realistic manner. Effective implementation of existing CBMs paves the way for more steps in this direction. Once again, these would reflect a wide spectrum, depending on the political dynamics of the relationship and receptivity of the other state. From reducing misperceptions and improving communications, India considers it possible to visualize movement towards reducing troop deployments or establishment of 'zones of restraint' once political dialogue on all issues is firmly established and security perceptions undergo changes; development of closer commercial and economic ties; improving communications and travel for the people through easing restraints; further strengthening cultural links; putting into place non-discriminatory and structural measures for curbing proliferation and contribution to global elimination of weapons of mass destruction; and eventually, moving towards open exchanges of security perceptions which will lead in turn to reduction of military expenditures.

Plurality is the true test of democracy and plurality requires openness and tolerance in social policy. Accepting the concept of cooperative security and enhancing it through confidence-building-measures needs political resilience based on democratic principles. India's initiatives for confidence building are rooted in the bedrock of these principles. Once a uniform degree of openness is established in each society, and a range of effective bilateral institutional mechanisms are put into place, applicability of regional approach in the area of confidence-building-measures will become feasible and productive. India is committed to seeking ways and means to improve its bilateral relations with all the states in its neighborhood and shall continue assiduously to pursue appropriate CBMs in keeping with the principles of Panchsheel which form a basis for India's conduct of inter-state relations.

Appendix 4

Statement of Government of Pakistan on CSBMs
between Pakistan and India

(prepared by S. Shafqat Kakakhel)

On May 28, 1990, the government of India conveyed to the government of Pakistan a two page document entitled "Confidence Building Package between India and Pakistan." On June 5, 1990, the government of Pakistan responded to India that, while it had reservations on the scope of the proposals, it was ready to engage in a purposeful dialogue and suggested that the foreign secretaries of the two countries meet that month at a mutually convenient venue to "begin a discussion to remove the causes of the present tension." New Delhi agreed, and the first session of talks between the foreign secretaries was held in July 1990 in Islamabad. These talks have served as the main forum for negotiating confidence- and security-building measures (CSBMs).

During the period July 1990–August 1992, Pakistan and India negotiated and signed three CSBM agreements, ratified an earlier one, and held detailed discussions on several others. These discussions marked the unfolding of a structured process that has been inspired by, and to a large extent modeled on, the provisions of the Helsinki Accord and the CSBMs finalized at Madrid (1983) and Stockholm (1986) and with the Vienna Document of 1990. It should be mentioned, however, that efforts by Pakistan and India to evolve what would today be called CSBMs actually predate the U.S.-Soviet and European processes. Moreover, for reasons that will be discussed later, the East-West and U.S.-Soviet models cannot be replicated in the South Asian context.

This statement will describe the progress achieved by Pakistan and India in negotiating a series of CSBM agreements, assess the significance and usefulness of these agreements, and will conclude by pinpointing the inadequacies of the arrangements already in place in promoting "confidence" and "security" between Pakistan and India. Ideally, the CSBMs in question would be studied within a historic narrative of the evolution of Indo-Pakistani relations since 1947. In view of the limitation of space and, more important in the interest of greater conceptual clarity, the process will be described and analyzed according to the categories defined by Ted Greenwood, namely, mutual security pledges, transparency, managing dangerous and potentially dangerous military activities, and crisis management.

Mutual Security Pledges

In 1949, soon after the first Indo-Pakistani war over Jammu and Kashmir and amid the preoccupation of the two countries with resolving problems such as the sharing of river and canal waters and the treatment of minorities, a correspondence began between the Indian and Pakistani prime ministers, Jawaharlal Nehru and Liaquat Ali Khan. The subject of the correspondence was Nehru's proposal for a joint declaration to "condemn [the] resort to war for the settlement of any existing or future disputes between [India and Pakistan]," and, instead, to pledge to resolve such disputes by "recognized peaceful methods, such as negotiations, mediation, arbitration, or by agreed reference to some appropriate international body recognized by both [countries]." Initially, Prime Minister Khan questioned the usefulness of what he called "a rather unnecessary repetition of certain portions of the UN Charter." However, in a letter to Nehru dated February 14, 1950, Khan proposed that the declaration should be supplemented by an agreement containing "a clear-cut procedure with an agreed timetable which would make it binding on both to carry out the settlement of the disputes to a peaceful conclusion." Khan further proposed that disputes be taken up one by one and resolved through negotiations, mediation, or arbitration. He also promised that Pakistan would be willing to accept the verdicts of a single jointly nominated arbitrator on all bilateral disputes. Prime Minister Nehru did not accept Khan's proposal, however.

In both conceptual and political terms, the "Pak-India Agreement on Bilateral Relations," signed at Simla on July 2, 1972, and generally referred to as the Simla Accord, constitutes a bilateral statement of mutual security pledges. The agreement declares the resolve of the two countries to "put an end to the conflict and confrontation" marring their relations and to "settle their differences by peaceful means mutually agreed upon." The two countries agreed not to use force to settle the situation. Paragraph 6 of the Simla Agreement reinforces these security pledges by identifying the major problem to be resolved amicably through negotiations: the status of Jammu and Kashmir. Unfortunately, the negotiations on Kashmir envisaged in the Simla Agreement never took place. Both countries reiterated their divergent substantive positions on the disputed state: India claimed that Jammu and Kashmir constituted an integral part of its sovereign territory while Pakistan asserted that the final status of Kashmir had to be resolved in accordance with the U.N. Security Council resolutions as well as in the spirit of Simla Agreement.

Continued differences over Jammu and Kashmir did not prevent the two countries from exploring additional mutual security pledges. In September

1981, Pakistan proposed to India "consultations for exchanging mutual assurances of non-aggression and non-use of force." After receiving a positive response from New Delhi, Pakistan presented a draft non-aggression pact in June 1982. In turn, in August 1982, India proposed a draft treaty of "peace, friendship, and cooperation." After protracted negotiations, the two sides agreed in May 1984 to integrate the two drafts in to one document, entitled "Agreement/Treaty on Good Neighborliness and Cooperation." However, the Indian government insisted that the text include a clause disallowing recourse to any third-party settlement procedure or to any international agency. India also demanded a commitment that neither country would offer military bases to a third country. Pakistan's rejection of these proposals led to yet another stalemate, and discussions on the agreement were interrupted in 1986. Prime Minister Benazir Bhutto, in a statement dated December 3, 1988, categorically opposed the idea of a new bilateral agreement, arguing that the Simla Agreement provided an adequate framework for bilateral relations.

Transparency

Both India and Pakistan have large standing armies that frequently conduct exercises. The need for a measure of transparency in these exercises should have been evident given the conflictual nature of the bilateral relationship. Yet the subject appears not to have become salient until October 1986, when India disclosed plans for holding the largest military exercises in its history, code-named "Brasstacks IV." Pakistan sought further information about Brasstacks and proposed that the countries discuss the exchange of advance information about troop movements and military exercises. In November of that same year, Pakistani Prime Minister Mohammed Khan Junejo reiterated the proposal for "mandatory procedures for prior notification of troop movements to prevent mutual misperceptions and apprehensions in future" at a meeting with Indian Prime Minister Rajiv Gandhi. But although Gandhi promised information about Brasstacks, he did not respond directly to Junejo's proposal for a bilateral agreement on prior notification of troop movements.

The Indian government did not fulfill Rajiv Gandhi's promise. In mid-November 1986, Indian newspapers reported that a total of 250,000 army, navy, and air force troops would participate in the exercises in the Sindh-Rajasthan and Punjab sectors. By the end of November, more than 50,000 Indian troops had been deployed in the Punjab. In response, Pakistan began to deploy its troops into the Punjab as well as in Sindh/Rajasthan.

On January 23, 1987, the Indian government asked Pakistan to withdraw to peacetime locations the forces it had deployed in the Punjab. Furthermore, Delhi warned that if Pakistan did not withdraw its troops, India would move its troops "into defensive positions." That same day, the Indian government announced that forward deployment of troops in the Punjab had already commenced, and added that if Pakistani forces did not redeploy, Indian forces would also take up positions in Rajasthan and Jammu and Kashmir. This threat caused much anxiety in Pakistan; the outbreak of hostilities appeared imminent. On January 24, Pakistan declared its readiness to hold immediate consultations to reduce the tension. India agreed the next day. On January 26, the prime ministers agreed in a telephone conversation that a Pakistani delegation would visit New Delhi. That delegation, headed by the foreign secretary and comprising senior military officials, reached New Delhi on January 30.

On January 30, the Indian newspaper *The Hindu* carried a report by G. K. Reddy, a senior journalist to whom the Indian government often leaked information that it did not want to disclose officially. Reddy's report stated that India wanted to "concentrate on the more immediate task of withdrawals by the two armies to their normal positions," and added that Pakistan realized that India would not at that state and forum discuss "issues like a balanced reduction of forces, procedures for exercises, and posting of observers on the prevailing pattern in Europe between NATO and Warsaw Pact forces."

At the talks, Pakistan pointed out that the tense situation could have been avoided if India had provided information about the military exercises. Pakistan proposed several measures to improve communication and effect transparency, including restraints on the introduction of additional troops, daily direct communications between the directors-general of military operations, regular contact between the foreign ministries, avoidance of flights by military aircraft, and timetables for the phased redeployment of troops. In view of the anticipated negative response from the Indian side, Pakistan did not formally introduce the proposal it had drawn up for an institutionalized system of prior notification of exercises and other military movements.

On February 4, 1987, an agreement was finally reached on the de-escalation of tension through several measures, especially the establishment of "hotline" communications between the army and air force operations chiefs to "prevent misconceptions, hasty reactions, and unfortunate incidents at a time when large numbers of forces have been deployed on the two sides of the border." This de-escalation agreement helped to disperse the clouds of war hovering on the horizon.

Significantly, the U.S. government promptly and warmly welcomed this agreement. In identical messages delivered to the Pakistani and Indian governments by the U.S. ambassadors in Islamabad and Delhi, Washington recalled that it had provided information on exercise notification procedures in effect in Europe to both countries in the fall of 1986, and expressed belief that "such procedures might have helped prevent the recent escalation of tensions." Further, Washington offered help "in ways both [countries] deem useful."

In the next two years, Indo-Pakistani relations were marred by sustained Indian accusations that Pakistan was encouraging and abetting the Sikh insurgency in Punjab by giving arms, training, and sanctuary to Sikh militants. Pakistan denied the charges and suggested that the interior secretaries of the two countries meet to discuss measures to halt illicit and undesirable border crossing. India agreed and several rounds of talks were held.

Other contentious problems between the two countries included the withdrawal of forces from the Siachen Glacier, where Indian forces had made incursions in 1984; India's construction of a navigation and water storage project (the Wullar Barrage/Tulbul Navigation Project) near Srinagar in Kashmir, which in Pakistan's view violated the Indus Waters Treaty of 1960; India's tacit support for the Soviet military intervention in Afghanistan; and New Delhi's hue and cry over Pakistan's nuclear program and its acquisition of military hardware from Washington. Despite these problems, however, the two countries maintained "normal" relations through regular high-level exchanges facilitated by SAARC, secretary-level talks on Siachen and on the Wullar Barrage Project, and meetings of the bilateral Joint Ministerial Commission. Prime Minister Rajiv Gandhi visited Islamabad for the SAARC summit in December 1988 and paid an official bilateral visit in July 1989. These high-level exchanges generated much optimism about a gradual improvement in relations and a peaceful settlement of the outstanding problems, especially Siachen and Wullar Barrage.

Yet although there were hopes of improvement in Indo-Pakistani relations, the situation in Jammu and Kashmir was heading downhill. In 1989, anti-Indian demonstrations spearheaded by Kashmiri youth in Srinagar became a recurring feature. Kashmiri Muslims refused to take part in the Indian general election. The Indian authorities tried to stem the demonstrations by force, which only caused the militants to step up their disruptive actions. The crackdown in occupied Jammu and Kashmir was accompanied by a vigorous government propaganda campaign portraying the uprising as having been provoked and sustained by Pakistan. New Delhi also started deploying troops along the line of control and near the international border. Pakistan in turn deployed forces and an "eyeball to eyeball" confrontation ensued. Fearing that the spiraling tension could lead to premeditated or inadvertent hostilities, the Pakistani foreign minister, Sahabzada Yaqub Khan, while visiting Delhi for SAARC discussions, called on Indian leaders to defuse the situation and enter into a dialogue to resolve the Jammu and Kashmir problem and all other outstanding issues. He called for the redeployment of troops to peacetime locations. Khan forcefully rejected Indian accusations of Pakistani support for the Kashmiri militants and asserted that the Kashmiri uprising was an indigenous, widespread, popular movement aimed at securing the right of self-determination pledged in U.N. Security Council resolutions. The two countries took sharply divergent positions, and Yaqub Khan's mission failed.

The foreign ministers met again in New York on April 25 but failed to bring about an improvement in the climate. On May 10 Indian Prime Minister V. P. Singh delivered a speech in parliament calling on the people of India to "steel their nerves" and "psychologically prepare" themselves for war.

The rising level of hostile rhetoric prompted the U.S. government to undertake a highly visible initiative to reduce tensions. Robert Gates visited Pakistan and India as a special presidential envoy. Gates arrived in Islamabad on May 19 and flew to New Delhi the next day. In meetings with senior political and military officials in both countries, Mr. Gates conveyed Washington's concern over the heightened tensions and called for immediate steps to reduce them. He proposed a "removal of deployments" and suggested that the two countries begin discussions on confidence-and security-building measures. He specifically mentioned CSBMs on prior notification of military exercises—a moratorium on military exercises at first, and subsequent holding of exercises away from the Indo-Pakistani border. He also suggested talks on the establishment of "cautionary zones," "military-free zones," joint border patrolling, and meetings between military officials. The Gates mission had a positive impact: the CSBM "package" proposed by New Delhi to Pakistan on May 28, 1990, included most of the suggestions made by Gates.

The importance of transparency in the Indo Pakistani context is indicated by the fact that the first three proposals in the Indian CSBM package pertained to "sharing of information regarding military exercises, . . . communications between military commanders, . . . [and] exchange of delegations of the armed forces." At the first round of talks between foreign secretaries, Pakistan presented a formal proposal on prior notification of exercises. At the second session of talks, India came up with a counter-draft. After detailed discussions between August 1990 and April 1991, an agreement on "Advance Notice for Military Maneuvers and Exercises" was signed. The instruments of ratification were exchanged during the sixth round of foreign secretary talks in August 1992. The agreement provides for advance notice on exercises, maneuvers, and troop movements by the army, navy, and air forces "in order to prevent any crisis due to misreading of the other side's intentions." It forbids holding of exercises in close proximity to one another, or near the border and the line of control. It contains details concerning the size, type, level, location, duration, etc. of exercises and provisions for addressing situations caused by any changes in the schedule, size, or location of exercises.

The second proposal in India's CSBM package called for "close communications between military commanders" of sectors jointly identified during mutual consultations. This proposal was meant to formalize the bilateral agreement of February 4, 1987, to establish "hotline" communications between operations chiefs of the army headquarters. During discussions, India proposed a multi-channel system extending the hotline facilities to air force and navy establishments, and also suggested the signing of a "memorandum of understanding" to institutionalize the procedures.

The third proposal in the Indian package called for "mutually acceptable understandings regarding exchanges of armed forces delegations from time to time." This was a precedent-setting suggestion because such exchanges had seldom taken place in the past. Pakistan responded positively and sent a high-level delegation to Delhi for five-day visit in March and April 1991. An Indian delegation visited Pakistan in September 1991. The visits helped in finalizing CSBM agreements on prior notice of military exercises, the prohibition of attack on nuclear installations, and measures to prevent violations of airspace by military aircraft.

In August 1992, during the sixth round of talks between the foreign secretaries, the Indian government formally invited the chief of army staff of Pakistan to visit India. The Pakistani army chief responded that, while Pakistan was in principle not opposed to the visit, it felt that the visit should take place within the context of the overall relationship. Moreover, he said, the visit should have a specific purpose and facilitate talks on specific issues rather than become a "ceremonial affair." These statements were later reiterated by the Pakistani foreign secretary.

Managing Dangerous and Potentially Dangerous Military Activities

During the visit of Pakistani President Zia ul Haq to India in December 1985, he and Indian Prime Minister Rajiv Gandhi agreed to conclude a bilateral agreement disallowing attacks on nuclear installations. The agreement was evidently prompted by press reports in 1984 about Indian plans for a strike against Pakistani nuclear facilities. At the time, Pakistan had warned that such an attack would trigger an all-out war. After detailed discussions, an "Agreement on the Prohibition of Attack Against Nuclear Installations and Facilities. . . " was signed during Prime Minister Gandhi's visit to Islamabad in December 1988.

The second CSBM to manage dangerous and potentially dangerous military activities was the "Agreement between Pakistan and India on Prevention of Air Space Violations and for Permitting Overflights and Landings by Military Aircraft," which was signed in April 1991. This agreement had been suggested by India as part of its CSBM package of May 28, 1990. Pakistan introduced a draft of the agreement at the first round of talks between the foreign secretaries. The Indian counter-draft was introduced during the second round of talks. The text was finalized during the third round and the agreement was concluded in April 1991, during the fourth round of talks. Ratification documents were exchanged during the sixth session of talks between the foreign secretaries, in August 1992. The agreement provides for measures to prevent air violations and calls for communications and prior notice of aerial survey and supply dropping, for mercy and rescue missions between the air force establishments, and for measures to promote safety of air operations.

The "Joint Declaration on the Complete Prohibition of Chemical Weapons," signed by the foreign secretaries on August 19, 1992, is the third CSBM for managing dangerous and potentially dangerous military activities. This agreement disallows the manufacture, import, deployment, and use of chemical weapons. The bilateral declaration preceded the international Chemical Weapons Convention in Geneva. During the sixth round of talks between the Foreign Secretaries, Pakistan also proposed a bilateral agreement prohibiting the acquisition, production, deployment, and use of biological weapons, on the pattern of the declaration on chemical weapons.

In Pakistan's view, an early solution of the Siachen Glacier issue would not only help avoid further human and financial losses, but would also settle a "potentially dangerous military activity," thus promoting confidence. India's large-scale operation in the area in April 1984, which enabled it to seize big chunks of high-altitude areas located near the northern areas of Pakistan, inevitably prompted the latter to move its troops into position on its side of the glaciers. This was the first "dangerous military activity" between the two countries since the East Pakistanû Bangladesh war of 1971. During the past ten years, both sides have lost hundreds of troops and spent millions of dollars stressing their competing claims on an area of doubtful military significance. Most of the human losses have been caused by the inhospitable terrain and punishing weather conditions at altitudes ranging between 10,000 and 22,000 feet above sea level.

In January 1986, at Pakistan's suggestion, the defense secretaries of Pakistan and India began talks to resolve the Siachen problem. Both countries agreed on the desirability of an early agreement on the withdrawal and redeployment of troops and subsequently on precisely demarcating the line of control. However, India insisted that the demarcation reflect the positions occupied in 1984, a demand that was unacceptable to Pakistan. In June 1989, the defense secretaries agreed that both countries would redeploy their forces to positions to be jointly identified by their military experts. The agreement announced in a joint press statement seemed to reflect the thaw in relations effected by Prime Minister Rajiv Gandhi's visit to Pakistan in December 1989; it was endorsed by Prime Ministers Gandhi and Benazir Bhutto during the former's second visit to Islamabad in July 1989. However, controversy arose on the interpretation of the agreement. Pakistan stated that the agreement would result in the restoration of the status quo prior to the incursion of Indian troops in 1984. This statement was contested by India. Further talks between military officials in August 1989 did not achieve any positive result. Subsequently, New Delhi's position hardened. In discussions between the foreign secretaries during 1990–92, New Delhi insisted that the redeployment of forces and determination of new positions must be based on the "new realities," a euphemism for positions occupied by it in 1984.

At the sixth round of talks between the foreign secretaries in August 1992, the Indians called for a meeting between defense secretaries and promised a more flexible attitude. When this meeting took place in November 1992, however, India reiterated the demand for an acknowledgment by Pakistan of the "new realities." The talks ended in failure.

Although no major military encounter has taken place in the Siachen Glacier zone, there is always the potential for clashes and conflict. Pakistan believes that an early decision on redeployment of forces would not only save precious human lives, financial resources, and military hardware, but would also serve as an effective confidence-and security-building measure.

Since the Indian nuclear explosion of 1974, which heralded the advent of the nuclear era in the subcontinent, Pakistan has ceaselessly worked for nuclear nonproliferation in South Asia. Its proposal for a nuclear-free zone in the region enjoys the support of a large number of countries in the United Nations. At the bilateral level, Islamabad has made seven proposals:

1. Simultaneous accession by India and Pakistan to the Nuclear Nonproliferation Treaty (NPT);
2. Simultaneous acceptance by both countries of full-scope IAEA safeguards;
3. A joint declaration renouncing the acquisition or development of nuclear weapons;
4. Establishment of a nuclear-weapons-free zone in South Asia;
5. A bilateral treaty banning all nuclear tests;
6. Convening of a conference on nuclear nonproliferation in South Asia under U.N. auspices, with participation of all regional parties; and
7. A regional conference on nuclear nonproliferation in South Asia, to be attended by Pakistan, India, the United States, Russia, and China (proposed by Pakistan in June 1991).

India has thus far turned down all these Pakistani proposals, saying that nuclear proliferation is a global problem that can only be addressed at the global level. In New Delhi's view, the NPT is a discriminatory treaty meant to perpetuate the positions of the nuclear "haves" and "have nots," and it cannot serve the cause of universal nuclear disarmament. India also asserts that Pakistan's proposals are "India-centered" and do not address India's concerns regarding China and the Central Asian states, which are brimming with nuclear arms.

Recently the United States, Canada, Japan, and the countries of the European Union have made concerted efforts to prevent nuclear weapons and missile proliferation in South Asia. Washington has reportedly suggested that Pakistan and India consider a CSBM regime that would preclude the acquisition and deployment of ballistic missiles. The U.S. government has imposed sanctions against Pakistan and China in retaliation for alleged missiles transfers from Beijing to Islamabad, which Washington claims violated the Missile Technology Control Regime. China and Pakistan deny the U.S. charge, arguing that it is based on flawed information.

Crisis Management and Conflict Resolution

Since the start of the bilateral discussions on CSBMs in July 1990, Pakistan has expressed the view that the process of building, sustaining, and promoting confidence and security between Pakistan and India would require much more than the various agreements for conflict avoidance aimed at bringing about greater transparency in the actions of the armed forces. Islamabad believes that the two countries should go beyond the avoidance and containment of crisis and summon the necessary political will to expeditiously and amicably resolve the "core," "major," and "serious" issues in Indo-Pakistani relations. The "core" issue is the final status of Jammu and Kashmir. The "major" issue is nuclear and missile proliferation. The "serious" problems comprise the redeployment of troops in and the effective demilitarization of the Siachen Glacier; the Wullar Barrage; the demarcation of land boundaries in the Sir Creek area, which would facilitate the final demarcation of maritime boundaries; the revision of border ground rules; and joint efforts to preclude illicit cross-border movement of persons and goods.

During the foreign secretary talks, Pakistan pointed out that the efficacy of the CSBM measures being negotiated would be strengthened significantly by an early dialogue on an amicable settlement of the Kashmir problem, which has bedeviled bilateral relations for nearly fifty years. During his visit to Delhi for the sixth round of talks in August 1992, the Pakistani foreign secretary delivered to Indian Prime Minister Narasimha Rao a letter from Pakistani Prime Minister Nawaz Sharif proposing negotiations on Kashmir. Unfortunately, New Delhi's response has been largely negative. India does not oppose talks on Kashmir in principle but it has made negotiations conditional on termination of Pakistan's alleged assistance to the Kashmiri militants.

Conclusions

In practical terms, the hotline communication between the directors-general of the Pakistani and Indian armies has been useful on both sides in clarifying positions on the movement of troops. The DGMOs speak with one another at least once a week—more often if either side desires to do so. The agreement on prior notice of military operations and the airspace violation agreement have also helped in averting possible difficulties. Similarly, the no-attack agreement and the chemical weapons declaration are desirable CSBMs.

Since early 1990, Indo-Pakistani relations have deteriorated to an all-time low, resulting in the indefinite postponement of the talks between the foreign, defense, and water resources secretaries. The meeting between the prime ministers of the two countries at the SAARC summit in April 1993 did not improve either the substance or the climate of bilateral relations. The Indian government's massive campaign to get the U.S. government to declare Pakistan a "state supporting terrorism"—which would have led to the imposition of wide-ranging political, economic, military, and other sanctions against Pakistan—has deeply hurt the government and people of Pakistan. The Indian campaign has been seen as evidence of an incorrigible, immutable hostility toward Pakistan.

The potentially dangerous state of Indo-Pakistani relations has been caused primarily by the Kashmiri struggle for self-determination. It underlines the fact that in the absence of a peaceful, just, and lasting solution of the Jammu and Kashmir problem, it would be virtually impossible to erect a durable edifice of constructive, tension-free, good neighborly relations between Pakistan and India. The Indian government's refusal to enter into a dialogue with Pakistan on the Jammu and Kashmir question suggests that while the CSBMs serve to avert the accidental outbreak of hostilities, they do not contain cast-iron guarantees against armed conflict resulting from unabated deterioration of relations. The absence of any substantial breakthrough on the vital question of nuclear and missile proliferation, which is inextricably linked with the unresolved political and territorial questions, is likely to undermine efforts aimed at the signing of additional military CSBMs between Pakistan and India.

About the Contributors

Šumit Ganguly is a Professor of Political Science at Hunter College and the Graduate Center of the City University of New York.

Ted Greenwood is a Program Officer with the Alfred P. Sloan Foundation, New York.

Kanti P. Bajpai is an Associate Professor in the School of International Studies, Jawaharlal Nehru University, New Delhi, India.

Pervaiz Iqbal Cheema is the Director General of the Academy of Educational Planning and Management, Islamabad, Pakistan.

Rosemary Foot is a Senior Lecturer in International Relations at St. Antony's College, Oxford University, Oxford, England.

Mark A. Heller is a Senior Research Associate at the Jaffee Center for Strategic Studies, Tel Aviv University, Tel Aviv, Israel.

Neil Joeck is a Senior Analyst at Lawrence Livermore National Laboratory, Livermore, California.

Shireen M. Mazari is the Editor of *Pulse Weekly*, Islamabad, Pakistan.

C. Raja Mohan is a Strategic Affairs Editor with the *Hindu*, New Delhi.

John Sandrock is a Senior Analyst at Science Applications International Corporation, McLean, Virginia.

Jasjit Singh is the Director of the Institute of Defence Studies and Analyses, New Delhi, India.

About the Book

Exploring the long history of conflict in South Asia, this book assesses the role of confidence- and security-building measures (CSBMs) in reducing tension. Utilizing a unique comparative framework, the contributors draw lessons for South Asia from the experiences of states in Cold War Europe and in the Middle East. Despite the significant historical, political, and geographic differences among regions, the contributors illustrate how the implementation of CSBMs elsewhere has important policy implications for limiting interstate conflict in South Asia.

DATE DUE

GAYLORD